East-West Technology Transfer

NATO ASI Series

Advanced Science Institutes Series

A Series presenting the results of activities sponsored by the NATO Science Committee, which aims at the dissemination of advanced scientific and technological knowledge, with a view to strengthening links between scientific communities.

The Series is published by an international board of publishers in conjunction with the NATO Scientific Affairs Division

A Life Sciences **B Physics**	Plenum Publishing Corporation London and New York
C Mathematical and Physical Sciences **D Behavioural and Social Sciences** **E Applied Sciences**	Kluwer Academic Publishers Dordrecht, Boston and London
F Computer and Systems Sciences **G Ecological Sciences** **H Cell Biology** **I Global Environmental Change**	Springer-Verlag Berlin, Heidelberg, New York, London, Paris and Tokyo

PARTNERSHIP SUB-SERIES

1. Disarmament Technologies	Kluwer Academic Publishers
2. Environment	Springer-Verlag / Kluwer Academic Publishers
3. High Technology	Kluwer Academic Publishers
4. Science and Technology Policy	Kluwer Academic Publishers
5. Computer Networking	Kluwer Academic Publishers

The Partnership Sub-Series incorporates activities undertaken in collaboration with NATO's Cooperation Partners, the countries of the CIS and Central and Eastern Europe, in Priority Areas of concern to those countries.

NATO-PCO-DATA BASE

The electronic index to the NATO ASI Series provides full bibliographical references (with keywords and/or abstracts) to more than 50000 contributions from international scientists published in all sections of the NATO ASI Series.
Access to the NATO-PCO-DATA BASE is possible in two ways:

– via online FILE 128 (NATO-PCO-DATA BASE) hosted by ESRIN, Via Galileo Galilei, I-00044 Frascati, Italy.

– via CD-ROM "NATO-PCO-DATA BASE" with user-friendly retrieval software in English, French and German (© WTV GmbH and DATAWARE Technologies Inc. 1989).

The CD-ROM can be ordered through any member of the Board of Publishers or through NATO-PCO, Overijse, Belgium.

Series 4: Science and Technology Policy – Vol. 3

East-West Technology Transfer

New Perspectives and Human Resources

edited by

George Bugliarello
Chancellor,
Polytechnic University,
Brooklyn, New York, U.S.A.

Namik K. Pak
Vice-President,
TÜBİTAK,
Ankara, Turkey

Zhores I. Alferov
Vice-President,
Russian Academy of Sciences,
St. Petersburg, Russia

and

John H. Moore
Director,
International Institute,
George Mason University,
Arlington, Virginia, U.S.A.

Kluwer Academic Publishers

Dordrecht / Boston / London

Published in cooperation with NATO Scientific Affairs Division

Proceedings of the NATO Advanced Research Workshop on
Human Resources and Leadership for Technology Transfer
between NATO Countries and Cooperation Partner Countries
Ankara, Turkey
July 18–21, 1994

A C.I.P. Catalogue record for this book is available from the Library of Congress.

DOI: 10.1007/978-94-009-0151-3

Published by Kluwer Academic Publishers,
P.O. Box 17, 3300 AA Dordrecht, The Netherlands.

Kluwer Academic Publishers incorporates the publishing programmes of
D. Reidel, Martinus Nijhoff, Dr W. Junk and MTP Press.

Printed on acid-free paper

TABLE OF CONTENTS

Preface

The NATO Advanced Research Workshop, and this book of proceedings, were made possible by a generous grant from the NATO Scientific Affairs Directorate, and generous support of the Scientific and Technical Research Council of Turkey (TÜBİTAK). In addition to the NATO Science Committee, we are particularly grateful to Dr. Jean-Marie Cadiou, Assistant Secretary General of NATO for Scientific and Environmental Affairs, for his encouragement, to Dr. Alain Jubier, Director of the Priority Area on Human Resources of the NATO Scientific and Environmental Affairs Division, for his guidance and advice, and to Dr. Paul Rambaut, Deputy Assistant Secretary General of NATO for Scientific and Environmental Affairs, for his personal participation in the Workshop.

The Organizing Committee of the Workshop consisted of Dr. Zhorev Alferov of Russia, Dr. George Bugliarello of the U.S., Dr. Namik K. Pak of Turkey and Dr. John Moore of the U.S. In Turkey, the Workshop was co-chaired by Dr. Pak and Dr. Moore. Dr. Pak also chaired the local Organizing Committee and provided generous and invaluable assistance to the Workshop personally and through the Scientific and Technical Research Council of Turkey.

A detailed program of the symposium is contained in Appendix 1 and a list of participants in Appendix 2.

Dr. Bugliarello, the member of the organizing committee who, with Dr. Pak, conceived the idea of the Workshop and proposed it to NATO and worked at its implementation, could not attend the Workshop because of illness, but assumed the main responsibility for editing these proceedings. In this, he had the invaluable assistance of his executive assistant Rose Emma, of Marcia Hawthorne, of his wife Virginia, and of his son David.

Introduction

1. THE RATIONALE FOR THE WORKSHOP

With the subsiding of the Cold War, the countries of the NATO alliance and those of the former Soviet block ("Cooperation Partners" or CP countries) face, in various degrees, two major technological challenges:

- how to convert military-oriented industries to the needs of a civilian economy;
- how to more effectively transfer technology across the frontiers of the former Cold War.

Both challenges are extremely complex. They involve, on the one hand, the need for the CP countries to build a new technological infrastructure suitable to the growth of a civilian economy, open to opportunities for technological investment from abroad, and to exchanges of technological expertise. On the other hand, the challenges require a much better understanding, by traditional market economy countries, of the situation in the CP countries and of what needs to be done to activate the East-West two-way flow of technological trade and opportunities. That flow offers to the participants from both sides considerable benefits and the hope of greater international stability.

The opportunities for both sides stem in large measure from the great richness in natural resources of most former Soviet Union countries, from the high level of technical and scientific education and skills of the potential partners from both sides and from the long experience that the market economy countries of the West have acquired in the commercialization of technologies.

An absolutely essential ingredient to transform these promises into reality is the presence, on both sides, of well-trained personnel, capable of managing the process of technology transfer in all of its complexity, and knowledgeable of the practices and potentials of the countries and institutions to and from which the transfers occur. The practices must encompass not only technical and scientific aspects, but also legal (e.g., intellectual property provisions), financial, economic, social and educational ones,

To help understand and respond to these challenges, an Advanced Research Workshop (ARW) was convened in Ankara, on July 18 - 21, 1994, with the joint sponsorship of NATO and the Scientific and technical Research Council of Turkey. The Workshop brought together a select group of leading scientists, engineers, managers and government officials with experience in technology transfer and technology policy from market economy countries, and from the Cooperating Partners.

The Workshop had four specific goals:

1. Identify key issues involved in preparing personnel in the CP countries for a more effective technology transfer to and from market economy countries, as well as within the CP countries themselves.
2. Identify corresponding needs in market economy countries with regard to transfer to and from CP countries and discuss mechanisms of proven usefulness in the market economy countries.
3. Identify priority actions required to respond to the issues singled out and suggest appropriate strategies and mechanisms for implementation.
4. Assemble, in book form, a précis of the proceedings of the Workshop, for wider diffusion in CP and market economy countries.

This book, edited by four members of the Organizing Committee of the Workshop of the Workshop - Z.I. Alferov (Russia), G. Bugliarello (U.S.), J. Moore (U.S.) and N.K. Pak (Turkey) - is the result of the Workshop. The book is organized in four parts. The first contains an introduction, opening remarks by N.K Pak who chaired the local organizing committee, and a summary of the Workshop's key findings.

The second part of the book (Chapters 1 to 3) contains a set of general background papers addressing the socio-technology of technology transfer, which encompasses prominently the question of personnel and leadership (G. Bugliarello), the legal framework within which a modern market economy operates (P. Newman and R.M. Sherwood), and a panorama of the specific legal issues involved in the protection and fostering of intellectual property V. DiCataldo, who unfortunately could not attend the workshop).

The third part (Chapters 4 to 11) is a set of pertinent issues as viewed by representatives of the Cooperation Partner countries, starting with a view of the current situation in Russia, by Z.I. Alferov. Another view from Russia is presented by M.V. Bratersky, a view from Siberia from J.P. Poholkov, and again a view from Russia by S.A. Arzhakov. These views are followed by several contributions from representatives from other CP Countries, arranged alphabetically by country. Included in this group is also a contribution by S. Raduscvic of the United Kingdom, addressing the technology transfer problems encountered by

Eastern European firms - problems that are relevant to the theme of the Workshop.

Lastly, the fourth part of the book (Chapters 12 to 19) contains accounts of experiences in several market economy countries. It starts with a paper by M. Macioti of the European Community, followed by a series of papers, arranged again alphabetically by country, recounting experiences in Finland (J. Kuusi), the Netherlands (W.A. deJong), Sweden (H.G. Forsberg), Turkey (N.K. Pak) and the United States (J. Moore, P.G. Katona and R.H. Rines). The paper by Dr. Katona deals with the spreading in the U.S. of a specific new technology (bioengineering).

The Advanced Research Workshop involved not only presentation of papers, but also in-depth discussion among the participants (listed in the Appendix). The results of those discussions are incorporated in the Summary Report in the Introduction.

The editors hope that this book will help accelerate the process of East-West technology transfer, as well as the process of industrial transformation from military to civilian economies. Both processes are urgent for a variety of reasons, foremost among them the fact that the economies of many countries of the former Soviet block are experiencing serious economic distress, and are thus in need of drastically accelerating their participation in the global economy, for which they are ill-prepared. In 1993, among former Soviet block countries, only Turkmenistan had a positive increase in its Gross Domestic Product (GDP) with respect to the year before (due largely to gas exports), while all the other countries had severe decreases in their GDP figure. Likewise, in 1993 nine of the 15 former Soviet republics had annual rates of inflation exceeding 1,000 percent.

It is clear that the transition to a market economy and the conversion from military to civilian economy are going to be very difficult steps for all the former Soviet block countries. However, it must be realized that today's market economies took a long time to develop into what they are, and that many of them too are facing - particularly the United States - major problems in the conversion of military industry to civilian purposes. The former Soviet block countries, however, have many positive elements that should bode well for their future in terms of technology transfer and economic conversion. Not only do many of them possess major natural resources, but also, almost universally, they possess a strong education in the sciences and engineering. What is now needed is to orient the results of that education and the thinking of the sectors that have the responsibility to direct the economy and transfer technologies, toward the creation of the new knowledge that will enable these countries to join the global marketplace, and to take full advantage of their resources.

2. WORKSHOP'S MAIN CONCLUSIONS

Through formal presentations and informal discussion, the Workshop focused on the requirements and opportunities for technology transfer between NATO countries and Cooperation Partner (CP) countries. It was recognized at the outset that human resources for technology development are abundant in the CP countries. Science and technology in general have been highly advanced in many parts of the former Soviet Union. However, because of its partial isolation in the past, technological development took a somewhat different path than in the NATO countries. Thus, there is a basis for mutual gains from technology exchange. However, many problems stand in the way of realizing that potential.

Problems

The first part of the Workshop discussions, following the formal presentations, focused on the identification of problems that impede technological transfer or exchange between NATO members and CP countries. Participants agreed that technology transfer should be understood as a transfer not only of hardware and technical information but also of organizational and other non-technological capabilities (such as human resources, marketing, and financial management). The meeting emphasized the latter aspects since they are essential for a successful technology transfer and seem to be a key bottleneck in the technology transfer between CP countries and NATO countries. In addition, certain sociological and psychological impediments need to be considered. It was agreed that in the context of the Workshop a precise definition of technology transfer was not of crucial importance.

Several issues in the CP countries were identified which need to be addressed by NATO and other international organizations if technology transfer activities are to be successful. The main issues include:

R & D System. Certain capabilities are lacking in the R & D system and in industrial enterprises: marketing skills, management techniques, financial management and internal/external communication. Those in CP countries who will have responsibility for implementing new technologies need training in innovation and technology management, so as to learn to manage in a market environment.

Inter-Institutional Cooperation. Problems arise from the lack of cooperation among different institutions (government, research, industry) in CP countries. These problems stem from dramatically changed new conditions as well as from institutional divisions inherited from the past.

Communication. There is a clear need to improve communications between NATO members and CP countries. NATO members need to become aware of the technological capabilities in the CP countries (including, in particular, technologies available openly from the research institutes of the former military-industrial complex). In addition, means of regular communication - probably via computer networking, among others - are needed. Face-to-face meetings of appropriate individuals are especially important. Attention should be paid to improving the accessibility of relevant databases.

Lack of Experience. Problems come from the lack of experience in CP countries in international cooperation ventures. These countries need to be assisted in realizing possibilities for cooperation through better networking of people and information.

Mentality. Both NATO countries and CP countries need to develop a better reciprocal understanding of their outlook, needs and capabilities. Although the development of market economies in the CP countries creates a common ground for understanding, there remains much that requires better understanding on both sides regarding this development and its relation to technology transfer.

Expectations. Early efforts at technology transfer have been characterized by unrealistic expectations on both sides - NATO countries and CP countries. Successful technology transfer requires a foundation in realistic expectations regarding opportunities and responsibilities.

Legal Institutions. The legal basis for a market economy and technology transfer is being developed, albeit unevenly, in the CP countries. However, its implementation requires additional knowledge and training in the CP countries. Law practitioners and government in those countries also need better knowledge and understanding of Western law. Intellectual property law is especially important.

Standards and Regulations. The exploitation of new technologies must ultimately occur through the development and marketing of new products. This requires that the products conform to international standards and comply with regulations in desired markets. Thus the development of standards and regulations in conformance with those of target countries is needed. Quality assurance is a necessary part of manufacturing and requires attention as well.

On the other hand, the Workshop participants agreed that the problems of production know-how, of the absence of some hardware technologies and of research competence are comparatively less important.

Principles to Guide Cooperation in Technology Transfer

A second part of the Workshop discussions endeavored to identify some general principles to guide the cooperation in technology transfer between NATO and CP countries. The most important principles identified include:

1. Technology transfer should be understood and implemented as a two-way transfer of skills and technologies.
2. Networking requires promotion. By networking it is meant the application projects that straddle institutional boundaries and in fact serve as catalysts in bridging the existing gaps between academies, universities, industrial firms and government.
3. In all cases, the transfer of complementary capabilities (organization, management, marketing and finance) should be included along with any other technology that is transferred.
4. The emphasis in technology transfer is commonly on advanced technology. However, it is important not to overlook the value of medium technology. In all cases, the domestic R &D communities should be actively involved.

Suggestions for Improving the Process

Next, in conformance with the principles above, the Workshop suggested several areas for cooperation in technology transfer between NATO countries and CPA countries:

1. Training. Training in the marketing of R & D based products and services on domestic and foreign markets should be considered. Training programs to assist CP managers in understanding and creating legal systems compatible with systems elsewhere are desirable. The combining of business oriented training (especially with regard to entrepreneurship) with engineering or technical education appears desirable. Where possible, existing training programs (such as the EBRD program in Siberia) should be utilized to provide such training.

Some large R & D institutes in a number of CP countries are in a difficult situation where they must restructure, change their profiles and attain a new balance among research, services and production. An essential component of the restructuring process is a significant change in attitudes and understanding of R & D managers.

Assistance in project management, restructuring of R & D, and R & D marketing are seen as important requirements. Training programs on these subjects should be designed for top level executives as well as for middle managers. As an example, a suitable subject would be assistance in managing complex projects on subjects such as environment, or remote sensing.

2. Communication. One approach to addressing the repeatedly stressed need for improved communication is the creation of a center that would provide information about available technologies and technical capabilities in the CP countries. This information would be furnished by the CP countries (the Ioffe Institute's compilation in Russia was cited as an example). The center should be prepared to provide this information in printed form and electronically to as wide an audience as possible. Further, it should advertise the availability of the information through various media and personal contacts.

In addition, a 'who's who' of scientists, engineers, and others engaged in technology development and transfer in the NATO and CP countries should be considered. Such a directory, if widely distributed, would provide much needed assistance to business and government personnel engaged in technology transfer.

3. Assistance to smaller firms (private and public) and entrepreneurs. Small and medium enterprises (SMEs) provide large fractions of new production and employment in many industrialized countries. Thus, it is highly desirable that SMEs and individual entrepreneurs be provided assistance in accessing sources of technology, both in CP and NATO countries. For example, infrastructural services such as innovation centers, cooperative projects, information services for small firms, etc., could be provided.

4. General recommendation. The concept of a joint technology transfer center should be explored. Such a center would facilitate technology transfer through a number of methods. For example, it could establish equitable 'rules of the game' for technology transfer. It could organize means of bringing interested parties together, for example through technology fairs featuring particular types of technology. The center should be non-governmental and non-profit. It could be established by an initial fund, perhaps contributed as a start-up grant, but would be expected ultimately to be self-supporting.

In this connection, a current proposal for a Montreal-Moscow center was discussed. It was suggested that this center be made accessible to countries of Western and Central Europe in addition to the CP and NAFTA (North American Free Trade Agreement) countries.

5. *Hard currency assistance.* Consideration should be given to international mechanisms that would address hard currency problems arising in connection with technology transfer programs of all kinds.

Suggestions for NATO Assistance

Lastly, it was suggested that NATO is uniquely positioned to further the development of the CP countries through technology transfer support programs. NATO Science Programs have an excellent reputation, enabling NATO to draw from a large group of international experts in many fields of science and technology.

The suggestions above indicate possible actions that are worth considering. Some actions might include:

1. Joint NATO-CP seminars related to the subjects mentioned above.
2. Focus groups meetings, in which parties from NATO and CP countries with common interests would be brought together. In general, there should be encouragement of mechanisms that contribute to direct, personal contacts.
3. Projects of the Science for Stability (SfS) type in which technology is transferred and the application of sound management principles is demonstrated. These projects should receive a high degree of priority. In this context, assistance to SMEs, existing or newly created, should be emphasized. It is desirable to combine the execution of R & D with assistance by experts from NATO countries, which is a key element leading to success in the current SfS program.
4. It may be strongly motivating to carry out large and highly visible projects which are of vital interest to CP countries. NATO could help in preparing proposals for such projects which would have to be funded from other sources.
5. Projects should fit into overall development strategy of a CP country. As in Science for Stability projects, foreign experts could assist in strategy development which would ultimately be decided by the CP country.

3. OPENING REMARKS BY NAMIK K. PAK (*Chairman, Local Organizing Committee*)

Science, being an international culture that reaches beyond the boundaries of countries, is crucial for the well-being of nations and for the further development of democracy. Organizations such as NATO, the European Community, and we, the scientists, are well aware of this and are seriously concerned about the present and future state of science and technology. We need to find realistic mechanisms of technology transfer, beneficial to all parties, focusing on sustaining the best in science and technology during the difficult times of transition for the Cooperation Partner countries.

The need for focusing on this issue originates from new radical organizational and economic transformations and the severe social problems and contradictions generated, after the restructuring processes in the science and technology systems in those countries. The large-scale dissemination of modern economic and social knowledge is very important, because rapid transition to the use of market forces without developing the necessary traditions and cultures generally introduces new obstacles in the way of solving problems. In the whirlwind of the transition to a market economy, heavy commercial pressure on science creates a danger of losing all the values that have been accumulated over many decades.

Political disintegration and/or economic collapses influence the structure of science and technology severely, especially where the science system is not tailored and structured for developing new products or new technologies that can be competitive in the world market. It is to be stressed however, that in such cases of crisis, the existence of a mature science and technology infrastructure is one of the most crucial elements for developing a self-sustaining, self-managing, and self-reliant national innovation system which could compete in the international markets. Since researchers are the most important assets of any nation's research enterprise, they represent a considerable long-term economic potential for their countries, if highly trained and equipped with intellectual and technical skills, and properly managed.

The main issue, then, is how to preserve these infrastructures and assets before they are lost altogether. The vital importance and responsibility of the international scientific community come on stage at this moment. Cooperative activities in all fields of science and technology, exchanges of scientists, promotion of networking among scientists and laboratories, improvement of libraries and information systems, as well as organization and implementation of joint projects become the utmost priority. No single society has been shown to be uniquely suited to a science culture; science is the common heritage of all mankind, which has been collectively created through the ages. It should be preserved with utmost care and affection, so that its benefits can be equally shared again by all mankind, regardless of geography.

This theme and the hope and faith we carry for the future of mankind brought us together from different parts of the world here to Turkey, which has always been the crossroads of civilizations and cultures. I do hope that our deliberations will produce fruitful ideas and suggest policies to help solve some of the problems occurring particularly in our part of the world, and will shed helpful light on other countries as well, in their way toward future progress.

1. TECHNOLOGY TRANSFER: A PARADIGM[1]

GEORGE BUGLIARELLO
Chancellor, Polytechnic University
Brooklyn, NY, USA

1. Introduction

Technology transfer began when, as we emerged as a distinct artifact-creating species, the knowledge of our inventions spread from neighbor to neighbor. Today, more than ever before, the future of nations, economies, industries, health-care, education and other key human activities is profoundly affected by the effectiveness of that process - a process that has become highly complex and at times spectacularly successful, at times replete with failures or disappointments. That complexity has led to questioning the very term "transfer," as conveying too simplified and linear a conception of the process [3].

In essence, technology transfer is a process shaped by the interaction of social and technical issues. Although this view of the process seldom has been explicitly stated and developed, some aspects of it have appeared for some time in the sociological literature, usually as critiques [6]. The emerging concept of national systems of innovation [10] stresses the influence of the socio-political system in which the innovation process is carried out in a nation. This helps underscore the importance of the socio-technological approach, which is, however, more general, as it applies not only at the national macro level but also at micro levels of the transfer, e.g., between industrial firms, however small, as well as to the transfer between disciplines.

Clearly, the process of technology transfer varies greatly with a number of factors such as the nature of the entities between which the transfer occurs, the kind of technology being transferred and the social climate under which the transfer occurs. Each of these factors involves in turn social and technological factors of considerable complexity - a complexity compounded when the transfer

[1]An earlier version of this paper was published as "Technology Transfer: A Socio-Technological Paradigm" in *Development and Transfer of Industrial Technology,* O.C.C. Lin and Y.C. Yang (Editors), Elsevier, Amsterdam, 1994 (by permission).

G. Bugliarello et al. (eds.), East-West Technology Transfer, 1-23.

occurs across national boundaries, as it is then affected by the characteristics of two or more national systems of innovation.

2. Definitions

Technology transfer is the process connecting two or more technological systems for the transfer of know-how, information, devices, etc.

To study the process, it is useful to view any technological system or entity (such as a factory, a design office, an airplane) as composed of two parts (Figure 1). One is the *techne*, i.e. the devices, both hard and software (meaning by the latter not only computer programs but also know-how, processes, procedures, design rules, etc.) created or used by the system. The other part of a technological system is the *social component* that produces the techne and operates it - the designers, manufacturers (be they of software or of hardware), operators, users,[2] as well as the financial systems that make the production of the techne possible. In addition to the primary interactions between the techne and its associated social components - such as between an automobile and its user or a milling machine and its operator - there are interactions within the purely social component of the system, i.e. among its users, designers, producers, etc. Furthermore, interactions connect with varying degrees of intensity a technological system with the rest of society. A technological system is an entity that is intrinsically shaped by scientific and engineering principles, whereas the rest of society is primarily the embodiment of other principles, complex social motivations, customs, laws and attitudes. From this intrinsic difference arise the issues, con-

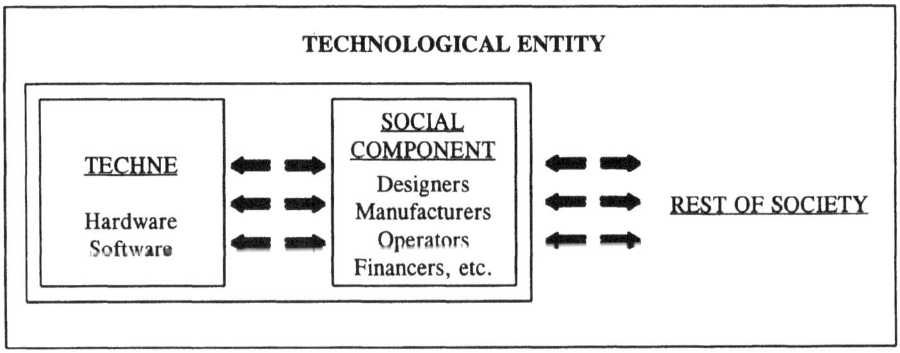

Figure 1. Interactions in a Technological Entity and Between It and the Rest of Society

[2]For many devices the user and the operator are the same.

flicts and opportunities associated with technology transfer. An example is how to transfer technology from a highly structured and technology-shaped military context to a civilian context which is much more loose and consumer-oriented.

In the technology transfer process the connections between the originating and the recipient entities involve a multitude of interactions among their components. Thus the operator of an entity which transfers technology to another entity, usually will be called to interact with the operator as well as the user of that entity, if the transfer is to be effective. For instance, the operators of a nuclear power reactor in Country A usually will be called to assist in instructing the operators of a similar power reactor being acquired by Country B. For a number of technologies, from nuclear power to biotechnology to aviation, also interactions among users or among agencies that represent them - including governments - are likely to become more and more influential. Examples are the interactions among airlines with a common interest in seeing developed a particular kind of aircraft, among health protection agencies with a common interest in the international diffusion of certain health procedures, or among departments of defense of allied countries with a common interest in acquiring a standardized weapon system.

This extremely simplified yet complex view of the transfer process becomes even more complicated if we consider that the interactions within each of the technological entities involved in the process are in turn the result of other socio-technological interactions. Thus, the designer of a technology to be transferred (more than one designer in the case of complex technes) is bound to interact with the designers of other technologies. In effect, the designer is in turn the user of a technology or techne - a computer, a piece of software, or of some other element of knowledge - produced by other technological entities.

To underscore the complexity involved, if the transfer occurs just between two entities, each respectively with ***m*** and ***n*** internal socio-technological elements (elements of the techne and of the social component) the total number of socio-technological interactions within and among two entities grows very rapidly with the number of elements involved (e.g., from 45 interactions among 10 elements to 4,950 among 100 elements). This is still, however, a very idealized view of the process, because it does not take into account the interactions within each of the ***m*** and ***n*** elements. This is the case, for example, when the producer of the technology is a factory with its own internal interactions, or when the designer is actually a team, again with its own internal interactions, or when a multiplicity of users leads to a multiplicity of interactions within the user community.

Luckily, not all of the socio-technological interactions have the same weight. According to the nature of the technology being transferred and to the goal of the transfer process, a number of them may be neglected, at least in first approximation, while other interactions may acquire an overwhelming significance. This is where technology transfer becomes an art as well as a science and requires a strong base of experience.

We need to note that technology transfer does not always occur between two specific entities. It may originate in one entity and be "broadcast," rather than targeted for a particular, single recipient. This, for example, was the case in the diffusion in Europe of printing and of silk manufacturing. In this century and particularly in its second half, an increasing world consciousness is impacting a growing number of technology transfer initiatives of this kind, leading to the creation of international not-for-profit agencies, such as UNDP. It also leads to some countries' decision to contribute to the advancement of technology for the whole world through the diffusion of science advances, through contributions to mega-science projects of global impact, such as the genome project, through collaboration on the development of fundamental technologies at a precompetitive level, or through technological efforts aimed at eliminating global shortages (e.g. the green revolution).

3. Mechanisms and Environments

Technology transfer, as a socio-technological interaction between two or more entities, requires appropriate mechanisms and is affected by the characteristics of the entities involved and the social environment in which it occurs (Figure 2).

The kinds of entities among which the transfer occurs are typically industry, government and the university. Often, the entity that is the source of the technology is of a different kind than the recipient entity. Thus, a university may transfer knowledge to industry or industry a piece of equipment to a university. The nature of the transfer differs markedly according to the entities that relate to each other in the process, as each has its own distinct socio-technological characteristics. For instancc, the fact that traditional industry and government tend to be hierarchical is a frequent source of frustration in their interactions with the university, which is not. The motivations of different entities may also vary, and even more so those of their myriad of sub-entities-departments, divisions, etc. As a result, the nature of the university-industry transfer process is different from

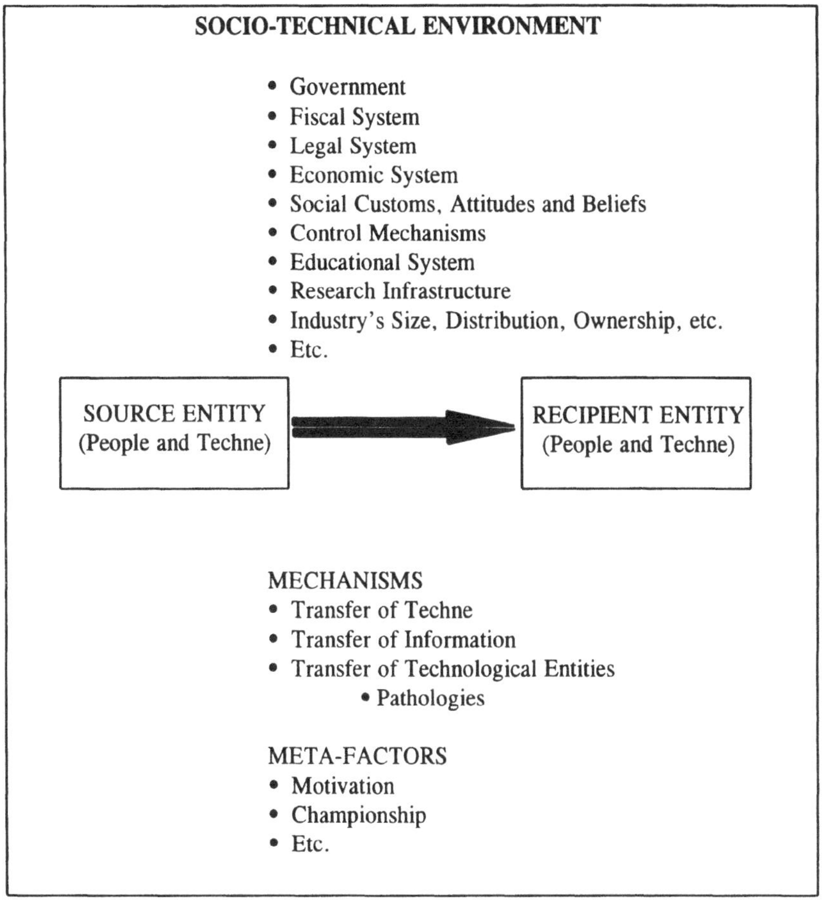

Figure 2. Components of the Technology Transfer Process

that between universities or between industries or between industry and government.

The transfer of technologies that occurs between sectors of the technological system of a given country is of importance to industrialized and developing countries alike. In either case, one hopes that a more technologically advanced sector will help transforming less advanced sectors. For example, in the U.S., the National Aerospace Plane research effort has been estimated as potentially benefiting some 4,000 leading technologies, such as automotive engine technology by weight reductions made possible by titanium aluminide valves [14]. Another example of potentially significant technology transfer from the military to the civilian sector in the U.S. is the Los Alamos light detection and ranging system for detecting gases in the atmosphere [1]. The system owes its existence to the Gulf War and could now be of significant service in the civilian economy. In the countries that were involved in the Cold War these kinds of transfer and the support of defense conversion are becoming an item of high socio-economic priority. But the transfers require the establishment of appropriate mechanisms - a difficult expertise. Many attempts to transfer fail not because of inadequacies of the techne, but because of inadequate mechanisms of commercialization and diffusion - again a socio-technological issue. Although at this moment there is more emphasis on the transfer of technology from the military to the civilian sector, historically considerable transfer of technology has occurred in the opposite direction also, from the civilian to the military sector. Dual-use technologies - technologies that can be of use to both sectors - represent an attempt, not always successful for a number of reasons, many of them again socio-technological, to bypass the economic inefficiencies associated with single-purpose technologies and to simplify the problem of technology transfer between the two sectors.

MECHANISMS

The mechanisms for technology transfer between two entities are all, intrinsically, socio-technological. The simplest, most straightforward mechanism is the **direct transfer of techne** (hardware and software) - by purchasing, by retro-engineering, or by other activities, legal or illegal. The mechanism has the advantage of immediacy and involves relatively few socio-technological complexities, other than how the decisions are reached to pursue it, and the possible resistance to change in the recipient entity. It is often the simplest stage of a technology transfer strategy, but it becomes counterproductive if the transfer process stops there, without generating a new attitude toward innovation and without triggering other forms of technological development.

More complex are mechanisms involving the **transfer of information**[3] in its many forms - students studying abroad, transfer of know-how and expert systems, exchange of expertise (a mechanism particularly effective, for instance, in universities through partnerships, sabbaticals and joint research projects), training programs, licensing, partnerships, indeed even espionage, etc. A particularly effective form of transfer of information - especially of the results of basic research - is the establishment of "windows," that is of observatories around entities that generate information, such as universities or research laboratories. In

[3]Transfers of techne, such as of machinery or of computer programs, are, of course also transfers of information, but it is convenient here to separate these two kinds of transfers.

the U.S., for example, universities have become an important source of patents, which increased from some 600 in 1986 to over 1300 in 1991 [16]. The perception that observatories of foreign industry around U.S. universities take unfair advantage of the basic investment by the taxpayers in such institutions has become a hot and complex issue that has pitted, at times, university managements looking for new sources of revenue against government and indigenous industry. Part of the issue stems from the perceived lack of symmetry or reciprocity among the countries involved. However, that lack of symmetry is also due to the limited interest and, consequently, lower efficiency of U.S. industry - in contrast to European or Japanese industry - in harvesting innovations from abroad, as evidenced by large imbalances in the exchange of technical and scientific personnel and by the relatively very limited U.S. purchase of patent and licenses from

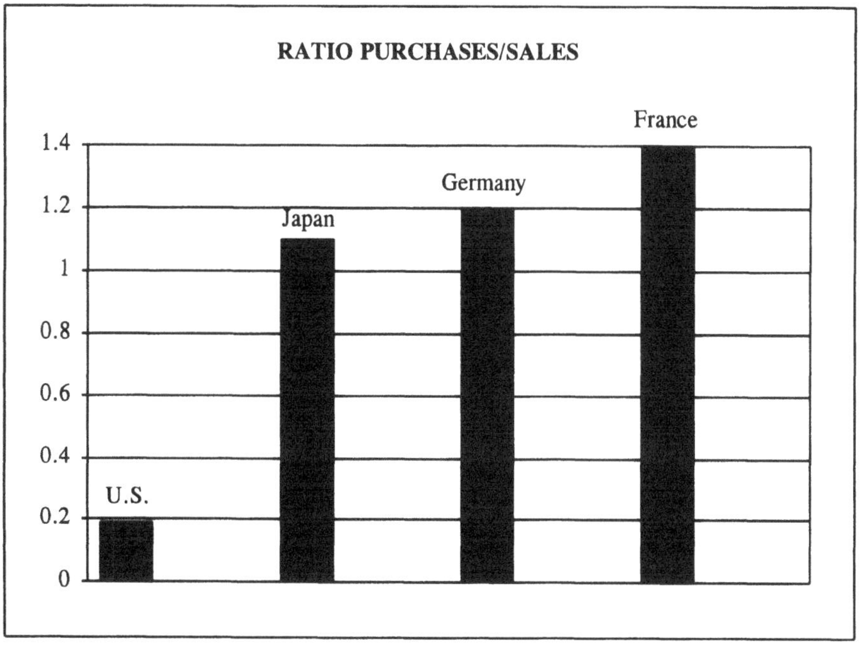

Figure 3. Patents and Licenses. Ratio of Purchases/Sales From/To Other Countries

abroad (Figure 3). This is, again, a complex socio-technological question with deep roots in the history and sociology of the country.

Mechanisms for transferring information include venture capital partnerships. For instance, participation by a country in a selective program of investments in another country that is a rich source of technology gives the investing country an inside track in following technological developments in the other country. However, it is often difficult to convince a country that seeks to upgrade its technology by attracting investments from abroad, that an investment in technological venture capital partnerships abroad helps in turn attracting technological investments from abroad.

Research parks and university-industry parks are yet another effective and relatively recent mechanism of technology transfer, primarily through information - through research and training interactions. They present a number of socio-technological challenges in their creation, ranging from the political will and understanding of local governments, to the assemblage of a critical mass of participants, the attitude of the surrounding community that often must cede a portion of its territory to the park and accept the relocation of part of its residents, the financing of the enterprise and the creating of an experienced organization to carry out the development (often through public-private-university partnerships), to the triggering of supporting elements of the community infrastructure (housing, shops, hotels, schools, public services, etc.) and the overcoming of barriers to an effective university-industry interaction. How these challenges are met has made the difference between successful and unsuccessful parks. Examples of the latter are many, because of simplistic views of the issues or the lack of socio-technological skills. The very complexity of the challenges often requires long lead times before a park can be built and made to function. For instance, Metrotech, a university-industry park created by Polytechnic University in New York City (Brooklyn) and currently, with over 17,000 industry jobs, the largest *urban* park in the U.S. [12; 4], required 14 years between initial conception and the first breaking of the ground - a telling example of the weight of social factors in a technology transfer enterprise.

Always within this category of mechanisms, the infrastructure represented by institutions such as ITRI in Taiwan, the Netherlands Organization for Applied Scientific Research (TNO), the National Institute for Science and Technology (NIST) in the United States, the Fraunhofer Institutes in Germany or the Faraday Institutes in the United Kingdom plays a significant part in technology transfer in those countries. For instance, the Fraunhofer Institutes, by receiving a substantial portion of their funding from industry and by training their students in part in an industrial environment and in part in an academic one, help lower the traditional barriers between academe and industry, facilitating the transfer of knowledge and technology between the two.

Among the many ad-hoc institutions involved in international transfer, the experiences, by way of example, of the Organization for Economic Cooperation and Development (OECD) in Paris provide many illustrations of the significance of socio-technological factors. Its national science and technology policy reviews are a powerful instrument of technology transfer by assessing critically and constructively through international experts a nation's science and technology policies [11] in the broad context discussed in this paper. However, the reviews are a mechanism usually available only to OECD countries.

A third category of mechanisms for the transfer of technology is the **transfer of entire technological entities** - e.g., the acquisition by entity *B* of a company or part of a company from entity *A*. This, like the previous kind of mechanism - the direct transfer of techne and the transfer of information - involves a large number of socio-technological issues that cannot be discussed within the confines of this paper. It is important, however, to underscore one such issue that often plagues transfer - namely the classic conflict between locating the technological entity being transferred in an area devoid of much economic development, so as to trigger that development, and the alternative of locating the unit in a more developed area, where it can synergize with other industries and technologies. The latter approach accelerates transfer and diffusion of new technologies; the former handicaps it, but is often pursued for social or political reasons.

All transfer mechanisms can be profoundly affected by a number of what can be called "**socio-technological pathologies**," such as the "not invented here" syndrome ("NIH"), the possessiveness about "turf," the egos of the parties involved, the strong obstacles usually encountered by interdisciplinary thrusts, or the failures of "technology push" approaches that do not take into sufficient account the nature of the market (as often experienced, for instance, in the context of economy conversions). Another set of pathologies has to do with organizational issues, the involvement of the wrong organizations, both in the originator and the recipient of the transfer process, to carry out the transfer and diffuse its results. At times, for instance, countries interacting with the U.S. look at U.S. government agencies as the main protagonist of the transfer process, rather than at private industry which in many cases has the real power to transfer, albeit within a framework of government regulations.

Although there are potential remedies for all of these pathologies, it is imperative for the management of the transfer process and for the setting of pertinent science policies that the pathologies constantly be kept in mind, as they often are major causes of failure of the process.

Among the pathologies, perhaps the most serious and insidious one, because it does not impede the process but stems from the consequences of its success, is associated with the fact that technology transfer not always has been beneficial. For instance, at the village level in many highly undeveloped countries, some pervasive new technology such as the internal combustion engine has at times proven counterproductive, by displacing more self-reliant, less technology intensive processes. The villages can become catastrophically affected by fluctuations in worldwide industrial systems, such as those associated with changes in oil costs, or by the breakdown of economies like that of the former Soviet Union that used to supply them with inexpensive machinery and technological assistance. An exasperated local expert of technology transfer at the village level in India went as far as stating that "all technology that comes from the North is neither superior, nor relevant, nor cost effective" [13].

To overcome pathologies of this kind, technology transfer activities - particularly those of global impact - need to be guided by a broader sense of ethics about the impacts that the transfer can have on societies and cultures. Unfortunately, that sense is far from being sufficiently developed and from providing guidance in the inevitable conflicts that arise with more narrowly motivated transfer activities. To compound the problem, even philanthropically-motivated technology transfer activities are not exempt from the typical socio-technological issues and pathologies of the transfer process. On the contrary, these are often exacerbated, e.g. when *pro bono* assistance to a developing country masks a different national purpose or is plagued by intercine struggles in the bureaucracies of both the transferring and the recipient entities.

ENVIRONMENTS

Technology transfer occurs not in a vacuum but in a very complex socio-technological environment, both in the transferring and the receiving entity, that can have an immense impact on the success of the process. It is hardly possible to overstate the importance of the nature, structure and practices of government, the legal and economic systems, the fiscal and educational systems, or the importance of social customs, attitudes and beliefs.

Thus, whether a **government** is a democracy or totalitarian, whether its power resides in parliaments or in a presidential leader, whether it is militaristic or trade-minded, whether it condones graft, whether it is stable, whether it is well organized and competent, etc., are fundamental aspects that can accelerate or decelerate the process. It is particularly important that a government be realistic in terms of what it expects from technology transfer and that it be able to asses its social and technological impacts. A government aspect of most immediate impact is the **fiscal system** - the treatment of innovation, the taxation of imported products, the specific facilitation of technology transfer activities, etc. It is, of course, important to recognize that a government is not monolithic. Different currents within the government, with different motivations, must be taken into account, as their shifts in power and orientation with time can radically change the context of the transfer process.

The way the **legal systems** of both the transferring and the recipient entity operate - their guiding principles, the protection they afford, how they penalize and facilitate - are of obvious significance. Among the myriad of issues involved, two of the growing importance are tort liability and intellectual property. The liabilities incurred by the entities involved in the transfer process vary substantially across legal systems, and can represent a formidable obstacle. For instance, in the United States, tort liability is by far the heaviest in the world - over 2,5% of the Gross National Product. This represents a burden on manufacturers, products and providers of service estimated to be five times that in the United Kingdom and seven times that in Japan [15]. Certification procedures are not necessarily more onerous in the U.S., but when they are they have favored the transfer of certain technologies abroad - e.g., in the pharmaceutical and health care fields, Even more important is the issue of the protection of intellectual property rights, which in the case of transfer between nations can become a significant irritant in international relations. Inadequate patent protection hampers transfer, in some industries more than others [8]. On the other hand, often insufficiently focused upon is the need for a recipient entity to have legal manpower adequately trained in patent and copyright law, to learn to protect and manage the intellectual property associated with the transfer activities.

Whether one deals with an **economic system** that encourages free initiative, or with a directed economy, or, as more often is the case, with a system between these two extremes, again influences the way the transfer process can be carried out. This was very obvious in the former Soviet Union, where the directed economy hampered a great deal of commercial technology transfer. Also significant is whether the system is more present- or future-oriented (as indicted e.g. by different rates of savings) and whether it encourages cooperation or competition. It is important to note that none of these different characteristics is necessarily more or less favorable to technology (e.g., the Soviet Union was very efficient in the acquisition of foreign military know-how). However, consciousness of the differences and the ability to tailor a technology transfer process to the different economic systems of the originator and the recipient are essential to avoid failure. In some respects, one such failure is protectionism, if viewed as the antithesis of technology transfer. Protectionism is a complex economic, political and technological issue. If, on the one hand, it lessens the stimulus of competition, on the other, it may foster considerable creativity in technology. A prime historical example is Japan, which, particularly in its early stages of modern development, followed a policy of limited imports and favored as much as possible the creation of a strong indigenous technological industrial capability stimulated by prototypes imported from abroad. That capability has now enabled Japan to move successfully toward the creation of totally new products.

An even greater but often not sufficiently stressed factor in technological transfer are **social customs, attitudes, and beliefs** - whether, again, the environment in which the technology transfer occurs is more present- or-future-oriented, whether it is more oriented toward cooperation or competition, whether it encourages entrepreneurship (the lack of an adequate number of well prepared entrepreneurs being often a major obstacle to the spread of innovation), whether it is characterized by a culture that is more humanistic or scientific-oriented, whether aspects of science and technology clash with religious beliefs, social customs or attitudes - e.g. toward the environment - and so on. A particularly difficult problem is the reluctance in some cultures to establish serious control mechanisms, including peer review, for assessing the effectiveness of the technology transfer process. Yet such mechanisms are essential if corrective actions are to be taken should the process falter. A not sufficiently used but effective mechanism for remedying the reluctance to peer review is to involve - gingerly - experts from other countries or entities.

The **education system**, both scholastic and industrial, is becoming more and more a crucial factor in facilitating or hampering technology transfer. A highly intelligent and well-trained work force greatly accelerates the adoption of new technologies, while a poorly trained one makes it much more difficult. A very limited knowledge of a common language also hampers the process. Conversely, in institutions like the Middle East Technical University in Turkey, adoption of English as the language of instructions cannot but encourage technology transfer. In a number of countries technology transfer is made more difficult by the absence of a well prepared force of skilled workers - mechanics, technicians, etc. - as well as by the too limited a production of engineers, often because of cumbersome curricula. This affects the ability to respond rapidly and flexibly to new technologies. Within an educational system, the separation of engineering and basic sciences as well as the politicization of education can have a serious negative impact. Such a situation in the former Soviet Union has been viewed as a significant contribution to the Chernobyl disaster [7].

The **research infrastructure**, of which the educational system can be a significant component, plays a major role in transfer, but a role that varies from country to country, as capabilities and orientation vary. Difficulties that often must be overcome in the transfer to a developing country are the isolation of many research institutions and the tendency to pursue research not appropriate to the immediately pressing problems of the country, which are perceived as less prestigious and less likely to produce international recognition. It is a major responsibility of countries that are sources of the technology to take a broad view of the transfer process, and provide encouragement and recognition for researchers in the recipient countries who focus their work on those countries' problems.

A problem hampering technology transfer to a number of former Soviet block countries and other countries that have followed their pattern is too exclusive and rigid a specialization of research institutions and production organizations. Several new technologies span diverse domains, such as multifunctional materials, or, looking ahead, intelligent materials - combinations of materials science and engineering with information science and technology (as well as, eventually, with the life sciences and bioengineering). Technology transfer cannot be effective for these new interdisciplinary fields unless different centers of research and production in the recipient entity can be integrated and made to act synergistically, overcoming "turf" possessiveness and the traditional sociological obstacles to interdisciplinary work.

Lastly, but of extreme importance in characterizing the socio-technological environment, are the **size distribution, ownership, thrust, and capabilities of industry** in the recipient entity (country, region, etc.). Typically, large companies, whether public or private, have the means within themselves to organize a technology transfer program respondent to their needs, although even here the influence of socio-technological factors, such as management self-interest or work force attitudes, cannot be over looked. On the other hand, very small companies - often no more than family concerns - seldom have the ability to take advantage of technology transfer, except in its simplest forms. It is primarily in the medium or medium-small size range that major economic advances arise from the transfer process, but also where sustained government assistance is usually needed, to facilitate the transfer and to diffuse and sustain it, through assistance centers, the development and enforcement of standards and quality approaches, the provision of capital, etc.

Finally, transfer of technology to a developing country or region becomes particularly difficult when in the recipient this middle sector is very small - as is the case of a country like Indonesia or a region like southern Italy - but also when it is embedded in a different industrial ecology than the transferring country. For instance, in the U.S., small and medium companies are a major source of innovation, but in many other countries they depend on the larger companies as sources of advanced technology and innovation.

META-FACTORS

Behind these more explicit mechanisms and factors, there are "meta-factors," such as motivation and championship, which can be either explicit or hidden and vary significantly according to the nature of the entities involved in the transfer process. It is imperative that these meta-factors be correctly understood. For instance, a government's motivation in engaging in technology transfer may be economic development, political expediency, or the enhancement of military strength. A frequent source of concern and friction between originator and recipient occurs when the motivation is disguised, e.g. when economic development is used to mask a military purpose, or vice-versa (such as the accusation some time ago by the U.S. government that Israel violated technology transfer agreement by shipping Patriot missiles to China).

Just as for government, the motivation of industry can be quite varied also - e.g. growth, or the desire to eliminate a competitive threat - with different motivations leading to different technology transfer strategies.

Motivation and championship are perhaps the single most powerful meta-factor of technology transfer. They are exemplified by some of the historic examples in Table 1 and, most often, they spell the difference between success and failure.

SOCIO-TECHNOLOGICAL TOOLS

A conceptually simple set of tools can help focusing on the socio-technological paradigm for technology transfer, but it is still far from being utilized in present practice:

A **socio-technological audit**, to identify systematically the most sensitive points of the process - both in the originating and the receiving entity, in the transfer mechanisms, as well as in the socio-technological environment of the process. The audit should be useful whatever the scale of the transfer process -

the macroscale between countries, or the microscale, at the extreme, between small organizations. To be effective, it needs to be performed with an open mind, and by persons or organizations removed from possible conflicts of interest.

A **socio-technological forecast**, to attempt to chart the future evolution and consequences of technology transfer as well as changes in its socio-technological environment, using, where appropriate, modeling, simulations and extensive data bases, in addition to the audit as a starting point.

A **socio-technological assessment**, to periodically review the progress toward the transfer's goals. Although a number of countries as well as large industries involved in the transfer process have instruments of performing some or all of these tasks (e.g., the U.S. Congressional Office of Technology Assessment), many more do not and are at greater risk of failure or inefficiency of the process.

4. Historical Examples

Historical examples of technology transfer are myriads. Unfortunately, ignorance and ethnocentrism often make us forget the variety of transfer that have criss-crossed the surface of the globe leading to the creation and applications of today's science and technology [5]. The few examples shown on Table 1 underscore the diversity of mechanisms, motivations and factors of success. It is worth noting that:

1) Different methods have been successful in different political regimes. Thus, under Peter the Great, a mixture of coercion and incentives brought to Russia new technologies, from shipbuilding to military organization. The sources of those technologies were the rest of Europe and China. Conversely, the decline of Ottoman power was accelerated by a failure of technology transfer in the XVIII and early XIX century (e.g. the rulers' imposed ban on books from the West). The United States is a very successful example of technology transfer in a democratic climate. Starting with the transfer of European knowledge brought by early settlers and by later immigrants, followed by a wave of European investments, of imports of advanced European technologies and of Americans studying abroad, the country progressed from being the recipient of technology transfer to becoming the largest global source of new technologies.

2) Geopolitical and military necessity have been throughout history major motivations for technology transfer. When coupled with favorable cultural

TABLE 1. Some Historical Examples of Technology Transfer

EXAMPLE	TECHNOLOGY TRANSFER	MOTIVATION: FACTORS OF SUCCESS
Roman Naval Fleet (260 B.C.)	Land fighting techniques to sea combat	Military necessity
European silk-making (VI Century)	Chinese silk-making	Commercial demand; smuggling
Orange grove irrigation in Southern Europe (VIII Century and beyond)	Arab irrigation techniques	Result of military conquest; improved techniques
Printing after 1453	Gutenberg's movable type printing press	Demand by scholars and general public
Russian developments under Peter the Great (XVIII Century)	Western European civil and military technologies	Ruler's ambition and championship; coercion, incentives
French Encyclopedie (XVIII Century)	Broad knowledge of science and technology	Social and economic improvement; literacy and social unrest
Japan after 1853	Western civil and military technologies	Geopolitical necessity
American urban water supply (Second half of XIX Century)	Water supply networks, pumps, etc.	Public Health: demands of urban concentration
U.S. Agriculture (XX Century)	Effective agricultural practices and innovations	Economic and social advancement: Agricultural Experiment Stations and university extensions
Italy's Vespa motor scooter (after WWII)	Small preheating engines for military airplanes	Military to civilian conversion; unfilled market niche
Nuclear technology in former Soviet Union (after WWII)	Key concepts and designs from the U.S. and U.K.	Military necessity; espionage and ruler's ambition
Personal Computer (1980s)	IBM-invented concept to many competitors	IBM's failure to protect its technology
Noiseless submarine propellers in former Soviet Union (1980s)	Precision machining technology from the U.S.	Military necessity; illegal sale from U.S. ally

traits, such as industriousness and inventiveness, specific transfers can trigger a much broader process of technical creativity and industrial as well as cultural transformations, as happened in Japan since 1853 and particularly after the Meji restoration.

3) A major mechanism of technology transfer has been military conquest, as shown in the case of transfer to southern Europe of Arab irrigation technologies. As another example, the Mongols were the bridge for much of the transfer of Chinese technology to Europe.

4) Espionage and smuggling - both military and industrial - also have been historically very significant mechanisms of technology transfer. They led to silk manufacturing in Europe and silent Soviet submarines. However, in the long run, they may become such an irritant as to block more effective and ethical means of transfer.

5) Some of the most effective examples of technology transfer have occurred and continue to occur in medicine and in public health, where, particularly in literate and well-to-do societies, popular demand and the self-interest of the ultimate users tend to press for a rapid transfer (in the form of information and artifacts such as drugs and devices) and to overcome bureaucratic impediments (at times imprudently, however, as in some dubious AIDS therapies). Similarly, commercial advantage has been a key motivating factor in the transfer of technologies such as silk making, the VCR or the personal computer.

6) Also very effective, in general, has been the transfer of knowledge among universities and research laboratories, which, particularly in a developing country, may become far more knowledgeable of scientific and engineering advances than the surrounding community, including industry. The diffusion of information from these institutions, however, is often hampered by the barriers that surround them, in perception or in reality.

Among the myriads of other examples of technology transfer not shown in the table, the one currently underway in China is historically one of the largest. It exhibits unique socio-technological complexities because of the coexistence of an authoritarian regime, a semiliberal market economy, and a highly enterprising and educated population with a cultural background that has been the foundation of success of Taiwan, Singapore and Hong Kong. Another contemporary example of great socio-technological complexity is the upgrading of the technological capability of the new German states in the East through an influx of technical and management skills from the rest of Germany. These examples also serve to demonstrate that the transfer is not always a one-way street, as, in the process, some significant technological skills are also being transferred in the reverse direction - from China and from the former East Germany.

5. Strategies

The strategies that guide decisions about technology transfer - why to transfer, what to transfer, how to transfer, when to transfer - are part of the broader context of science and technology policies, both in the originator and in the recipient entities. The strategies are, of course, very complex when the entities involved are countries, but they are not trivial in the case of other entities, e.g. large global or high tech companies.

The progression from prototype reproduction to total new product technology that has been so single-mindedly and successfully pursued in the last century and a half in Japan characterizes a strategy of technology transfer adopted or hoped-for by some developing countries. It was followed to some extent by the United States in its formative years, although without much government intervention. The strategy is a difficult one, as it requires a highly skilled work force, an extraordinary ability to do reverse engineering and, initially, engineers and technicians trained abroad or by teachers from abroad. To be feasible, often it also demands protectionism for fledgling new industries and products - a negative in terms of international relations. Yet, when successful, the results can be spectacular. This was the case with the Japanese victory in the 1904-05 war with Russia. The war showed how rapidly and effectively if it had been possible for Japan, within fifty years of its opening to the West, to build modern armaments based on Western prototypes, often improving them.

Another not mutually exclusive strategic progression followed by many countries is to focus at first on the sales of products from abroad (in which case the major technology transfer occurs between the technology of the provider and the operators and users of the recipient). This is followed by the development of the ability to produce components of varying degrees of technical sophistication for the original producers of the technological products being imported. The last stage in the progression is integration, that is the ability to reverse the situation and create new products that may rely in turn on components from other countries.

The advantages of this approach are graduality and reduction of risk. It is often the only possible avenue of development, when the human resources need to be developed and capital resources are not available. On the other hand, it requires complex international agreements (e.g. to establish joint ventures) and it provides less control over the technology. There have been instances when, in order to gain access to a new foreign market, a producer has agreed to purchase some components from that market, but has kept the level of such purchasing low by changing the design of the product. The changes require new components to come, again, from the producer's country.

Often the strategic dilemma is whether to transfer technologies to upgrade a weak sector, or to reinforce an already strong sector (an easier strategy), or to create a totally new peak of excellence through a targeted national project (e.g. airplane building, participation in space projects, particle physics research). The latter is a tempting but costly strategy that makes international financing agencies like the World Bank nervous. However, from the socio-technological viewpoint, it may be an important approach to giving a recipient country a boost in confidence and pride.

"How to transfer" strategies obviously include decisions about mechanisms, in which, again, socio-technological considerations often must predominate over pure organizational logic. For instance, in mainland China, the establishment of some interdisciplinary management programs in universities, to be successful, required the creation of separate institutes [2].

The formulation of appropriate science and technology policies is the most difficult and central issue in technology transfer, as the policies must be based on all the factors discussed in this paper. Because of their socio-technological essence, the policies are as much an art as they are the result of prescribed models. They must judge the forces that will help or impede the transfer, and carefully modulate the process accordingly. Obviously, strategies will vary greatly from situation to situation. However, some of the most salient caveats to be taken into account formulating a strategy can be summarized as follows:

1. As one of the paramount factors of success, motivation must be clearly understood. Transfer fails or disappoints either the transferring or the recipient entity if the motivation is not clear to all the parties involved and mutually agreed upon.

2. Every socio-technological interaction involved in the transfer process is a potential source of difficulties if overlooked. Although we have gained sophistication in the last four decades of scrutiny of the process, this point is still far from fully appreciated, and the major source of failure.

3. As a corollary, failure is virtually assured if mechanism used in a given setting are uncritically applied to a different setting - e.g. one with a very different national system of innovation.

4. Conversely, a good understanding of the complex socio-technological interactions involved can produce results that exceed the expectations of the source or the recipient. Thus the United States was surprised by the ability of Japan to absorb electronic and quality control technology after World War II.

5. It is the joint responsibility of the transferring and the recipient entities to see to it that the transfer of technology, in responding to specific objectives of both entities, does not create problems that in a broader context make the transfer counterproductive. Such are the encouragement of the production of environmentally taxing products, or of technologies such as canned beverages or fast foods that absorb economic resources of an impoverished population without providing a comparable nutritional advantage, or the training of scientists or technicians who, finding limited opportunities for their newly learned skills, emigrate.

6. The mirror image of the transfer and diffusion of technology - and one of equally complex socio-technological nature - is the regression of ignorance. That regression, unfortunately, is not automatically or proportionally correlated with the introduction of new scientific and technological information, know-how and products. It often needs to be addressed first, before the transfer becomes feasible, by overcoming inertia, psychological defensiveness, cost of replacing obsolete practices and equipment and other factors. That a reservoir of ignorance can endure for a long time is dramatically underscored by the permanence of the AIDS epidemics in spite of clear knowledge of the causes and of the transmission of the disease.

7. Technology transfer is not always a one-way street. A good transfer strategy needs to explore and utilize what the recipient of the transfer has to offer. The great historic example of what was transferred from America to Europe at the time of the discoveries - mainly agricultural products - is also an example of a failure to take seriously many other indigenous products and technologies - such as herbal remedies or ecologically sound approaches - that only today are we beginning to appreciate in their importance.

6. Conclusion

The technological history of the second half of this century is one of enhanced importance of the technology transfer process. That process, coupled with intrinsically strong national capabilities, has led to a very rapid upgrading of the technological prowess of the European Community and of the nations of the Pacific

Rim. On the other hand, it has not worked for a number of nations in Africa, and has worked only in a lopsided way for several other nations.

The key to both the successes and failures of technology transfer is its socio-technological nature. It is a process that transcends technical consideration and operates across different cultures and systems with different receptivities and modes of receptivity about technology. The need for a much greater and more systematic focus on the multiple and complex interfaces between the technical and social factors of the process could only be briefly outlined within the confines of this paper. That focus, however, will be determinant for our ability to make technology transfer more predictably successful. A globally effective technology transfer is needed to address the problems of the gap between rich and poor countries, of environmental remediation, of the conversion from military to civilian technology, and of other threats to world stability, as well as to capture the opportunities for further human progress.

References

1. *Aviation Week and Space Technologies* (1992), Los Alamos Lidar research demonstrates military, civil uses, **December 7**, 57-58.

2. Baruch, J. (1993) *Verbal Communication*.

3. Bodde, D.L. (1993) On guns and butter: reflections on technology transfer from federal laboratories, *Technology In Society* **15**, 273-280.

4. Bugliarello, G. (1993) Metrotech: an urban university-industry park, *Journal of Urban Technology* **I-2**, 41-48.

5. Edwards, M. (1971) *The Travel of Ideas, Arts and Invention Between Asia and the Western World*, Taplinger, New York.

6. Goulet, D. (1977) *The Uncertain Promise*, IDOC/North America, New York.

7. Kapitza, S.P. (1993) Lessons of Chernobyl - the cultural causes of the meltdown, *Foreign Affairs* **Summer**, 7-11.

8. Mansfield, E. (1993) Unauthorized use of intellectual property effects on investment, in M.B. Wallerstein, M.E. Mogee and R.A. Schoen (eds), *Global Dimensions of Intellectual Property Rights in Science and Technology*, National Arcade Press, Washington, D.C.

9. NAE (National Academy of Engineering) (1993), *Mastering a New Role*, National Academy Press, Washington, D.C.

10. Niosi, J., Saviotti, P., Bertrand, B. and Crow, M. (1993), National systems of innovation: in search of a workable concept, *Technology In Society* **15**, 207-227.

11. OECD (Organization for Economic Cooperation and Development) (1992), *Reviews of National Science and Technology Policy (Italy)*, OECD, Paris.

12. Post, N. (1992) High technology grows in Brooklyn, *Engineering News Record* **December 16**, 25-28.

13. Roy, B. (1991) Ethics of technology transfer, *Engineering News Record* **December 16**, 932.

14. Scott, W.W. (1992) NASP spinoffs already making positive impact on U.S. industries, *Aviation Week and Space Technology* **July 27**, 54-55.

15. Spencer, L. (1992) The tort tax, *Forbes* **February 17**, 40-42.

16. Thayer, A.M. (1992) University technology moves to market via patenting, licensing, *Chemical and Engineering News* **August 24**, 17-20.

2. LEGAL FRAMEWORK OF THE INDUSTRIAL ECONOMY

Incentives for Technological Development — Judicial Systems and the Laws of Intellectual Property

PAULINE NEWMAN
Judge, United States Court of Appeals
for the Federal Circuit
*Washington, DC, USA**

and

ROBERT M. SHERWOOD
International Business Counselor
*Alexandria, VA, USA**

The economy of nations operates within a legal framework that governs commercial activity. The systems of law that implement this activity can sustain or, conversely, inhibit economic growth and development. Whether a nation's legal institutions are founded in the common law or the civil law tradition, economic growth requires effective laws that foster industrial development. We shall discuss these laws, with particular attention to the laws of intellectual property and their role in technological development, as applied to countries in transition to an industrialized free-market economy.

1. The Rule of Law and the Missions of Commerce

The rules of commerce exist in the larger framework of the rule of law. The term "rule of law" embodies the principles of representative government; it characterizes the institutions of a democratic society. By the rule of law we mean that the power of government arises through laws that are enacted by the people, and

*The authors' views are their own, and are not to be attributed to any institution with which they are or have been connected.

G. Bugliarello et al. (eds.), East-West Technology Transfer, 25-41.

in turn are objectively and fairly applied by the institutions charged with their administration.

Legal systems both implement the rule of law and are governed by it. Indeed, the rule of law implies economic freedoms under law. Thus the term is particularly suited to an open, market-based economy wherein commerce is served by the classical principles of enterprise, property rights, and justice. The legal and judicial institutions that benefit industrial innovation and technology transfer are not different from those that serve the other commercial and societal purposes of a nation. The common aspiration is the consistent application of just law.

The principles of the rule of law are as essential to a competitive industrial economy as to a democratic society. Nations in transition to a market economy have the opportunity to adopt innovative approaches not only to the technological and commercial aspects of economic growth, but also to the institutional and legal framework of an industrial economy.

THE MISSIONS OF LEGAL SYSTEMS

The legal systems of nations have been described as having three "missions" with respect to commerce and industry: (1) to establish the rights and rules of property ownership; (2) to protect the rights thus established from illegal disposition by guarding against both civil wrongs and crimes; and (3) to provide and enforce the rules of exchanges and transfers of property [3]. Implementing these missions, legal systems also establish rules for entering and leaving commercial activity, such as by company law and bankruptcy law; and rules that promote investment and competition and establish open and stable markets, such as antimonopoly codes and the laws of intellectual property [6].

The economic consequences of effective legal systems are pervasive. In an open market economy effective systems of commercial law reduce the need for intrusion by government into the workings of business. Legal systems constitute an industrial policy in that commercial development depends not on directives from government officials but on market forces, human energy, and legal institutions [16]. A nation's economic vigor is directly correlated with its legal and judicial systems. The structure of the law, the ease or difficulty of financing and conducting business, and the adequacy of remedy when legal rights are violated, all contribute to that vigor.

To be effective in supporting commercial activity, laws require a high degree of certainty in their application. There must be confidence that the law will be respected, that it will be administered expeditiously by officials, and, when called for, applied objectively and fairly by the courts. It is fundamental that redress is readily available to those who have been wronged by violation of the law. Deficiencies in any of these aspects have not only societal consequences, but economic ones. Particularly when financial commitments are needed from investors, uncertainty about the commercial rules that will apply, coupled with the risks inherent in technological enterprise, can defeat the taking of investment risk.

2. Judicial Institutions in a Market Economy

We need not stress the value of effective judicial systems in connection with all aspects of political and economic life. Recognizing the diversity among nations of their legal institutions [8;19;7], we identify some major attributes of judicial institutions in the administration of commercial law in a market economy. These are basic principles, for the fundamentals of the judicial institution are constant.

THE JUDICIAL PROCESS

The development of a technology-based commercial economy requires that the rules are known and are conscientiously enforced. Thus we start with the premise that the purpose of judicial institutions is the efficient and effective application of law. The various forms that the judicial process can take vary with the history and tradition of nations [10]. There is a common thread, however, for all judges share the assignment of consistent application of the law, and the even-handed imposition of remedy for infractions of the law.

Although judges represent the authority of the state, this authority is itself limited by the law. In addition to the personal integrity and wisdom that are essential to judicial activity, judges must exercise care to avoid abuse of their authority. Judges apply the law as enacted, within the range of discretion that is applicable in the circumstances. The judicial duty to render equal justice applies to both private sector and government-private relationships.

AN INDEPENDENT JUDICIARY

The optimum judicial structure and the appropriate degree of separation of the various powers of government are subjects of great interest as nations review their constitutions and reorganize their polity. Whatever balance a nation chooses, the independence of the judiciary is a premise of democratic systems.

Judges serve best when they are independent of political or economic pressures. In the United States we do not have a uniform system of judicial selection, for although judges in the federal court system are appointed for life, judges in many state court systems are elected by popular vote. However judges are selected, the integrity of the judiciary is fundamental to any legal system. In the United States there has been developed an elaborate structure of codes and canons for judges, and systems of discipline for infractions.

THE LAW SHOULD BE CLEAR, AND CLEARLY STATED

It is often said that a great strength of the United States Constitution is its brevity. Details of interpretation are left to the courts, enabling adaptation of its basic principles to changing circumstances. However, for the details of commercial relationships there is much value in law sufficiently comprehensive that its application raises no uncertainty and requires no resolution by judges in lawsuits. Law is written to encompass the behavior that is its central object, and not the behavior at the edges. However, the legal difficulties and human misunderstandings tend to arise not at the center, but at the edges.

Most lawsuits occur in the grey areas where statute and precedent do not quite reach, where the policy served by the law abuts other policies served by other laws. It is these grey areas of conflicting policies and uncertain applicability of the law that characterize intellectual property litigation in the United States. Resolution of disputes often requires the courts to balance the public policies that are involved in integrating intellectual property law into a competitive economy. Such situations test the wisdom of judges and indeed may test the law itself. Further, although basic legal principles with respect to commerce, such as the laws of contracts and sales, have currency in all nations, new areas continue to arise, such as laws relating to space exploration and the new fields of computer-managed information and communications.

THE LAW SHOULD BE CONSISTENTLY APPLIED

The rule of law has been described as a law of rules [14], tempered by the search for justice [18]. Stability of the rules of commerce is essential to industrial activity, accompanied by confidence that the law will be fairly applied. Illustrated by the field of patent law, the history of United States jurisprudence shows changing economic and judicial attitudes about patents, as we progressed from an agricultural to an industrial nation [12]. To enhance stability in the law, in 1982 all appeals of patent cases were assigned to a single court, the Court of Appeals for the Federal Circuit, in the expectation that the law would thereby be more consistently applied throughout the nation [13].

APPELLATE REVIEW

Confidence is added to the rule of law when dispute-resolution through litigation includes the right to a second judicial look, particularly when the law or the issues are complex. A system of appellate review can smooth out any errors in the initial decisions, and impart greater uniformity to interpretation and application of the law. Appellate review is particularly useful when the law represents a balance of social, commercial, and economic policies, since the balancing of these policies is performed by a multi-judge court that is more likely to have broad exposure to the issues in litigation.

PUBLIC AND PUBLISHED JUDICIAL PROCEEDINGS

An open judicial process is implicit in the rule of law; not just because the ways of justice benefit from public scrutiny, but because the open trial and publication of judicial decisions show how the law is being interpreted. Whether in the common law or the civil law tradition, the way that judges have applied the law in specific situations will guide those who come later. From the perspective of economic activity, the resulting predictability is an important guide to industrial investment decisions. For the laws of intellectual property, which partake of so many interrelated policies, the application of the law to particular factual situations may be of extreme economic importance. An example of current interest is that of computer software, which is affected by both copyright and patent laws. The way that judges balance conflicting policies may aid commercial interests to provide for controversial issues, thus avoiding misunderstanding or facilitating resolution of disputes.

The publication of judicial proceedings opens them to public scrutiny and criticism, and legislative adjustment if needed. Although stability is vital to the rule of law, legislative adaptation to changing economic, technological, or policy circumstances is an important aspect of a living law.

ADEQUACY OF THE REMEDY

When those injured by wrongdoing do not have adequate remedy, the law is of scant value. As applied to industrial innovation and technology transfer, the taking of commercial risk and the making of financial commitments includes calculation of a risk factor based on the availability and the sufficiency of remedy should things go wrong.

Most commercial disputes are resolved better by compromise than by litigation. However, when settlement is not possible, the nation's institutions must provide fair and expeditious decision of disputes. In some instances the ability to obtain injunctive relief is the only effective remedy. Efficient and prompt enforcement of the law serve to reduce the diversion of time and resources to litigation, surely an unproductive use of resources, and is an additional factor in estimating investment risk in technological innovation.

THE ROLE OF LAWYERS

The lawyers of a nation are often the guardians of the rule of law. By nature or training argumentative and skeptical, lawyers have in the United States made the courtroom a forum for debate of the important issues of the day, constantly testing the effective functioning of the rule of law in democratic institutions.

Further, in today's complex economic and commercial arrangements it is not realistic to expect all businesspeople to be expert in all things. Lawyers are used to the style of legal documents, know the rules of trade and commerce, and today are as much a part of commercial enterprises as are the accountant and the salesman.

INTERNATIONAL DISPUTE RESOLUTION

International arbitration and mediation are often favored in commercial arrangements involving nationals of different nations. We take note of the possibility of regional cooperation in industrial innovation, and encourage the creation of regional tribunals to adjudicate disputes related to international technology transfer and trade. Although the dispute-resolution mechanisms in the GATT and the new World Trade Organization are applicable when the disputants are governments, they do not extend to commercial disputes involving private parties. An accessible mode of international dispute resolution would add stability to technology transfer among nations.

3. Incentives for Technological Innovation

New technology contributes in major ways to a nation's growth over the long term. In the diversity of nations and their institutions, the sources of state and private sector contributions to technological advance vary greatly. Experience shows that a greater diversity of output of useful technology, and more effective and efficient procedures, result from competitive, market-oriented efforts. In this context we turn to the laws of intellectual property, for these are the primary legal systems supporting the creation and utilization of new technology in open market economies, whereas intellectual property plays a reduced role in closed or state-dominated economies [4]. By establishing exclusive rights to the products of creative activity, the laws of intellectual property act as a commercial incentive for investment in the financial, technological, and human capital that support industrial innovation.

FORMS OF INTELLECTUAL PROPERTY

Intellectual property is the general term for property rights in the products of human creative effort, technologic and artistic. This property takes the legal forms of patents, trademarks, copyrights, and trade secrets. The attributes of this property are established by laws that take into account its intangible nature, thereby facilitating commerce in its tangible embodiments. Intellectual property systems coexist with other mechanisms for fostering industrial growth, and the details of the legal framework may vary among nations.

Patents

For most fields of technology, the principal form of intellectual property is the patent, which provides the legal right to exclude others from use of the technology for a fixed term of years. Patent laws require disclosure of the technology to the public, as a condition of the grant of the patent. Patents are public documents, published in some countries before grant, and in some countries only after grant.

Trade secrets

Proprietary technical information is often of great practical value, even when the information is not patentable, for it reflects the accumulated efficiencies of experience. It includes the "knowhow" that is often critical to successful technological operations, and thus is important to technology transfer. The laws of trade secrecy and proprietary information protect such information from misappropriation.

Trademarks
Trademarks, service marks, and trade dress, are an important underpinning of a market economy, for they designate the origin of a product, and thus foster quality, uniformity, and commercial responsibility. By providing brand distinction they contribute to a diverse and competitive marketplace.

Copyright
The law of copyright bars copying of creative, artistic, and other subject matter. This law provides the foundation of publishing, music, film, sound recording, the arts, and the media. Some fields of industrial technology, such as computer software and data bases, are protected by copyright principles. Considerable attention is being given today to the appropriate balance of the rights of originators and users in connection with international information networks made possible by advances in technology.

Computer Chips
A special law in the United States relates to the circuitry and design of semiconductor chips. This law contains some elements of patent law and some of copyright, and several unique features: it provides protection against copying but not independent development, sets a shorter term than either patent or copyright, and authorizes reverse engineering for learning purposes. The purpose of the law was to meet the commercial needs of the creators of chips while facilitating improved design.

Plants
The development of new plant species is encouraged in various ways in different countries, and by international treaties. Indeed, most intellectual property is the subject of international treaty, adapted to the forms and purposes of the property and designed to secure orderly and fair commercial practices.

4. Contributions to Economic Development

There are two themes fundamental to the contribution of intellectual property to national economic development. These themes apply to economies in transition as well as to industrially mature economies and, indeed, to developing countries [15]. The themes are (i) the reduction of investment risk in innovative technology, and (ii) the provision of commercial stability through the legal and judicial institutions that implement these laws.

RISK REDUCTION IN INDUSTRIAL INNOVATION

Investment capital in a competitive economy is concerned with the risk that is assumed, weighed against the potential return. The creation and commercialization of new technology generally involves higher risk than many other uses of capital; thus there have been designed various systems of risk reduction, in order to implement the larger purpose of economic growth. Incentives to industrial innovation have ranged from direct governmental subsidy to the enactment of laws that favor a particular technologic interest. The creation of a legal environment that supports the commitment of capital and human resources, whether through internal development or by technology transfer, is the dominant role of intellectual property law. The reduction of commercial risk that is thereby achieved provides an economic incentive to this commitment of resources.

The major risks in technological innovation include those risks inherent in investment in scientific and technologic research, for research results are rarely predictable. Commercial-scale development of new products is expensive and often technologically challenging. There is the risk of rapid obsolescence of successful innovations, and the risk of imitation before the investment has produced a commensurate financial return. Intellectual property laws do not eliminate these risks, but they do reduce the risk of immediate imitation, and thus can increase the financial prospect sufficiently to support investment in the creation and development of new technology in a competitive economy.

The intellectual property laws provide the innovator of a new product or process with a shield from competition with the same product sold by others. Imitation pursues commercial success. Indeed, it is only the profitable products that inspire imitation, usually by those who have borne neither the cost of the development nor the risk of failure. Intellectual property laws provide an enhanced incentive at the threshold and throughout the development. By reducing the likelihood of early competition the potential return on investment is stabilized, thereby supporting higher investment risk, or stimulating investment in products whose payout is longer term or that have a lower profit margin or a smaller potential market. Although there are many factors that affect the risk/reward ratio in technological innovation, when intellectual property rights exist the right to exclude others can impart significant risk-reducing weight.

The ways in which the laws of intellectual property may serve economies in various stages of development have been discussed by many thoughtful commentators. Some argue that intellectual property laws primarily benefit foreign firms, and that countries in transition are better served by the unencumbered opportunity to use known technology [17]. Others urge that a nation's own technological future will be inhibited without the added stimulus to building local technologic industry, providing career opportunities in science and engineering, and facilitating technology transfer into the country [15]. Brunetti et al. [2] report a study of twenty-eight countries that shows a high correlation between economic growth and investor belief that economic policy will not be capriciously altered by unrestrained governmental authority. We do not pursue this debate in these pages, other than to point out that our experience in the United States and other countries weighs well on the side of the longer view, as intellectual property systems have served the goals of the introduction of advanced technology, a more productive economy, a greater diversity of goods, and enhanced trade opportunities.

THE INSTITUTIONALIZING OF LEGAL AND ECONOMIC THEORY

The system of laws brings stability to business planning, by providing standard rules of commerce and trade. Stable rules of all sorts are central to a commercial economy. Such stability is achieved through the institutions of the nation: legislative, executive, and judicial. We reiterate the role of law and legal institutions in providing the stability that generates public and commercial confidence. A measured evolution of all areas of law provides for both flexibility in response to new conditions and stability for business and economic planning. Again we shall use the laws of intellectual property as our model, to illustrate how the theory of the law is adapted to national interests.

There are many facets to intellectual property theory. For example, some theorists see patents and copyrights primarily as an economic tool; some as founded on principles of natural right and fairness. Some are concerned lest these laws impede the flow of ideas and knowledge; others suggest that without them fewer ideas and less knowledge would be available, or used for public benefit. The details of these laws as adopted by various nations vary with the value that the nation places on particular facets of theory as applied to that nation's economy.

Intellectual property theory has been generated for the most part in connection with patent law, but many of the legal concepts address other forms of property. Much modern theory arose as the countries of the West industrialized, based on a combination of principles of natural right, and recognition of the incentive value of property ownership. Little attention has been given, however, to the relevance of this theory to the various stages of industrial development. Although much has been written for and against the actions whereby some nations have adjusted the scope of intellectual property laws, for example by excluding selected subject matter from the patent or copyright laws, empirical study is sparse, particularly with respect to providing commercial incentives for significant transfer of advanced technology [11].

Intellectual property rights have been much discussed in connection with conversion to an open, competitive economy. The various philosophical constructs that surround intellectual property can be correlated with their practical effect, for the rich diversity of theories that underlie intellectual property laws has contributed to institutionalized understanding, and illustrate how legal theory can be adapted to support a nation's technological and economic goals:

Property Theory

The essence of the concept of property is the right to exclude others from its possession and enjoyment. Intellectual property law is founded on this principle, with adjustments to accommodate the intangible attributes of intellectual endeavor. By their intangible nature, once ideas and knowledge have been disclosed they no longer are in the sole possession of their creator. After they have been shared with the public, control derives not from possession, but by operation of law. The knowledge is released, but the right to profit therefrom is restrained by operation of law.

The Theory of Natural Right

When new knowledge is created, it is initially possessed solely by the creator. That right of possession does not arise by statute, but by the act of creation. The laws of patent and copyright secure this right—"secure" is the word in the United States Constitution—to the creator of the knowledge. This invokes the theory of natural right, a theory that underlies much of property law, and that was dominant at the time our Constitution was written. On this theory, the patent law permits the creator of an idea, by natural right, to continue to control the use and profit of the idea—the attributes of property—even after the idea is disclosed to the public.

The theory of natural right is equally applicable to copyright. It is said that copyright "subsists" in a work when it is created; that is, the right arises not by statute but by the act of creation. A few countries require that legal formalities be met to create copyright protection, but the great majority by international treaty have done away with registration formalities as prerequisites to copyright.

Labor Theory

Implementing the premises of human right and fundamental fairness, the labor theory holds that those who have labored in the creation of property are entitled to own the things that they created. It is an ancient theory, formalized by John Locke and others. Although today complicated by the complexities of modern industry, the basic principle is often pointed to as manifesting an important philosophical difference between capitalism and socialism. On the premises of the labor theory, the creators of technologic or artistic property have earned the benefits of ownership. Proprietary information and trade secrets also arise by the act of creating the information. The protection of trade secrets has a long common law tradition, derived primarily from the labor theory.

Social Welfare Theory

Technologic innovation and artistic creation produce social and economic benefits in the form of jobs, goods, trade, and social stability, thus adding to the quality of life and the public welfare. Insofar as intellectual property law contributes to the allocation of human and capital resources to creativity and technologic innovation, it is said to serve the social welfare.

Investment Incentive Theory

This theory derives its theoretical validity from its practical consequences, which in turn are grounded in basic attributes of human and economic nature. The incentive value of intellectual property varies with the technology, the market, the competitive situation, and other factors typical of commercial endeavor. Indeed, it is obvious that some exclusive rights will be of greater value than others, and that their utility as an investment incentive will depend on the particular situation. The right to exclude others from practice of patented or copyrighted subject matter is always a positive factor in the calculation of investment risk.

Monopoly Theory

All property functions through the right to exclude. Monopoly theorists distinguish between the classical monopoly that restrains trade to the disadvantage of the consumer, and the role of patent and copyright law in creating new property and new trade. Belief in a competitive marketplace accommodates the contributions to creativity and innovation that are supported by intellectual property laws, while the details of these laws reflect the policy balance that appears best to serve a nation's economic and cultural needs.

Market Regulation Theory
Theorists have described the patent right as a form of market regulation, achieved by operation of law instead of by governmental management. It is often pointed out that all free markets are regulated to some extent, and that nascent or marginal industries can be shielded from competition in various ways without a patent. However, the patent right itself is driven by market forces, not be government regulation. The ensuing private sector efficiencies, potential for diversity, and freedom from bureaucratic intervention, are long-term benefits of the market influences that flow from intellectual property principles.

Diversity/Competition Theory
An innovator's success often encourages others to develop competing products. The creator of a new product or process may show the way to new markets, or new economies of production, or occasionally entirely new industries. Others may build on this knowledge and compete in the field thus opened. The result is a more productive economy, a greater diversity of goods, increased competition, and overall technological and economic growth.

We cite the example of agricultural research in the United States. Before 1970 the United States did not protect what were called breeders' rights—unlike most other countries. The law then was changed. It is estimated that over three thousand new varieties were developed by private industry after enactment of the law, compared with 150 in the prior ten years, despite the extensive research activity of the United States Department of Agriculture.

The Prospect and Reward Theories
Economists today call the contribution of intellectual property systems a "rent seeking" function that serves to allocate economic resources. Today there is a burgeoning volume of theoretical analysis relating to questions of efficiency, patent and copyright scope, societal cost and benefit [5]. Although some modern economic analysis is controversial as applied to intellectual property, we mention two of the more interesting economic theories.

The "prospect" theory states that protection from competition, by staking a claim to the subject matter that has been discovered or created, provides an economic incentive to take entrepreneurial risks, while avoiding duplication of effort and the need for secrecy [9].

The "reward" theory views the patent or copyright as a reward for the creative or technological contribution, which reward is reaped through exercise of the right to exclude. Some proponents of reward theory presume that the technological or creative contribution would have been made anyway, without the "reward." Economic studies—and common sense—confirm that expensive R&D may not be done at all without an economically sufficient profit opportunity. Bentham [1] observed that "he who has no hope that he shall reap, will not take the trouble to sow."

Contract Theory
According to this theory a patent is somewhat like a contract between the inventor and the government, wherein the patentee's part of the contract is disclosure of the invention. Although disclosure is only one of the purposes of a patent system, a significant body of technical information appears only in the patent literature. Without the opportunity for patenting, information that is amenable to secrecy would surely be so kept. The disclosure of technical information is a significant public benefit of patent systems.

The relinquishment of secrecy is an important consideration in the need for reliable judicial interpretation and enforcement of patents, for the inventor complies with this part of the bargain at the time of disclosure, and can not recover the lost secrecy should the patent later be invalidated or held unenforceable. This explains the reluctance of some in the United States to adopt a system of publication of patent specifications before our examination process is completed, for this forces an uneven bargain should the subject matter be held unpatentable. The concern is that a required early publication may weigh against participation in the patent system for inventions that are amenable to secrecy, thus depriving the public of technical knowledge.

Taken together, this rich diversity of intellectual property theory, developed over centuries of innovation and creative activity, illustrates the interaction between law and practice in contributing to the wealth of nations.

5. Summary

Experience has shown the importance of effective legal institutions in economic development. Well-written laws of themselves achieve little public benefit absent public confidence that the judicial system is available, when needed, to sustain the rights created by those laws. An effective judicial system requires impartiality, consistency, predictability, and adequacy of remedy. The laws of intellectual property in turn contribute to economic development by providing for orderly risk reduction in technology transfer and industrial investment, but only to the extent that the judicial system works to enforce the laws, effectively and impartially.

References

1. Bentham, J. (1962) A manual of political economy, in J. Bowring (ed), *The Works of Jeremy Bentham* **2**, Russell & Russell, New York.

2. Brunetti, A. and Weeder (1993) *Credibility and Growth, WWZ Discussion Paper No. 9316*, University of Basel.

3. Epstein, R.A. (1991) All quiet on the eastern front, *University of Chicago Law Review* **58**, 555.

4. Gould, D. M. and Gruben, W.C. (1994) *The Role of Intellectual Property in Economic Growth*, Federal Reserve Bank of Dallas Research Department Working Paper No. 94-09.

5. Grady, M. F. and Alexander, J.I. (1992) Patent law and rent dissipation, *Virginia Law Review* **78**, 305.

6. Gray, C. W. and Associates (1993) *Evolving Legal Frameworks for Private Sector Development in Central and Eastern Europe*, World Bank Discussion Paper No. 209, Washington, D.C.

7. Hartwig, M. (1992) The institutionalization of the rule of law: the establishment of constitutional courts in the eastern European countries, *American University Journal of International Law & Policy* **7**, 449.

8. Juelke, R. C. (1993) The economic causes and consequences of constitutional reform in eastern Europe, *William and Mary Law Review* **34**, 1367.

9. Kitch, E.W. (1977) The nature and function of the patent system, *Journal of Law & Economics* **20**, 265.

10. Kuzmik, A. M. (1993), Rule of law and legal reform in Ukraine: a review of the new procuracy law, *Harvard International Law Journal* **34**, 611.

11. Mansfield, E. (1994) *Intellectual Property Protection, Foreign Direct Investment, and Technology Transfer*, IFC Discussion Paper No. 19, The World Bank, Washington, D.C.

12. Newman, P. (1990) Intellectual property in the courts, in *Proceedings, Events, and Addresses of the Bicentennial of the United States Patent and Copyright Laws—May 1990*, Foundation for a Creative America, Washington, D.C.

13. Newman, P. (1992) The federal circuit—a reminiscence, *George Mason University Law Review* **14**, 557.

14. Scalia, A. (1989) The rule of law as a law of rules, *University of Chicago Law Review* **56**, 1175.

15. Sherwood, R. M. (1990) *Intellectual Property and Economic Development*, Westview Press, Boulder, Colo.

16. Sherwood, R. M., Shepherd, G. and de Souza, C.M. (1994) Judicial systems and economic performance, *The Quarterly Review of Economics and Finance* **34** (Special Issue), 101.

17. Soltysinski, S. (1992) The uneasy development of intellectual property law in Poland, *Journal of Proprietary Rights* **5**, 2.

18. Tribe, L. H. (1989) Revisiting the rule of law, *New York University Law Review* **64**, 726.

19. Utter, R. F. and Lundsgaard, D.C. (1993) Judicial review in the new nations of central and eastern Europe: some thoughts from a comparative perspective, *Ohio State Law Journal* **54**, 559.

3. A NECESSARY EVOLUTION OF THE PATENT SYSTEM

A Jurist's Suggestion for Improving the International Transfer of Technology

VINCENZO Di CATALDO
Professor of Business Law
University of Catania, Italy

1. Introduction

A jurist participating in a meeting which aims to draw up guidelines for facilitating technological exchanges between the participating countries in particular and the world in general could direct his contribution along various lines. In the first place, he could draw up a comprehensive picture of the existing regulations on this topic, in order to propose a revision of these to make them more functional; and indeed this could seem to be the most congenial task.

In the present case, however such an operation would excite little interest. There are no pre-existing regulations for the transfer of technology between NATO countries and countries of the ex-Warsaw Pact (the former system was based on the principle of non-transfer); in order to create a system it is therefore necessary to bear in mind the regulatory models for exchanges existing in different geographic contexts. For the existing models there is already sufficient information available; moreover their functionality has already been tested and some suggestions for modernization have been made. And there has already been considerable discussion over the case, still unsolved, of the "Code of conduct on international transfer of technology."

It seems more useful therefore, rather than repeating what has already been said by others on other occasions, however important and however relevant these ideas may seem, to suggest a new line of thought: to apply to the present case a well-known idea, namely that there always exists a limit to the modification of a subsystem, and that therefore it is not possible to modify that subsystem

G. Bugliarello et al. (eds.), East-West Technology Transfer, 43-52.

beyond that limit, unless the basic structure of the wider system of which it constitutes a part is altered first.

This means, in the present case, that it is not possible to think only of adjustments, whatever the entity, in the regulations governing the international transfer of technology; it is necessary rather to make major changes in the structure of the patent system, which constitutes the basic framework of protection for the technological innovations of the Western countries.

The existing patent system is in many ways out of date and therefore needs substantial revisions, especially in areas of significance to the transfer of technology. But in order to move in this direction, it is necessary first of all to define what changes have occurred in the field of research over the last few centuries.

2. Science and Technology Occupy Different Worlds: Effect on Inventions

One basic characteristic of yesterdays world is the separation of science and technology. Formerly these two were two different worlds, involved in different activities, barely if at all in contact with each other.

Another characteristic of yesterday's world was its geographical fragmentation. With the necessary generalizations and approximations inherent in a brief outline of a complex picture, we can say that each of yesterday's "regions" lived in a world of its own, albeit experiencing a few moments of contact, even of a certain importance, with the other worlds (commercial, cultural, political exchanges) but on the whole considering itself autonomous.

These two characteristics greatly affect the rules which have developed over the centuries regarding inventions. The second is quite well-known, and I therefore do not intend to discuss it here. The former, on the other hand, is less familiar to us. Let us examine it more closely.

3. Scientific Inventions and the Scientific Community

The world of science, in Western countries, has always attributed great importance to the communication of ideas. From the beginning of history there has always been a scientific community with a universal identity, thinking in universal terms without national barriers, interacting freely. Newton's remark "if I have seen farther, it is by standing on the shoulders of giants" expresses at once a sense of indebtedness to the common heritage and a recognition of the essentially cooperative and cumulative quality of scientific achievement.[1]

The scientist knows that he owes a debt to the scientific community, which has given him a necessary basis for his further achievements. The scientist knows that his discoveries depend, not only on his own contribution and good luck, but also on a good series of earlier acquisitions, of which the new discovery will become a part. Above all, he is aware that the new discovery will not put an end to all research, that research will continue beyond the life-span of those currently involved in it; he knows that the development potential (in final analysis, the importance) of a discovery is measured above all by its capacity to provide a starting-point for further discoveries.

Scientific progress, and this has always been acknowledged, depends on the cooperation of whole generations, past, present and future.

There is a strong connection between the universality of the scientific ethos and the recognition of a cultural heritage which conditions all research activity and to which nobody can claim an exclusive right. Substantial discoveries in the scientific field are a collective product and are therefore available to all, becoming a collective heritage.[2]

4. The Technological World and the Patent System

The world of technology, on the other hand, has always given great importance to exclusiveness. The author of a new invention has the right to keep it to himself. Technology is private property. And the Western countries have built up over the centuries a complex system of regulations (known as the "patent system") with the precise object of guaranteeing the exclusive ownership of inventions.

Naturally, even in the existing patent systems there are opposing tendencies to be found. These systems tend to justify their existence by occupying a positive role within the flow of innovations. They have also given rise to regulations to guarantee that the new invention will become part of the collective heritage (above all, the expiration of the patent in a limited term and the regulations which demand an "adequate disclosure" of the invention must not be forgotten). But, as we know, no empirical test has so far been able to confirm that the patent system has had a really positive role in favoring technological progress. The effective power of the regulations tends to be somehow diminished by a number of technical details (it is well-known, for example, that the expiration term of a patent tends to be fixed as a period longer than the period of interest of third parties in the utilization of the invention).

5. Today's Patent System

If it is difficult to draw a picture of yesterday's world in a few lines, it is much more so to define the characteristics of today's; perhaps some of the most important of these elude us, and will be fully appreciated only by those who come after us. But I must draw attention to two aspects of the problem under examination: the first is that science and technology are growing closer and closer together; the second, that the distances between the different countries are growing smaller.

The world of science and that of technology, which have been separated for centuries, are tending to coincide today (in many fields at least, if not in all). Of course this is merely the result of processes which began long ago, have continued underground, and are now coming to maturity. Technological innovation, today far more than in the past, depends on scientific innovations. The way things are changed derives more and more directly from the way things are viewed; it derives more and more directly from the newly acquired knowledge. The immediate derivability of medicines, therapies, and instruments for various uses, from scientific achievements is clearly visible to all.

The words we use reflect, often without our being aware of it, the reality of the situation. They reveal this new relationship between science and technology. In fact, when the collecting of "information" is indicated as a typical characteristic of our times, a new meaning is attributed to a familiar word (which is different not only from the one used for centuries to indicate scientific achievements (always denominated "knowledge") but also from those used to indicate technological innovations ("technology")). The "information" we speak of today is at the same time one and the other; the frontier between science and technology is no longer so clear-cut as it was. The world of research, which is today a result of the "merging" of the two worlds up to now kept separate, tends to assume what has always been characteristic of the world of science: the existence of worldwide informal exchanges of ideas and information.

The creation of connections between researchers from different parts of the would, operating as an interactive network, is further encouraged by other factors: by the increasing sophistication and costs of research, and by the need to make use of procedures, materials and instruments which are ever more complex and costly.

Contacts between scientists, which in yesterday's world consisted mainly of a flow of information regarding the final results of research projects carried out on an individual scale, have today been promoted to a level "in advance" of research, so to speak, becoming contacts with a view to carrying out the research itself in a better way. A "trip abroad," once viewed as an exciting but unique moment in the life of the scientist, has now become a repeated and routine stay in research structures or overseas laboratories.

6. New Role of Patent Systems

Patent systems too are no longer what they once were. Indeed, conspicuous developments have occurred. For example, through a process of trial and error, they have begun to solve the problem of diversification of the sectors of technology, that is of the development of sectors other than that of mechanics.

The patent system has become aware of the increasing interaction between countries, and, above all, of the need to rationalize the numerous different national patent systems. As a result of the big international conventions of the seventies, an attempt was made to define transnational collaboration procedures at various levels between the different national systems. Examples are the unified procedure for the granting of a European patent, the cooperation between Patent Offices for the granting of patents in accordance with the Treaty of Washington and the launching of supranational patents (such as the European patent for the European Economic Community).

In substance, much attention has been paid to the increasingly international nature of the exchanges of technology (that is, of the fruits of research activities). It is interesting to note how certain new regional regulations take into consideration also the transfer of technological innovations which do not constitute inventions subject to patent but are pure know-how: realities which until now have been totally outside the realm of the patent system (such as, for example, the regulations for international transfer of technology in Latin America; the E.E.C. regulations on know-how licensing).

On the other hand, the patent system has not noted as yet the loss of importance of the frontier between science and technology. Nor is there yet much awareness of the deep changes which have taken place in research activities, that is in the very methods of carrying out research, which have become collective and international.

7. Major Changes in the Organization of Research and the Patent System

Some major changes in the organization of research have already been noted. In particular, it is accepted today that the inventor is generally no longer a single person working alone, but is more often a group of researchers. This awareness has led jurists to become interested in problems (regarding the collective ownership of inventions and the collective ownership of patents) which once were not worthy of note, and for which there are still not adequate written regulations.

Nevertheless, it is necessary to go a step further. The novelty lies not so much in the fact that the single inventor has become a group of inventors, as in the fact that the inventor (whether single or a group) is no longer isolated, but lives in ever closer contact with other inventors.

8. Applying the Patent System to the New Realities

This awareness, in fact, leads us to think in particular about one of the crucial points of the patent system, which attributes the patent to the first inventor or to the first inventor to file an application for the patent (in the case in point it is not necessary to distinguish between the two rules), and does not afford any kind of recognition to any other person.

The second to file, and all those following him, not only receive no acknowledgment, but are even "punished" by being deprived of the possibility to continue to reap the benefits of the investments they have made, because they too have to respect the "exclusive" right issued to the winner.

This rule is clearly the offspring of that world in which inventors are involved in different activities, without particular contacts between them, without exchanges of information, and without a predetermined setting of objectives for their activities.

As I have said, in today's world, increasingly, research is no longer an isolated, occasional activity. The world of research has become a "system", a network of interconnections, of concerted aims and shared functions, of interactive cooperation. In reality, it is the very mobility of today's researcher which permits the research of the various operators to develop in a context of regular consultations to select the objectives to be reached and the procedures to be followed. In this context, cases regularly occur of "independent" inventions, that is, of an invention made simultaneously by more than one operator, as a result of separate research projects. This circumstance, formerly very rare, now occurs with increasing frequency, precisely because in reality these inventors are no longer strictly "independent." It may appear paradoxical, but the great effectiveness of this mutual interaction between researchers clearly emerges also in those cases where different groups of researchers are placed in position of mutual competition, rather than in one of willing collaboration (the research on the AIDS problem is a very evident example of this [3]). Also, in these cases, it is possible to trace profound mutual debts between one group and another, which are objective proof of the unplanned circulation of information.

The direct consequence of this is that the rule assigning a patent to the "first" inventor, and denying any form of recompense to the second and all the others, appears more and more difficult to justify and therefore inadequate in today's world ("unjust" in the deepest sense of the word).

Instead, a balanced rule should aim at a distribution of the invention rights within the whole area of researchers who (independently of one another) followed that line of research, and contributed in a significant way, though only partially, to its realization; it should aim to quantify the contribution of each of them to the completion of the research project, and share the patent between the different researchers in proportion to their contribution. This is the line, in effect, followed spontaneously more and more often in cases of conflict between two or more (independent) inventors.

This line of thought opens up a prospect full of difficulties and uncertainty. It is necessary to find a solid criterion by which to define the group of researchers among whom the patent is to be distributed. (It must not be forgotten that the "first to file" rule is still preferred, in many countries, to the "first to invent" rule, simply because of the difficulty involved in identifying the first person to invent. And simplicity of application is a value in law.) Then, criteria must be established for the distribution of the proceeds of the invention among the members of the group previously defined, through the constitution of a joint ownership (even with different ownership quotas between the researchers, or of instruments, such as licenses, or of newly-coined institutions).

9. The Transfer of Inventions and the Patent Licensing Systems

A second line of development of the patent system should direct attention to the transfer of inventions, and, more generally, of technological information focusing, above all, on the licenses and the acts constituting co-ownership.

In the original logic of the patent system, there is no reason to entertain the idea of operations such as licenses. Indeed, they appear antithetical with respect to the original requirements of the system, and therefore to its rules, because they lead to a splitting of the exclusive right, whereas the object was rather to create an exclusive right which was as complete and compact as possible.

In the modern world, licenses become important (both on an intra-state level, and, especially, on a transnational one), because various circumstances lead to the substitution of the circulation of goods with the circulation of the know-how required to produce them.

But in the phenomena listed above, there is a further and in some ways deeper reason for interest in the institution of licensing. This reason (even when present only at the intra-state contact level) depends on the very fact that today a new need exists for contractual contacts between different researchers for the distribution of the fruits of their inventions. As I have said, the instruments most suitable for this purpose are, alternatively, licensing and the joint ownership of patents.

In this sense, instruments and institutions (joint ownership of inventions and patent licenses), once an occasional occurrence, tend to become more general. It is therefore necessary to examine the system with more attention than it has been afforded up to now, refining the regulations which today are practically nonexistent. The regulations controlling patent licenses, if we discount antitrust measures, remain entirely at the discretion of the autonomy the negotiations possess.

10. The Need for New Regulations for Shared Patents

In this perspective, the study of a new regulation for the "sharing" of a patent between a number of independent researchers and the study of a more refined system of rules controlling patent licensing are not two distinct operations. They are two aspects of a single line of investigation, which aims to review the core of the patent system.

The natural laboratory for the examination of the regulations in terms of technology remains a series of different national patent systems. It will remain so for a long time until the institution, if and when it occurs, of a global patent system. It is therefore within these systems, above all, that the suggested revolution will have to take place. If it produces results, it will be possible to extend them to the field of international transfer of technology, which would certainly represent a ground where they can be tested and developed.

Others[4] have said that the patent system (whose traditional role as incentive and stimulus for technical progress has never been supported by convincing empirical results) may today find a new legitimacy as an instrument for the collecting and spreading of information of technological importance.

This prospect offers a role which is surely in tune with our times; but, as always happens when a new function is attributed to an existing system, we cannot ignore the fact that the definition of a new role inevitably implies an alteration of the rules. A modification in the function cannot but lead to a modification in the structure. In my opinion, the modifications to be sought should be along the lines of those outlined here.

Footnotes/References

(1) Merton, R.K. (1957), *Social Theory and Social Structure*, The Free Press, Glencoe, Illinois, 558. The aphorism appears moreover to go back in time to a period and to figures of whose existence we will never know if Newton himself was aware. On this subject see the exhilarating work by R. K. Merton, *On the Shoulder of Giants*, The Free Press, New York, 1965.

(2) For a similar view see the *Convention for the Protection of Scientific Discoveries*, signed in Geneva on 3rd March 1978 under the aegis of the World Intellectual Property Organization (WIPO), but not yet enforced.

(3) I refer to the famous dispute between the Pasteur Institute in Paris and the U.S. Department of Health and Human Services over the ownership rights of the invention regarding a test-kit for the research of AIDS antibodies. The dispute was solved with the acknowledgment of a joint paternity for the identification of the AIDS virus attributed to the research groups of the two institutes (directed by Prof. Luc Montagnier and Dr. Robert Gallo respectively), and with the acknowledgment for the two of a joint paternity for the invention of the test-kit. For details of the dispute and its solution see C. Norman (1986), "AIDS Patent Negotiation Breakdown," in *Science* **232**, 819, and D.M. Barnes (1987), "AIDS Patent Dispute Settled," in *Science* **236**, 17.

(4) Beier, F.K. and Straus, J. (1977), The patent system and its informational function - yesterday and today, *International Review of Industrial Property and Copyright Law* **8**, 387 ss.

4. SCIENCE AND TECHNOLOGY POLICY IN RUSSIA: A VIEW FROM THE RUSSIAN ACADEMY

ZHOREV I. ALFEROV
Vice-President, Russian Academy of Sciences
St. Petersburg, Russia

1. Introduction

Russian Science and Technology policy is formally regulated by the same bureaucratic organizations as in the former USSR. The Russian Academy of Sciences, as successor to the USSR Academy of Sciences, is responsible for the organization of fundamental research. The Ministry of Science and Technical Policy of the Russian Federation (successor to the USSR State Committee of Science and Technology) determines the subject and budget of the State R & D Program and selects scientific research institutions (mostly industry oriented) for the role of State Scientific Center. In reality, however, the state science and technology policy in Russia is totally different from that of the former USSR.

2. Transfer of technology from the Laboratories of the Academy of Sciences to Industry: Past and Present

The Russian Academy of Sciences (as in the former USSR) is the largest scientific center of the country, uniting more than 300 research institutes in the fields of natural sciences, technology and the humanities.

Basic research had always been the primary task of the Academy of Sciences of the USSR, resulting in important applications and forming the basis of new technologies.

Among numerous examples of research results, one can mention the invention of laser-maser principles (by N. Basov and A. Prokhorov at the Lebedev

G. Bugliarello et al. (eds.), East-West Technology Transfer, 53-61.

Physical Institute) and the discovery, in the fifties, of semiconductor properties of the A3B5 compounds (by A. Regel and N. Goryunova at the Ioffe Physico-Technical Institute). Later, pioneering research on semiconductor heterostructures at Ioffe Physico-Technical Institute defined today's development of optoelectronics and high speed microelectronic components.

All of the Nobel Prizes received by Soviet scientists in various fields of science were awarded to scientists of the Academy of Sciences, who carried out their work at the Academy laboratories.

The St. Petersburg Scientific Center of the Russian Academy of Sciences is the oldest, some of its institutes dating from the time of Peter the Great, founder of the Academy.

At present, the St. Petersburg Scientific Center has about 40 research institutes with a total of more than 15,000 employees including 7,000 scientists. The largest institutes, the Ioffe Physico-Technical Institute, the Konstantinov Institute for Nuclear Physics, the Steklov Mathematical Institute, the Pavlov Institute of Physiology, to mention a few, have won well-deserved world recognition. The centers of humanities research, the Institute of Russian Literature, the Institute of Ethnography and Anthropology, and the Institute of Oriental Sciences are a repository of world culture and history.

Our national research institutes, particularly those in the physical and chemical-biological fields, have always been keenly interested in cooperating with industry. Today, in the transitional period to a market economy, this has become vitally important for the very survival of the institutes.

FROM A LABORATORY OF THE USSR ACADEMY OF SCIENCES TO SOVIET INDUSTRY - EXPERIENCES OF THE CENTRAL ECONOMIC PLANNING SYSTEM

In the terminology of the USSR administrative command system, the term "implementation" - the transfer of technology from laboratory to industry - defined the forcible implantation in industry of something new, not typical of industry.

On paper, the process of transfer looked well-structured and impressive. A new device, a technological process, or a material developed at a laboratory of the Academy of Sciences, was transferred to an industrial research laboratory, where the technology was being completed up to the level necessary for experimental production, and a production study was prepared. Thus, a laboratory of the Academy of Sciences carried out not only research, but also an industrial development study.

However, the case was somewhat different in practice. In the industrial ministries, their branch of science was carried out by a system of specialized institutes, where both research and development could be carried out according to the plan of each ministry, and introduced into industry at a factory defined by the same plan. Well-balanced circuits did exist - e.g., from industrial laboratory of semiconductor lasers to pilot line of semiconductor lasers to factory or industrial laboratory of LED, to pilot line, to factory. The electronic industry, for instance, had "head" laboratories for components of different types which were responsible for the level and volume of production. Since the "head" laboratories were usually one of a kind (to avoid duplication and expenditure of scarce resources), they, by definition, developed the country's best technology. In any case, the minister of each entity always knew who was responsible for the shortage of one kind or another of product.

However, research and inventions carried out at the Academy of Sciences were always outside this system. New discoveries were always unplanned, and a monolithic system of "head" industrial institutions had no need of them.

Lack of competition adversely affected the development of industrial production, including the war industry, where the main stimulus became orders from the high authorities, usually dictated by the information that the Americans were far ahead in this field. One can give many examples of pioneering research and inventions carried out in this country, but eventually we found ourselves far behind.

I will give you an example close to me. In 1968, our laboratory was the first to create semiconductor lasers on the AlGaAs heterostructures operating at room temperature. At the beginning of the 70s, together with an industrial laboratory, we carried out R & D in sufficient volume and set up small scale industrial production. We were ahead of the R & D in the West for some years. But at the end of the 70s the USA and Japan gained an overwhelming advantage in industrial assimilation of this most important semiconductor device, a device that determines progress in communications, information displays, new audio and video systems, etc.

Here is another classic example from the same field. At the end of the 60s to the beginning of the 70s, our laboratory developed highly effective AlGaAs LED successfully applied to optical pumping of solid state lasers. These studies were carried out in tight collaboration with an industrial laboratory of the electronic company "Positron" in Leningrad, where there was a pilot line and everything was ready for serial production. But, according to the ministry structure, "Positron" should not have been engaged in LED. Another company in Moscow was chosen for this purpose. As a result, production was launched several years later.

However, this centralized system did have positive features. As soon as the authorities of a ministry were convinced of the efficiency of joint work with an institute of the Academy of Sciences, a long-term scientific program was usually created for the development of a certain direction of applied research and industry. This was finally directed by the ministry who took upon itself the financing of this research in the Academy. Usually this financing is beyond the power of a separate industrial institute. Besides, investigations carried out at an Academy laboratory are more broad than the competencies of an entire industrial institute.

FIRST ATTEMPTS TO TRANSFER THE SOVIET (RUSSIAN) TECHNOLOGY FROM THE ACADEMY TO THE WORLD MARKET: WE WERE GOOD SCIENTISTS BUT BAD BUSINESSMEN

Under the present conditions of this transitional period, when the centralized system of ministry leadership of industry is destroyed, and a new one has not yet been established, laboratories of the Academy conducting applied research - or fundamental research giving a sudden applied result - found themselves in a worse financial position than before.

Industrial laboratories and companies do not show interest in long-term scientific programs, and are in a difficult financial condition themselves. On the other hand, our country lacks intermediary companies who offer to the market "raw" technology from the academic laboratories. Often, these technologies entered the world market but required here a great deal of development to prepare even for the pilot line. What is of great importance here is that our scientific achievements were implemented in the industrial developed countries and then, in return, entered into large scale production in Russia.

3. Concepts of Scientific and Technological Development in the USSR and their Absence in Russia

Scientific and technological progress in the former USSR was regarded by the central authority as playing the dominant role in a planned economy. The abundant militarization of the economy and the immense expenditures for the armed forces - including research - contributed to the breakdown of the economy in the

USSR. On the other hand, one cannot ignore the prestigious position of Soviet research centers, and the fact that the state cherished Soviet science and accepted a scientific-technological model as the way toward a progressive state.

At present, there is not any scientific-technological concept of development in Russia. It is, virtually, the "raw materials" model that is being implemented now, which makes the output and sale of raw materials (oil, gas, nonferrous and rare-earth metals) of primary importance. Incidentally, the development and manufacture of equipment for the subsequent technological treatment of these materials takes place in the West, ignoring the great potential of our defense-based industry.

The enormous economic damage caused by the disintegration of the USSR is now being multiplied by this policy, and can but inevitably result in dramatic consequences for Russian science.

4. Transition from a Centralized to a Multiple Sources System of Financial Support.

The reductions in military budgets have had a strong impact on scientific research centers. State funding of scientific centers in Russia is negligible and does not allow for the continuation of research. The money is hardly enough to keep existing laboratories operating.

This is why we see one of our major tasks as diversifying the financial sources for the continuation of research work. At present, we can keep only a limited number of high-class laboratories in operation. By the efforts of the Russian Academy of Sciences (RAS), a Fundamental Research Fund has been established. This fund is supposed to support the most promising work and research. Applications for participation are considered by a commission of experts. State financing through the Ministry of Science will continue, but these means will be used to support first of all applied technological research through State Science and Technology Programs (SSTP).

At present, in Russia, 41 state science and technology programs are being realized. In our country, such state programs are rather a traditional support mechanism, and we intend to keep it.

In 1993, about four thousand projects are planned for realization within these programs. They were selected by competition out of thirty thousand proposals.

The largest grants are:

"Development and application of space vehicles for science and the economy" (1993- 39,000 million rubles) ;

"Development of civil aviation" (1993 - 30,220 million rubles) ;

"New materials" (1993 - 1,568 million rubles) ;

"Prospective processes for agricultural production" (1993 - 1,275 million rubles).

By their status, the SSTP of Russia are highly rated federally targeted science and technological programs. They are developed with a view toward promoting the most promising fundamental research and, thereby, developing science-intensive branches of the economy.

Except for the programs "Development and application of space vehicles in science and the economy" and "Development of civil aviation", the state customer or the government procurement agency of SSTP is the Ministry of Science and Technology of Russia. For these two programs, the state customers are the Russian Space Agency and the Ministry of Transport of the Russian Federation.

Special scientific councils are being established to organize and implement these programs. The programs are selected as a result of competitions which are open to everybody and are conducted by scientific councils who submit the results to the Ministry of Science and Technology of Russia together with recommendations for inclusion of projects in a program. The programs are financed by the budget of a republic, as well as by ministries, departments, associations, enterprises and customer organizations, including those on a shared participation basis.

In 1993, in the course of realization of these projects within the SSTP, new machinery, technologies and materials from practically all branches of science and technology were developed and tested as mock-ups, pilot units and full-scale prototypes. Some of these developments rank with or even surpass world levels. Research efforts are aimed at solving essential social problems, resource management and enhancement of labor productivity and product quality; at solving problems of creating substitutes for imported products; and at developing export potential by producing competitive domestic products.

The funding for these programs has been reduced very sharply due to the creation of a large number of new State Research Centers sponsored by industrial institutions and financed by the same source.

The financial situation, even for the best research institutions of the Academy of Sciences, can be seen from the structure of the expenses of the Ioffe Physico-Technical Institute (Figure 1).

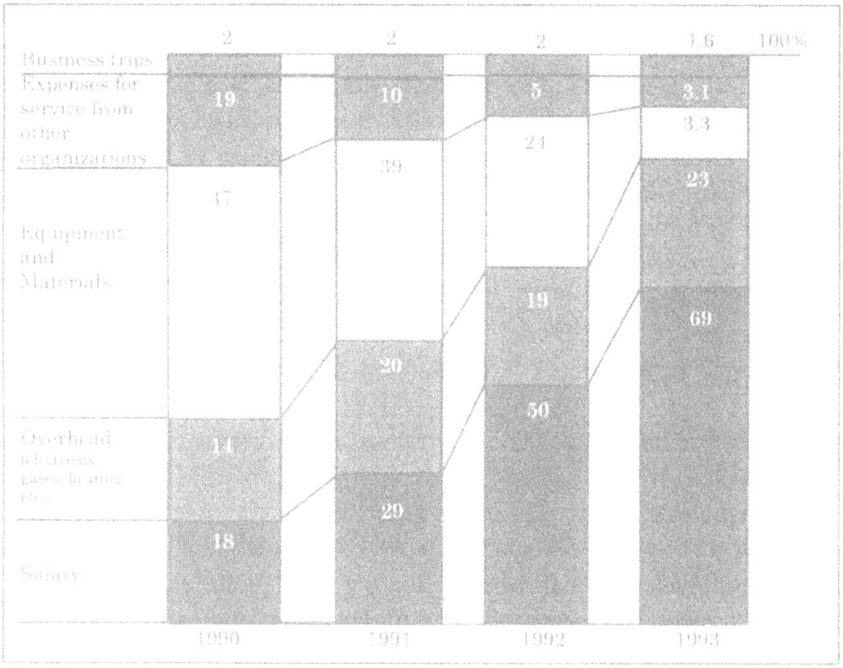

Figure 1.
Structure of the expenses of the Ioffe Physico-Technical Institute in 1990-1993

A situation must be created so that Russian scientists can effectively operate in their own country, because if the brain drain exceeds a certain critical level, the Russian scientific schools will collapse. This would be an irreplaceable loss for our country.

I have raised strong objections when the question of help for Russia is raised during discussions concerning scientific cooperation. It is true that we receive much help, but often not through real involvement. However, when the conversation turns to joint scientific research, equal partnership in which both sides are interested is necessary. In some respects, this partnership might turn out to be more helpful to "them" than to "us" because, by taking advantage of the economic crisis in Russia, foreigners can buy the results of our research more cheaply than they could on the world market. It is only natural that we are taking some protective measures. I have a new position on my staff, an economic aide, who is responsible for working out economic policies. However, nothing yet has changed and we are continuing to sell the results of our research to Western companies for a song: even these low prices help us to increase our troubled budget considerably.

Unfortunately, this plus is almost neutralized by a huge minus. Should this situation continue, we risk becoming just an appendage to Western civilization. In the former USSR, programs for the development of high-tech industry according to world standards were determined by the work of academic institutes such as the Ioffe Institute. At present, Russian industry is not capable of fully paying for our research. Therefore, our laboratories must turn to the West.

5. The Role of International Scientific and Technological Partnerships

It is obvious from the above that international collaboration is of utmost significance for the survival of Russian science, The importance of this collaboration is not only financial in nature. The moral aspect is essential, too: Russian scientists should realize their well recognized intelligence, creative abilities and experience. The cut in international collaboration is a result of the taxation policy of the government. Taxes and custom-duties imposed on any agreements and research grants - except the charitable ones - make the situation quite hopeless. The State has an insignificant financial gain from the laboratories of the Academy of Sciences (which is likely not to exceed $10-20 million a year) while for the strongest of our research laboratories there is little chance of having the active support of their intellectual potential.

Due to the mutually complementary structure of Russia and some foreign countries like Turkey and Korea, our collaboration in science and technology is particularly valuable.

The Russian side is strong in its fundamental projects and raw material and these countries have accumulated immense experience in technological progress.

Today, as has been noted by John W. Kiser, President of Kiser Research Inc. in Washington in his essay (The Christian Science Monitor - February 28, 1994):

"The battle of Leningrad is being fought again. This time Russian scientists are under siege, and the enemy is not Germany, but Moscow..."

Revival and then development of the scientific and technological potential of Russia depends first and foremost on the chosen model of State development - on whether the science-technology model is chosen -on the tax policy of Russia's President and Government, as well as on successful international partnerships in the field of science and technology.

5. SOCIAL AND POLITICAL IMPACT ON RUSSIA OF THE TRANSFER OF TECHNOLOGIES FROM NATO COUNTRIES

M.V. BRATERSKY
Russian Public Policy Center
Moscow, Russia

1. The Role of Technologies in Social and Political Transitions

In the second half of the twentieth century technological development became the mainstream of the progress of civilization. During the past several decades technologies have emerged as a major factor of societal and political change, not only in the developed world, but in the Third World as well. The examples of South-East Asian and many Latin American countries are quite obvious. Russia and other post-Soviet countries are no exception to this tendency. Technologies are coming to the forefront of Russia's development now that Russian society is starting to develop more or less naturally, without the domination of a state ideological policy.

Technological development appears to be only one side of development, and is closely connected with deep changes within society, the economy and policies. Parallel to the technological progress, changes take place in the structure of society and within social groups. Domestic policies are being transformed and the foreign policy of the country is seeking new priorities.

New technologies are beginning to play a role which was not typical of them in the past. The flow of technologies to developing countries and to those countries that are now in transition, is bringing along with it new values and knowledge; it influences the structure of employment, establishes new professional and social groups and changes the economic model of development. Since new technologies can be economically effective only in certain social, political and legal conditions, they start acting as a catalyst of economic, social and political change.

G. Bugliarello et al. (eds.), East-West Technology Transfer, 63-76.

Development in general does not rely on technology alone. A more important role is played by social factors. It is people, after all, who change their life-style, their attitude to work, and the organization of their society. An undisputed fact, however, is that, having been put in a certain technological framework, a man changes. Russian examples prove it: those who work in Western-style banking are using international banking technologies, and they work, behave and expect much in the same way a Swiss banker does.

In practical terms the first to focus on the relationship between technical progress and social development were American scholars at the beginning of the fifties. An assumption was made that the future of civilization is inseparably connected with technological progress. In order to concentrate on the related issues of technical, political and social progress a special concept was developed, which later became known as the concept of modernization. One of the authors defined modernization as a "comprehensive process of economic growth, social mobilization and the development of culture" [2]. This school of thought formulated the concepts of progress and that of the development of traditional societies [1;3;4;7].

In the period of the Cold War amid competition between the two political camps for influence in the world, this concept tried to solve more practical issues as well. American experts concluded that the logic of technological development would give the developing countries an impetus to seek closer cooperation with the developed world, since only there the former could find stimuli for development. The theory also stated that the imperatives of technological development would guarantee rapprochement of the developing and developed countries in different areas and on all levels. In turn, closer cooperation would bring about a transformation of the developing countries' policies and societies in a direction acceptable to the West.

The experience of world development showed later that the process is much more complicated than the theories assumed. Still, along with failures, the theory of modernization scored some victories as well.

Today, a whole new world - the former Soviet block split into two dozen nation states - is starting the transition from what it was previously into something it will become. In discussing programs of technical cooperation and technology transfer from NATO countries to the former Eastern block, one has to be aware of the potential political and social effects of this process. Moreover, one can try to forecast the impact of certain technologies on societies and adjust technology transfers correspondingly.

2. NATO Countries' Technical Aid to CIS and Russia: Mixed Priorities

The Concise Oxford Dictionary [6] treats "technology" as *mechanical arts and applied sciences collectively*. It is a relatively recent phenomenon in which people have begun to speak not only of welding technology, but also of communication technologies, banking technologies, social technologies etc.

In terms of foreign policy problems in general, the traditional issues to be raised only a few years ago were control over technology exports to the countries of the Eastern block, the problems of double-use technology or forecasts of probable technological developments and their impact on Western security [5].

It has taken the profound change in the former USSR and Eastern Europe for the Western countries to start thinking about technology transfer as the means of technical aid aimed at transforming post-communist economies and societies into modern ones. NATO countries are involved in technical assistance programs both on a bilateral basis, and within the framework of international organizations. So far NATO has not been an important player in technology transfer through technical aid. Though there are signs that after the Partnership for Peace Program is launched the situation may change, thus far the major flow of expertise and technologies has been coming to Russia from NATO countries through EC and national technical assistance programs.

Let me briefly review three programs: TACIS (EC), USAID (USA), and Canadian, representing respectively an international organization, a big donor, and a typical medium-size program. Since the problem addressed in this article deals with political questions, private technology transfers are not discussed here.

The three programs formulate their priorities and even their reasons for providing technical aid to the former Soviet Republics differently: For the EC the TACIS program is a follow-up of the decision taken by the meeting of the European Council in Rome in December 1990, when EC decided to support the authorities of the former Soviet Union in order to bring about economic reform and recovery. TACIS is supporting the respective countries' efforts to build up a market economy and the skills needed for its operation, and a democratic society. With regard to the Russian Federation, TACIS chose as its focal sectors 1) Enterprise Restructuring and Development and 2) Human Resources Development, which is understood as cooperation aimed at reforming the institution of public administration and retraining the economic and business management of an economy run on market principles" [8].

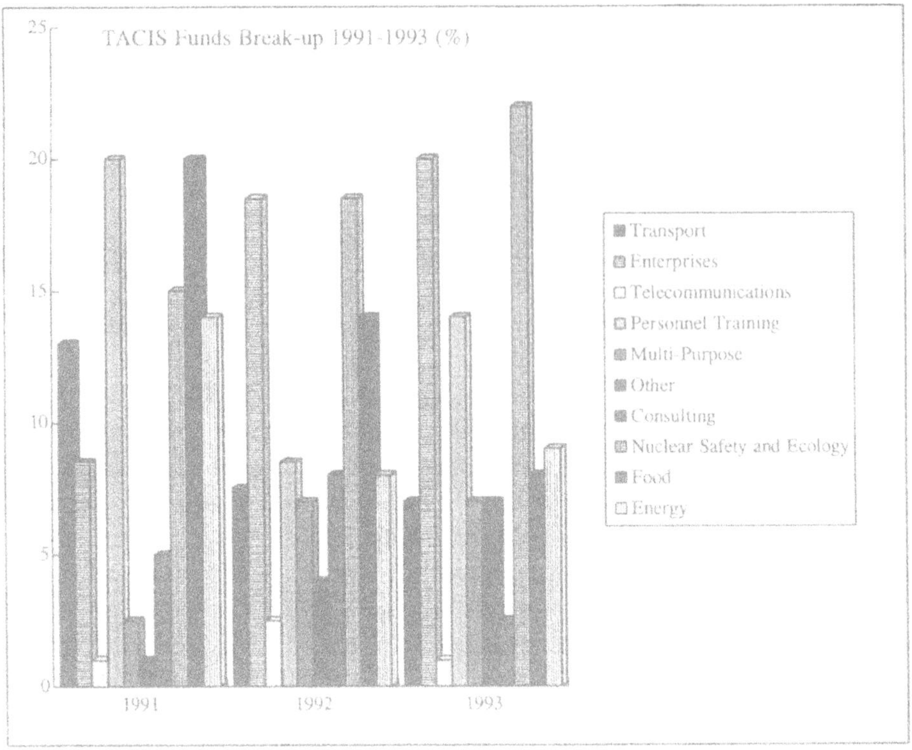

Figure 1. Commission of European Communities Technical Aid to the Commonwealth of Independent States (TACIS) (Source: *Europa* No. 3, May-June 1994, pp. 41-42)

USAID is building its activities on the basis of the Freedom Support Act passed by US Congress. In its strategy paper USAID defines the goal of its technical mission to the New Independent States (NIS): "We wish to achieve enduring, normal and productive bilateral relations with each New Independent State, and to encourage such relations among them, and between them and their partners in the world community. We believe that this kind of partnership will ultimately require stability and prosperity, and international relationships based on mutual recognition of reasonable security interests, normal economic relations, and free movement of people, goods, and ideas" [9].

Canada's program of technical assistance to Russia was first announced at the London G-7 Economic Summit in July 1991. The program has three objec-

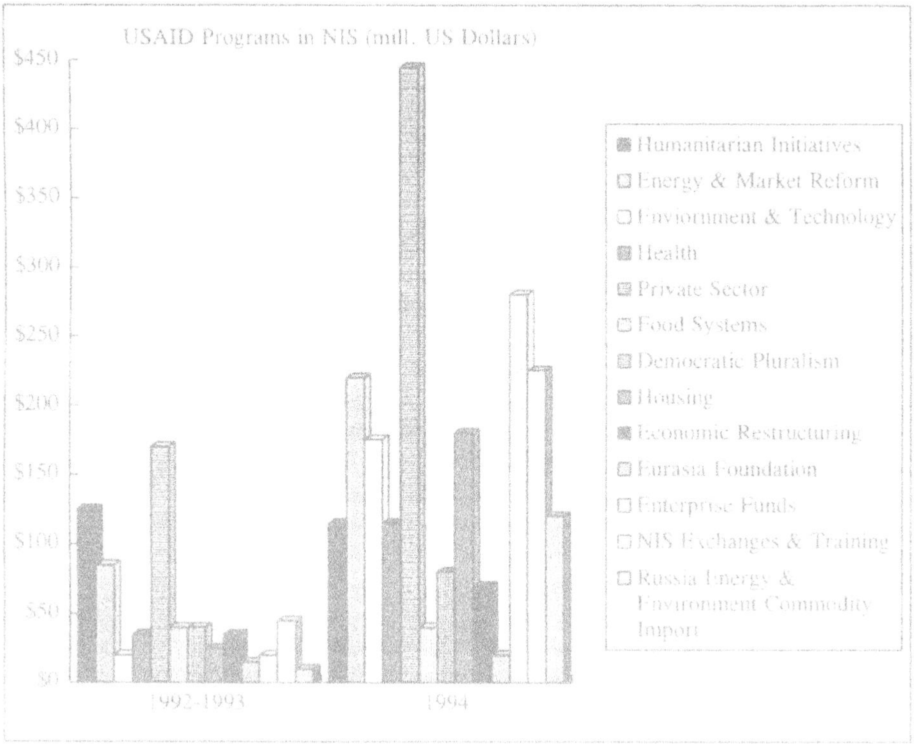

Figure 2. USAID Programs in the New Independent States
(Source: *U.S. Agency for International Development Fact Sheet #94-06*, Washington, DC, January 1994)

tives: to promote the transition to market-based economies, support democratic development, and increase Canadian trade and investment.

The strategies cited above, the nature of technical aid distribution between projects together with a study of the nature of projects undertaken within the framework of technical aid programs (the latter part of this analysis is too bulky to be presented here) lead to some conclusions:

1) There is no coordinated "Western" strategy of technical aid to Russia and CIS.
2) There seems to be no "positive" understanding among the Western countries of the nature of Russia's technological needs. COCOM demonstrated a "negative" understanding, by listing technologies not to be

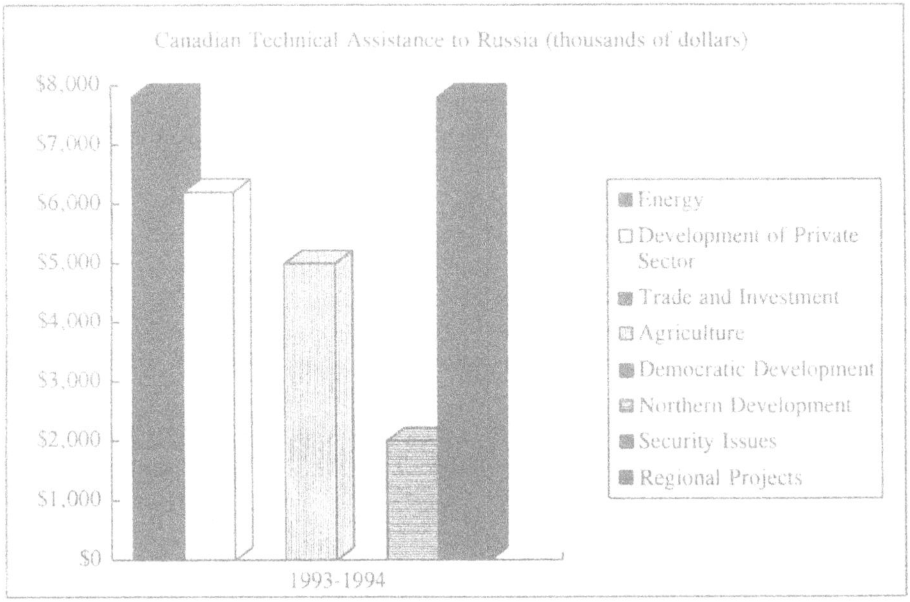

Figure 3. Canadian Technical Assistance to Russia
(Source: *Canadian Technical Assistance to Russia - Project Listing*,
April 1994, Bureau of Assistance for Central and Eastern Europe,
Department of Foreign Affairs and International Trade)

exported to Russia. There is no Western authoritative body which would formulate what technologies are a priority for the transfer to Russia in the present transition period.

3) Western technical donors are still focused on the economic and security consequences of technology exports and pay much less attention to the social and political spin-off of technology transfer to Russia. Though all Western governments made a strong point of helping the "evolving Russian democracy" through technical aid, the main focus of their programs was directed elsewhere.

3. Technologies Relevant to Social and Political Change in Russia: Four Empirical Cases

In order to show how technologies, or the lack of them, influence political and social developments in Russia, this article focuses on four distinct areas: privatization, telecommunications, plastic currency and farming. They are not really case studies, and no data was available to apply more scientific quantitative methods to such studies. These areas by no means exhaust the list of politically relevant technologies; a political scientist would quickly add to this list such technologies as political campaigning, public administration and applied computing in certain areas. However, the impact produced by the technologies considered here on society and politics will help to illustrate the ideas advocated in this article, and will hopefully draw the attention of experts and politicians to the need of further research in this field.

3.1. PRIVATIZATION

Unlike any other East European country - Poland, for example, where clearly the primary goal of privatization was to restructure the Polish economy and to assure future economic growth - Russia was guided by opposite priorities in its privatization program: 1) Russia emphasized the political consequences of the privatization program, and 2) in historic terms, Russia aimed at completing the program rapidly.

The concept of privatization in Russia was totally dominated by political reasons at the cost of economic effectiveness. After coming to power "democrats" had no guarantee of staying in power, and were looking for a social basis to serve as an anchor for "democratization" and "capitalization" of Russia. As there was no sizable social basis of this kind in the country, they decided to create one artificially through privatizing the economy and cultivating "a class of owners." Moreover, not only was the economic effectiveness not a priority, but the fathers of Russian privatization sacrificed the common rules of social justice as well.

This predominant idea also made it necessary to complete the privatization in one year - while the authors still control the government machine and there is no organized political force to stop the process.

The results of the privatization in Russia can be briefly described in a few points:

a) There is now a class of owners in Russia who are a guaranteed obstacle against the return of communism. However, the target had been to create a large middle class of independent entrepreneurs. Instead, Russia today has a small class of "nouveau riches" married to criminal structures and corrupt government officers.
b) Common people feel cheated. Their misery becomes more evident with every new financial scandal over "privatization funds."
c) Economically, Russian privatization was a catastrophe. The state budget received no revenues at all for all the property that passed to the hands of the "nouveau riches." This has undermined production and contributed significantly to the unprecedented economic recession. It strangled production capital and stimulated the growth of speculative capital.

Some technical aid programs including TACIS did transfer some privatization know-how to Russia. The results of privatization in Russia might have been much better had technical aid been more consistent and persuasive.

3.2. TELECOMMUNICATIONS AND MAIL

If in the Soviet era information flows within and outside the country were carefully filtered and blocked, right now they are open but totally chaotic. Experts do not know what their colleagues are doing, businessmen do not know what the prices and opportunities are in neighboring regions, and government does not have a complete picture of the situation in Russia's regions.

It is difficult to make a call to another city and electronic networks, barely developed, do not offer even the most basic services they offer in the West such as managing your banking account, booking tickets or shopping. Even mail does not work well: it is unreliable and takes too long.

The lack of telecommunication networks increases the cost and time span of virtually every activity in the country. It hinders the development of a home-based self-employed middle class which could bring more stability to the country. It hinders the integration of Russia in the world economy and labor markets, and makes the Russian economic behavior and lifestyle incompatible with Western ones, threatening to keep Russia forever in the backyard of civilization. This situation may become dangerous even from a security perspective, but already now it adds to the discontent of intellectuals, preserves economic and technological backwardness in other areas, and maintains an excellent shelter for illegal activities of Russian and foreign criminals.

The Russian government recognizes this problem, though it views it mostly from an economic perspective. It is trying to promote international cooperation in this area, but so far Russia lacks adequate technologies and investment in this field.

3.3. PLASTIC CARDS, TAXATION AND CRIME

For more than a year sociological surveys in Russia indicate that the biggest concern of the citizens in this country has become crime and corruption, not political instability or economic difficulties. Having initiated the Federal Anti-Crime Program, President Yeltsin has also assigned the highest priority to this problem. Peotr Fillipov, former head of the Presidential Analytical Center and one of the authors of the Anti-Crime Program, believes that up to 90% of retail trade and small businesses in Russia pay bribes and pay for protection. A real war is being waged against businessmen and bankers on the streets of Russian cities, with dozens of casualties every day. Many people believe that the country is run by a "Mafia," not by the government or regional elites.

Though there is hardly a technological panacea against this disease, some measures can definitely improve the situation.

The biggest source for the growth of corruption and organized crime is the nature of money transfers in Russia — an important part of it is in cash. Cash payments allow businesses to conceal their income from the Internal Revenue Service, thus creating large amounts of illegal unregistered money. This money, in turn, makes these businesses vulnerable to rackets and to the pressure of corrupt government officers. The system has become a circle: you cannot operate a business without concealing your income; but you have to pay the required bribes and pay off the racketeers, and to afford this you must conceal your income.

The introduction of plastic cards for all forms of payment in select towns proved to be an effective instrument for breaking this circle. So far plastic currency is the privilege of the rich, and it is accepted only by a few stores and services. A countrywide introduction of plastic cards alone will not solve the problem of crime and corruption, but with the support of adequate tax legislation and police measures it is capable of making the criminal situation much healthier.

3.4. FARMING

Traditionally Russia has been a peasant country, and its economic strength and the morale of the people relied on the peasantry.

One of the declared priorities of economic reform in Russia is to give a second birth to farming. If successful, this policy will solve the food problem of the country. More importantly, it will create a layer of politically and economically independent people who will enhance political stability and bring back a work ethic to Russian society.

The problem here is that Russia lacks adequate technology for individual farming and small-scale food-processing, because for decades all technologies have been developed for large-scale state or collective farms. This specific area attracted Western technical aid. It seems that right now, when land reform is entering a critical phase in Russia, Western efforts in this field should be continued.

4. Impact of Uncoordinated Efforts on Russian Society and Policy - The Need for a Technology Transfer Policy from NATO to Partner Countries

There is a long dispute in scholarly literature, in art, and in Russian society about the roots of Russian national political psychology. Many have addressed the question of whether Russians can form a democratic society. It seems that the answer will have to come much later, because there is barely a democratic society in Russia at the moment, and few Russians are totally satisfied with what they have in their country.

Some things are evident, though: for the majority of the population democracy did not appear to emerge according to their personal aspirations. In other words, they were not prepared for it internally, and it was imposed on them.

Historically, democracy was introduced into society by economically free and active individuals. They demanded a certain organization of society to secure their economic freedom and develop society further in line with what seemed natural to humankind. Russian reform did not start from economics, and an economically free individual did not exist when political liberties were declared. As a result, in the course of reforms Russia has to solve two gigantic problems simultaneously: to bolster democracy and to help its people make a new economic start.

In this respect the flow of technologies from the West and from NATO countries in particular-both "hard" such as producing ones and "soft," such as economic and political know-how - becomes very important. One should admit that, though the efforts of the Western countries in this direction were never properly coordinated, they initiated some positive political and social changes in Russia.

4.1. "SOFT" TECHNOLOGIES IN POLITICAL AND SOCIAL LIFE

The biggest impact in this sector of technology transfer was produced by the adaptation of **Western political know-how, non-governmental organization know-how, polling technology and marketing know-how.**

All programs conducted in Russia are based on the assumption that the political system is being supported by two processes: firstly, the participation of citizens in the political process and, secondly, the development of democratic institutions. A series of workshops, seminars and publications has managed to inform practically all active Russian politicians of senior and medium level in Moscow and in key other regions of the basic concepts and technologies of political campaigning, party-building and parliamentary work. This knowledge has contributed to a certain extent to the stabilization of the political situation in Russia and to the adoption of common rules of the game by the majority of participants in the political process.

The concept of non-governmental organizations (NGOs) was not alien to Russia even before, but modern NGO technology - including organizational principles, fund-raising know-how, and lobbying methods - were brought to the country from the West. Self organization of the citizens is the key element of the development the civil society in Russia. The number and influence of NGOs - ranging from consumer associations to policy-oriented groups -are growing very quickly now and it is important to continue the education of new emerging groups.

Polling technology became an important tool for the government in establishing a feedback from the people. Traditionally in Russia the government has been and often remains separated from the people. Today, politicians have to seek the support of the voters, and for that purpose they have to know their opinion on dozens of questions.

Marketing ideas were totally alien to the Soviet economic system. Now we see that business starts to work for the customer; this means a radical change in Russian mentality.

4.2. "HARD" AND "SOFT" TECHNOLOGIES IN ECONOMIC BEHAVIOR

The biggest change regarding the patterns and standards of the world civilization in attitudes, decision-making, consumption modes, lifestyle as well as in ideology can be seen among people involved in banking, insurance and financial services, media, private farming, tourism, private hotel business, international transportation and communications.

The key technological elements here are: **applied computing, telecommunications with a special role played by electronic networks,** knowledge of financial markets and instruments, application of international standards in services and work in general, and knowledge of foreign languages. At the same time, when at least one of these components is missing, one will expect from the people economic and intellectual failures, dissatisfaction, absence of initiative and stimulus for work, a relationship of dependency on the state, etc.

4.3. THE NEED FOR A TECHNOLOGY TRANSFER POLICY FROM NATO TO PARTNER COUNTRIES

This article has attempted to argue that technology transfer from NATO countries to Partner Countries should not be viewed exclusively from a technical point of view. The process generates profound changes in the societies and politics of Partner Countries; the impact produced by it should be taken into account by NATO and Partner Countries while they work out their technology transfer policy.

The problem outlined above is of a political nature and needs a political decision taken on the advice of experts in technology, economics, sociology, and political science. It is closely connected with the changing role of NATO and the current revisions of its policies.

As shown above, very little precise quantitative information relating to the social and political impact of technology transfer on the Partner countries from is available so far. The first step in formulating proposals for NATO and Partner countries would be to collect and process such information.

A body best fit for the coordination of this research would be the NATO Committee on the Challenges of Modern Society. As the problem of the impact of technology transfer falls within one of the four priority areas of NATO International Scientific Exchange Programs — more precisely within Human Resources/ Science and Technology Policy —the organizational form of such a research could be either a NATO Advanced Study Institute (ASI) or NATO Advanced Research Workshop (ARW). Since the problem of the social and political impact on Partner countries from NATO is being addressed at this Advanced Research Workshop on Human Resources and Leadership for Technology Transfer, it is of great importance to utilize the expertise and organizational experience accumulated by this research body.

There is a need to focus on several issues:

1) Collect and process data on the social and political impact of technology transfer from NATO countries to Partner Countries.
2) Identify technologies contributing to "positive" social and political change in general and in regard to specific Partner Countries.
3) Prepare proposals on the use of technology transfer for supporting democracy, civil society and societal infrastructure of economic reform in Partner countries.
4) Submit its scientific findings and recommendations to the NATO Committee on the Challenges of Modern Society, to be discussed and presented for the consideration by NATO and Partner Countries at the political level.

References

1. Binder, L., Coleman, J., LaPalombara, J., Pye, L., Verba, S., and Weiner, M. (1971) *The Theory of Prismatic Societies*.

2. Francis, A.M. (1980) *Perspectives on Modernization: Toward a General Theory of Third World Development*, 215.

3. Halperin, M. (1963) *The Politics and Social Change in the Middle East and North Africa*.

4. Huntington, S. (1968) *Political Order in Changing Societies*.

5. National Academy of Sciences (1985) *Technological Frontiers and Foreign Relations*, National Academy Press, Washington, D.C.

6. Oxford University Press (1990) *Concise Oxford Dictionary*.

7. Riggs, F. (1964) *Administration in Developing Countries*.

8. TACIS (1995) *Summary of Indicative Programmes 1993-1995*, TACIS Information Office, D.G.I., Commission of the European Communities, 39.

9. U.S. Agency for Economic Development (1994) *United States Assistance and Economic Cooperation Strategy for the New Independent States*, Approved January 14, 1994 by the Coordinator of U.S. Assistance to the New Independent States, 2.

6. THE PERSONNEL NEEDS OF SIBERIAN INDUSTRIES AND INSTITUTIONS FOR EFFECTIVE TECHNOLOGY TRANSFER

JURY P. POHOLKOV
Rector, Tomsk Polytechnic University
Russian Federation

Introduction

The modern world is characterized by a high dynamism of development in its social, economic, scientific, technical and cultural spheres.

Moreover, a society trying to create comfortable conditions and surroundings from time to time faces problems, the solution of which allows it to rise to a new state of development. Currently, one of such problems is technology transfer. It leads to contradictions between old and new, between designers and producers, between producers and consumers. Despite the need, the expediency and effectiveness in the use of new technologies are often insufficient for a quick progress to mass production

Apparently, such a kind of problem depends not only on the development level of science, education, production, and the economy in general, but also on the social system, on peculiarities of culture and even on the geographical position of one region and its demographical situation at the given time.

Undoubtedly, at the center of these problems there is a person with his or her characteristics and an official with all his or her connections, interests, abilities and opportunities.

This paper endeavors to analyze the problems in the transfer of new projects (technologies, materials, devices, etc.) from designers to producers using examples from the real life of a big region such as Siberia.

G. Bugliarello et al. (eds.), East-West Technology Transfer, 77-97.

1. The Siberian Region of Russia
(brief characteristics of the economic situation)

1.1. GEOGRAPHICAL AND HISTORICAL INFORMATION

Siberia is a vast territory of Russia to the east of the Ural mountains (Figure 1). It is divided into Western Siberia and Eastern Siberia. Western Siberia includes the Omsk, Tomsk, Tyumen, Novosibirsk, Kemerovo regions and the Altai territories. Eastern Siberia includes the Irkutsk region and Buryatia, Khakasia and Tuva Republics. The Tyumen region and other regions have a number of national structures (autonomous regions): Khanty-Mansi, Yamalo-Nenets, Evenk, Taimyr, Ust-Ordynsk Buryat and Aginsk Buryat [6].

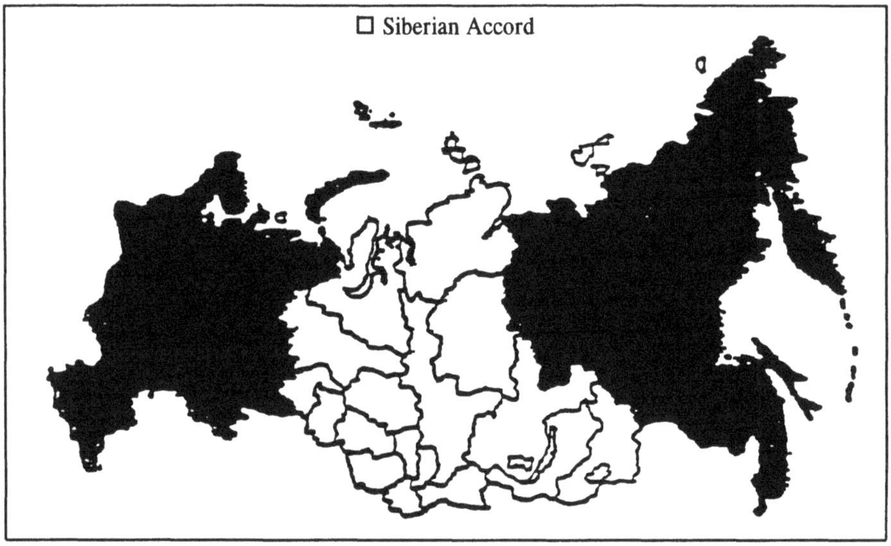

Figure 1. Siberian Accord

In November 1990 during events called later on in Russia "a parade of sovereignties" the association SIBERIAN ACCORD was set up. Twenty-four million people live on the territory of the Siberian Accord, which has an area of 10 million square kilometers.

The development of Siberia began in the XVI - XVII centuries. Especially after the reform of 1861 and during the Transsiberian railway building in 1891-1905, the stream of migration to this region increased substantially.

The development of Siberia after the October Revolution 1917 in connection with the opening up of prospecting for natural resources proceeded rapidly, and from an agrarian region, Siberia turned into an industrial-agrarian one. The population increased three times over that of the pre-revolutionary period. At the same time, in terms of economic development, before the revolution the agrarian sector had priority; after the revolution the branches of extractive industry were given priority; and for the last 25-30 years Siberia became a fuel-power complex. The processing and consumer industry including light, food, and above all the everyday infrastructure are still insufficiently developed [8].

1.2. CHANGES IN ECONOMIC POLICY OF SIBERIA

Today Siberia is considered to be one of the most important regions of Russia because of great stocks of natural resources. These are 85 per cent of Russian stocks of gas, 75 per cent of coal, 65 per cent of oil, and great stocks of the other important natural resources [11].

The policy of economic development of Siberia was not constant. Even for the last 8-10 years there have been three qualitatively different stages of socio-economic development.

I Stage - before 1988

The territorial priorities were defined using the directives of centralized plans.

The characteristic feature of economic policy in Siberia in these years was priority development of the West-Siberian oil-and-gas complex and of the Krasnoyarsk territory. Both played an important role in the economic progress of the country on the whole.

The documents guiding such a policy were various territorial and district development programs which were not part of the plans for the national economy, and so they were not balanced by material, finance and other resources. Measures for achieving the economic policy goals were limited. So, in oil-producing districts personnel enjoyed regional coefficients multiplying their salary, "north privileges," extra payment for long experience of work, etc.

On the whole, by the end of the period the indices of economic development of Siberia looked rather well at the All-Republic level. The economic policy of this period had a pronounced pro-Siberian character. The rates of growth of

Siberian industry, on the whole, slightly exceeded the average for the republic. The regional share both in production and non-production investments increased continuously, and standards of living approximated the average for the country, but slowly and irregularly.

II Stage - 1989-1991

The beginning of economic reforms, the non-participation in state economy control, and the introduction of new enterprise forms have adversely affected the economic situation of Siberia; the period of contracted birth rates began.

The share of national investment in Siberia declined from 28 per cent in 1988 to 25 per cent in 1991. As a result, the rates of decrease in industrial production in Siberia were considerably higher than the average ones. According to all production and consumption indices, by the end of this period Siberia had the lowest values for the last years compared to the national Russian ones.

III Stage - since 1992

The economy development is mainly defined by market regulators, while state management reduces rapidly. The period is characterized by strong reduction in manufacturing, especially for the last months (for five months of 1994 the volume of production in Russia decreased by 25 per cent compared to the analogous period the previous year). The same tendencies are observed in the industry of Siberia. But there is one important distinctive feature of the Siberian economy: the dynamics of investments. During 1992 in comparable prices investments decreased by 31 per cent in Siberia (versus an average by 45 per cent in Russia). In 1992 the investment peculiarities of the Siberian economy are shown by the "Tyumen phenomenon:" the investment reduction in that region was 19 per cent while in the south regions of Western and Eastern Siberia it was 39-40 per cent and differed only slightly from the All-Russian level.

In 1991 Western Siberia's share of gross output was 10.8 per cent of that of the Russian industry as a whole, and in the fourth quarter of 1992 it increased to 17.4 per cent, the main reason being the rise in prices of oil-and-gas industry products.

The dynamics of the Siberian share of Russian economy is given in Table 1 [5].

TABLE 1. Share of Siberia in Important Indices of the Russian Economy (%)

Indices	1985	1988	1990	1992
Population	16.0	16.3	16.4	16.4
Consumption fund	15.9	16.2	16.0	15.9
Accumulation fund	23.0	24.3	21.3	23.8
Basic funds	19.3	20.3	21.2	21.8
Industry products	17.3	17.6	17.5	17.5
Capital investments	26.1	27.8	25.2	32.0
Agricultural products	16.8	16.9	16.5	15.9

The rates of change of industrial production in Siberian regions compared to Russian ones are given in Figure 2 [5].

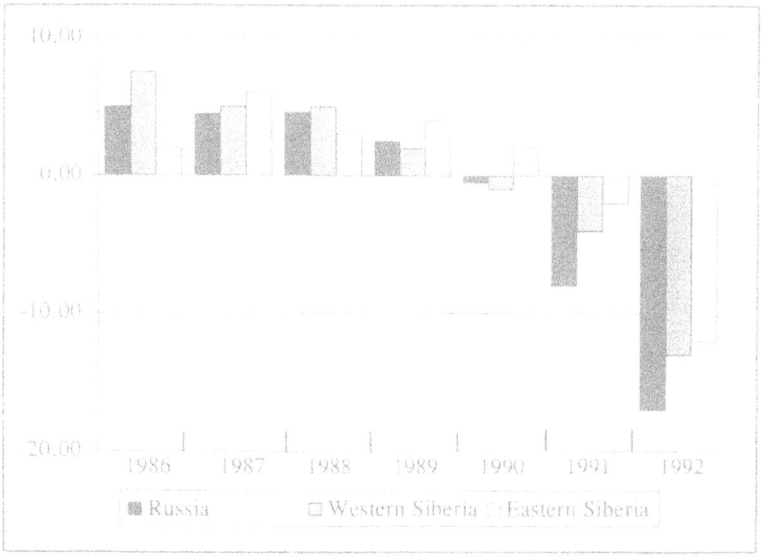

Figure 2. Rates of Change in Industrial Production (%)

The average monthly pay of industrial personnel - as per cent of pay for Russia as a whole - for the Siberian regions and for the participants of the Siberian Accord is shown in Table 2 [5].

TABLE 2. Average Monthly Payment of Personnel as Percent of Payments for Russia as a Whole

Regions, territories	1986	1988	1989	1990	1991	1992
Siberia	117.4	117.0	117.8	117.8	125.1	151.3
Western Siberia	115.4	115.3	115.9	117.3	122.6	148.1
Altai territory	101.7	99.8	98.2	97.7	96.4	87.5
Kemerovo region	122.9	121.6	123.3	126.3	146.4	202.4
Novosibirsk region	104.1	102.6	103.2	105.2	98.9	78.5
Omsk region	102.0	99.1	97.3	95.6	90.7	95.1
Tyumen region	152.7	160.2	162.3	161.9	173.6	274.3
Eastern Siberia	120.8	120.0	120.8	118.6	129.2	156.6
Krasnoyarsk territory	125.2	122.2	122.7	119.8	139.5	176.2
Irkutsk region	124.3	123.9	124.7	123.1	131.1	153.7
Chita region	106.9	107.3	110.1	108.7	109.1	118.2
Buratia	110.4	114.3	115.7	112.1	111.5	109.3
Tuva	93.2	99.0	94.6	94.0	84.0	104.4

1.3. MAIN FEATURES OF SIBERIAN INDUSTRY AND ROLE OF SIBERIA IN THE ECONOMY OF RUSSIA

The extracting branches of industry are leading in the Siberian industrial complex. The share of Siberia in Russian oil output is 75 per cent; gas output, more than 90 per cent; coal, 64 per cent; wood stocks and commercial timber production, 32 per cent. Only 20 per cent of Russian oil is reprocessed in Siberia.

The data concerning the role of Siberia in the manufacture of different kinds of products are represented in Table 3 [10].

At present, oil is extracted in the Tyumen and Tomsk regions. Its maximum output occurred in 1988, 415 million tons (oil and condensate). In 1989 the output decreased by 10 million tons, in 1990 by 29 million more, and in 1991-1992 by more than 10 million tons every year. The crisis of Western Siberia proved to be greater than that of the other Siberian regions [9].

TABLE 3. Economic Specialization of Siberia

Industry	Region										
	Share in Russia, %	Altai territory	Kemerovo region	Novosibirsk region	Omsk region	Tomsk region	Tyumen region	Krasnoyarsk territory	Irkutsk region	Chita region	Burytatia
Machine-building	30	+	+		+	+		+	+	+	+
Chemical	40	+	+	+			+	+	+		
Light	30	+		+	+			+	+	+	+
Food	30	+		+	+	+	+	+	+	+	+
Construction materials	10	+	+	+		+	+	+	+	+	+
Energetic	42		+						+		
Wood	17					+	+		+	+	+
Timber	32								+	+	+
Pulp and paper	24							+	+		
Mining	12		+						+	+	+
Coal-mining	64		+								
Metallurgic	36		+	+				+			
Shipbuilding	8							+			
Radio engineering	15							+			
Agricultural machine-building	26			+							
Machine-tool manufacture	34			+							
Aviation	32			+							
Metal-working	28			+	+	+					
Electrical	40			+		+					+
Electronic	12			+							
Oil-processing	20				+			+			
Oil-extracting	75				+	+	+				
Gas-extracting	90				+	+	+				

This branch of industry is supposed to organize 10-12 holding companies which, as united production-economy complexes, will operate in the whole production cycle, including search and prospecting of oil fields, oil production and processing and realization of oil products as well.

In Western Siberia oil-producing enterprises have already organized three companies: "LUKoil," "Yukos" and "Surgut oil-and-gas." Not long ago the "Eastern Oil Company" was also registered. The former three companies produce oil and oil products supplying mainly the European regions, the latter one Siberia.

In 1992 in Russia natural gas extraction amounted to 640 billion cubic meters, 445.4 billion cubic meters being used for inland consumption, and 90 billion cubic meters for export.

Gas consumption per head in Russia in 1992 was 2.97 thousand cubic meters/year, against 2.4 thousand cubic meters/year in the USA. It is the highest consumption level in the world. Natural gas extraction in the Siberian region in 1992 was equal to 556 billion cubic meters, including 549.8 billion cubic meters in the Tyumen region [12].

The gas industry, probably, is the only sector of the Russian economy where the economic crisis has not led to a sharp recession in production. However, the rates of gas extraction decreased to a considerable extent. At present, furthermore, this sector of industry has great difficulty in maintaining production volumes. The same conditions are encountered in the oil sector.

Also very difficult is the situation in the wood products sector, which is considered to be the oldest industrial branch of Siberia. Without exaggeration one may say that it is on the verge of breakdown. There are no young people living in the forest settlements, only pensioners live here - the wealthy, according to our present criterion. Nobody can envy their life because woodworking enterprises have no means to maintain forest settlements and their social infrastructure. Due to the rise in the cost of stock and transportation rates in Russian and abroad there is no market for the best timber of the Irkutsk region and Krasnoyarsk territory, not only in our country but in the whole world. The wood conveyor is being stopped. [2; 3; 7].

The branches of the defense complex have a very important place in the Siberian economy. Approximately 11 per cent of the total number of working people in the military industrial complex and more than 10 per cent of defense enterprises of Russia are in Siberia. About 18 per cent of all the people engaged in industry in Siberia work in defense. Of this number, 20-24 per cent are concentrated in sectoral and academic research institutes and design bureaus, approximately 25 per cent are engineering staff and professional, a statistic that underscores the high intellectual potential of the Siberian military industrial complex [1].

Siberian defense enterprises have 14 per cent of the total regional production output; in the total volume of machine-building products their share exceeded 50 per cent by the end of 1990. This complex includes more than a half of all the basic production assets and of the industrial production personnel of Siberian machine-building.

The main kernel of Siberian military industrial complex comprises the enterprises in machine-building, instrument-making, radioelectronic and aviation industry, which indicate the complex specialization of the production of high technology products.

2. Technology Transfer in Siberian Industry
(issues, experience, needs)

2.1 TYPES OF ORGANIZATIONS INVOLVED IN TECHNOLOGY TRANSFER

Organization structures play a major role in technology transfer. There is a large number of such organizations. Among them we can single out four main types involved in technology transfer (Figure 3).

1. *Integrated Sectoral Research-Production Associations (RPA)*
This is the most conservative and cumbersome organization under the control of a united center. Its strategy on technology transfer is developed, as a rule, by RPA workers. Sometimes associations of this sort are customers of the Research Institutes of higher educational establishments and the Academy of Sciences and customers of foreign firms as well. Such organizations are still existing but the role of Research Institute and design bureau is decreasing.

2. *Separated Branch Organizations*
Separated branch organizations are systems of branch Research Institutes, design bureaus connected by cost accounting ties with industrial enterprises. They carry out research and development work tasked to them. As industrial production falls, this group of organizations has decreased considerably.

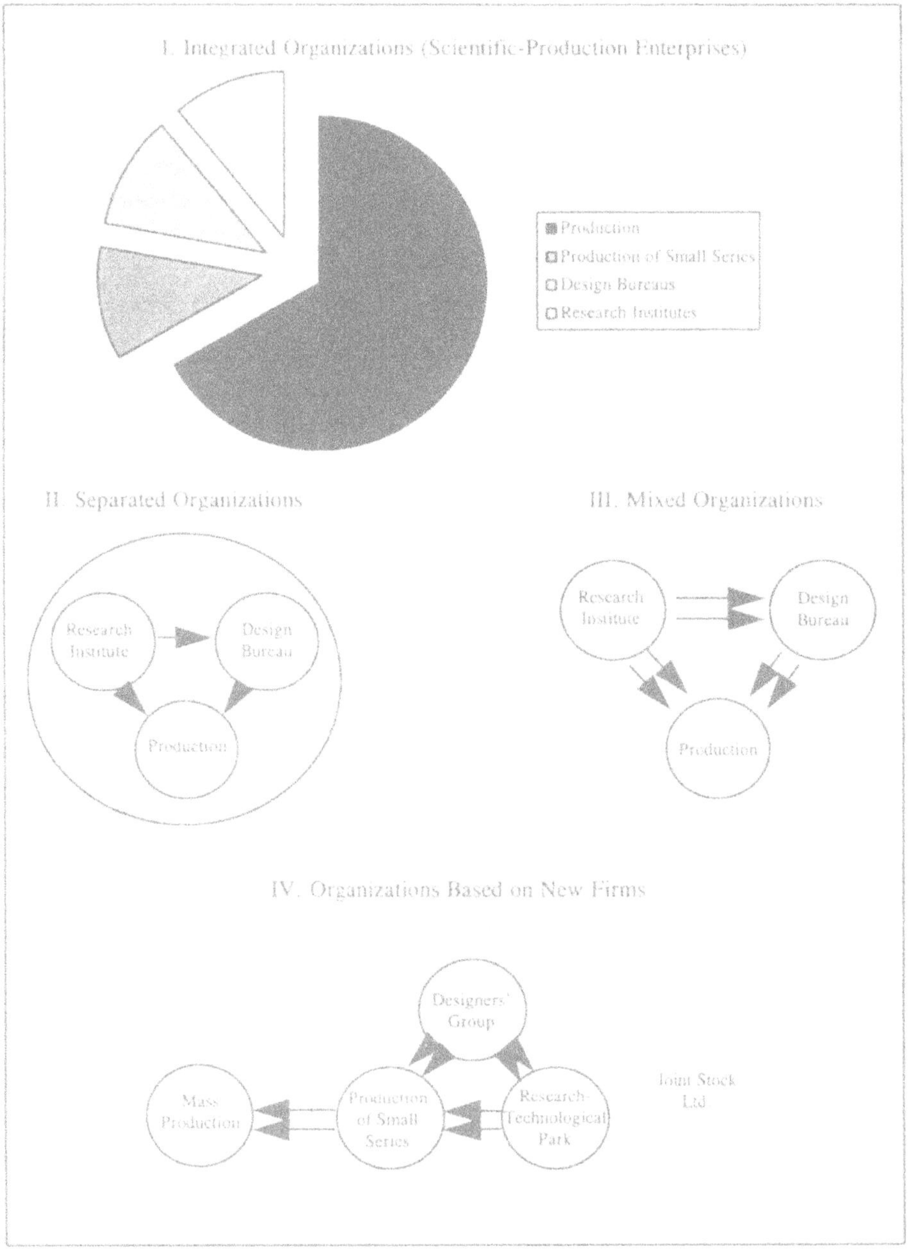

Figure 3. **Basic Types of the Scientific and Industrial Organizations Which Support Technological Transfer**

3. *Mixed Organizations*
These organizations may include the Research Institutes of higher educational establishments, Academy of Sciences, design bureaus of the same systems or branch, and large plants. The hierarchy of the partners may differ. Their relations are determined by economic contracts between them. The personnel in this group of organizations is decreasing.

4. *Small Firms*
At present this is the most rapidly developing type of organization; it includes different sorts of limited liability companies, either small joint-stock companies or individual private enterprises. Newly-created Research-Technological parks, which often represent joint-stock companies as well, begin to play the role of accelerators of technology transfer, by offering services in elaboration of patented designs, certification, experimental production. Sometimes these parks play a role of incubators of new high technology production.

The designers in this kind of structure, as a rule, are the people who worked in the State Research Institutes and design bureaus in the past, and who are the authors (or co-authors) of inventions [4].

2.2. THE MAIN PROBLEMS IN TECHNOLOGY TRANSFER

The problems occurring in technology transfer can be divided into several groups, according to their causes (Table 4).

In the table these problems are represented only partially. It should be especially noted that at present the instability of the Russian economy has a decisive influence on the process of technology transfer. Two main factors play a role.

A deep decrease in production, inflation, the absence of money resources for technologies' purchase prevent the flow of foreign technologies to Russia. At the same time, the flow of capital from abroad is strongly kept back by a weak legal basis, and an unstable political and economic situation which does not assure the repayment of capital to investors.

The second factor, however paradoxical, is competition on the world market. Russian products and technologies, although inexpensive because of cheap manpower on the Russian home market, are not permitted by competitors to enter the world market though they are of good quality.

For the Siberian industry these factors are even more serious, given the remoteness of Siberian enterprises from the Russian borders and the higher cost of any contacts with foreign partners (scientific, business, production).

TABLE 4. Classification of Problems in Technology Transfer (TT) and Their Causes

Cause	Production falling, inflation	Absence of training specialists for field technologies transfer	Contradictions between personnel and leadership	Absence of certification system	Shortcomings of patent system	Absence of technologies' transfer system
Problem	1. Absence of money for new developments payment. 2. There is no necessity to improve products. 3. Going away of experienced specialists (completely or partially) "Intellects going away."	1. Absence of specialists in TT field. 2. Absence of personnel and additional training in TT field.	1. Aspiration to independence by separate groups of designers and individuals. 2. Potential washing-out. 3. Low salary. 4. High overhead expenses (prices for energy inflation). 5. Poor copyright protection (collective and individual).	1. Absence of regional certificate centers. 2. Absence of demands for quality production on the part of society. 3. Poor procedural and laboratory basis. 4. Uneven demands for certification in Russia and abroad.	1. Few patenting centers. 2. Poor legal basis in patenting.	1. Absence of data banks on required technologies. 2. Absence of special structures in the enterprises. 3, Absence of data banks on developed technologies. 4. Absence of special national program by technologies' transfer.

2.3 NEEDS OF SIBERIAN RESEARCH INSTITUTES AND INDUSTRIAL ENTERPRISES IN TECHNOLOGIES' TRANSFER

An analysis of the changes taking place at Siberian institutes and industrial enterprises today - their nature and the problems connected with a transition to the market economy - shows that the use of new technologies is an even greater necessity for Siberian industry than for the industry in the rest of Russia. These needs are defined, mainly, by the fact that the basic Siberian industry is an extracting one (oil, gas, coal, wood, minerals, metals). New directions are required.

Firstly, there is a need for technologies for raw materials processing. Secondly, the most effective new technologies of raw material extraction, wood stock and mining are needed; and thirdly, technologies concerning nature protection, ecology, sewage treatment, waste utilization. The needs of some Siberian enterprises in technology transfer are given in Table 5.

A great research-technological potential is concentrated at present in the Siberian region (Research Institutes of the Siberian Department of the Russian Academy of Sciences, Research Institutes of the Academy of Medical Sciences, branch Research Institutes, higher educational establishments, Research Institutes at higher educational establishments). In the transition to a market economy, with at the same time decreasing budgets and sharp reduction of orders by indus-

TABLE 5. Needs of Siberian Enterprises in New Effective Technologies

Enterprises	A group of necessary technologies		
	Technologies of raw material processing	Technologies of extraction, mining	Technologies in the field of ecology, nature protection
Siberian Chemical Group of Enterprises		Technology of rather pure silicon separation	Technology of organic radioactive waste material processing
Joint-stock company "Tomsk Oil"	Technology of natural and accompanying gases' cleaning. Technologies of oil processing	Technology of oil well output increase	Technologies of oil waste collection and processing
Tomsk timber - industrial group of enterprises	Technology of deep timber processing	Technologies allowing to keep the undergrowth	Technologies of river-bed cleaning. Technologies of artificial wood restoring
Joint-stock company "Siberian turf"	Technology of turf processing	Technology of turf output	
Joint-stock company Tomsk Electric Lamp plant			Gases' cleaning from hydrogen sulfide
Production association "Kemerovo Wood"	Technology of activated charcoal production		Technology of antismoke additives for motor fuel and oils' production
Joint-stock company "Norilskgasindustry"	Technology of cleaning of heating surfaces of steam boilers from contamination		Optimization technology of process burning in boiler rooms and central heating-power plant
Association "Nizhnevartovsk oil-and-gas"	Technology of deep oil processing	Development technologies of small low-productive deposits	Technology of drinking and circulating water decomposition

TABLE 6. Examples of Transfer Technologies Developed in Western Siberia (Tomsk)

Technologies († - conversion)	Designers (institute, enterprise)
1. Ecological	
1.1 Economic control systems for admixtures and cleaning of air, gases, water, substances	Tomsk Polytechnic University (TPU), Tomsk State Architectural-Building Academy (TSABA), Tomsk State University (TSU), Institute of Oil Chemistry (IOC), Siberian Department of Russian Academy of Sciences (SD RAS), Research Institute of Semiconductors (RIS), others
†1.2 Control technologies for radiation, radioactive waste materials storing and reprocessing	Siberian Chemical Enterprise, TPU
2. Medical	
†2.1 Precision electromechanical technologies for manufacture of prostheses, stimulators, instruments for microsurgery	Instrument Plant (TIP), Siberian State Medical University (SSMU)
2.2 Prosthesis, medical instruments of alloys	Siberian Physico-Technical Institute at TSU (SPTI), Russian Materials' Centre (RMC), SD RAS
2.3 Production technology for radio-pharmaceutical preparations, isotopes for medical diagnosis and treatment	Research Institute of Nuclear Physics at TPU (RINP), Research Institute of Cardiology RAMS (RIC)
2.4 Early diagnosis of oncologic diseases, atherosclerosis using laser methods on genetic markers	Research Institute of Oncology RAMS (RIO), Research Institute of Medical Genetics RAMS (RIMG)
2.5 Economic, fast devices, analyzers for diagnosis of various pathologies	Research Institute of Biology and Biophysics at TSU (RIBB), Research Institute of Applied Mathematics and Mechanics at TSU (RIAMM), RIC, SSMU, TPU, Design-Technological Centre "Optics"

TABLE 6. Examples of Transfer Technologies Developed in Western Siberia (Tomsk) (cont'd)

3. Technical		
†3.1	Production technologies for ultradispersed powders for powder metallurgy, creation of new sorbents, getters, catalyzers, pigments	TPU, SCE, RMC, IOC SD RAS
†3.2	Fluoride Technologies for uranium reprocessing, creating of ozone-safe refrigerants, high-purity metals, fluoroplastics	SCE, TPU
†3.3	Technologies for design, fabrication of high-strength ceramics (construction, electrotechnical, piezo-, etc.	Institute of Strengthening Physics and Materials (ISPM) SD RAS, TPU, SCE
†3.4	Ion-beam technologies for isotope separation (U, Os, etc.); hardening and obtaining of high-resource, corrosion-proof cutting tools, pipes, etc; testing, modification of materials of cosmic, atomic technique	SCE, TPU, RINP, RMC Institute of Heavy-Current Electronic SD RAS (IHCE), Research Institute of Applied Mechanics (Krasnoyarsk)
3.5	Certificate units for products' defectoscopy	Research Institute of Introscopy at TPU (RII)
†3.6	Robotized technologies for high-speed materials' cutting (including underwater), casting treatment; small-sized high-safety electric drive for almost inaccessible objects	Research Institute of Machine-Building Technology (RIMBT), RIAMM at TPU, Research Institute of Automatics and Electromechanics at TACSRT
†3.7	Diagnostic systems for atmosphere composition, waste gases' visualization in fuel burning and other substances' consumption	Institute of Atmosphere Optic (IAO) SD RAS
3.8	Systems of noise-insensitive and digital small-sized radio-relay stations for closed communications lines "Delta-3"	Tomsk Academy of Control Systems and Radioelectronics (TACSR), SPTI at TSU
†3.9	Electronic-digital, remote-controlled transmitting transducer of movement, direction, rotations, temperature, pressure; economical flowmeters of gases, liquids	Scientific-Production Association (SPA) "Polus," Joint-stock Company "Manotom," TIP, RIS, TPU, RII at TPU
3.10	Technologies for new construction materials using natural raw material and technogenic waste	TSABA. Research Institute of Communal Economy at TSABA
3.11	Complex of means for elimination of oil products' overflow	Research Institute of Construction Materials at TSABA; IOC SD RAS
3.12	Catalyzers and methods of complex reprocessing of accompanying gas to liquid and solid hydrocarbons, stratal water removing from oil pipelines	IOC, ISE SD RAS, TPU
3.13	Computer-aided systems of remote control and processes' regulations in oil pipelines	RII at TPU, Cybernetic Centre TPU

TABLE 7. The Main Export Contacts of Siberian Regions in 1991, $ USA

Region	Volume of export operations		
	more than 10 mil	more than 5 mil	more than 4 mil
Altai territory	China Hungary		Japan
Kemerovo region	Italy France Turkey Hungary	Spain	Great Britain Greece
Omsk region	Sweden	USA China	
Novosibirsk region		China Poland	Germany Netherlands
Tomsk region	Finland Germany China Japan	Afghanistan Viet-Nam	
Tyumen region	Italy Cyprus	Hungary Great Britain	Finland
Krasnoyarsk territory	China Germany Netherlands Yugoslavia Italy Singapore	Korea Republic Hungary	
Irkutsk region	France China Japan Cuba Italy	Belgium Finland Korea Republic Austria Poland Mongolia	Yugoslavia Bulgaria Morocco
Chita region	China		
Buryaria	China Mongolia		

trial enterprises place a great stress on this potential, which is used very ineffectively. The main problems are the following: loss of enterprising young people to commerce; intellects migrating abroad; aging of material resources; reduction of volume of fundamental investigations.

In spite of all this, today many Siberian institutes have generated new developments, and new technologies which may be beneficially transferred to industry [4].

Examples of new technologies which may be used more widely are given in Table 6.

2.4. INTERNATIONAL CONTACTS AND TIES IN TECHNOLOGY TRANSFER

Siberian Research Institutes and industrial enterprises are constantly developing contacts and ties with foreign partners both for the export of products, developments and the import of consumers' goods and different technologies.

The main export ties of different Siberian regions and their volumes are given in Table 7. China is more often seen among the partners [13].

At present, many businessmen come to Siberia from the USA, Canada, Germany, France and other countries. Among the proposals these businessmen make are the creation of enterprises on the Siberian territory which use new technologies. Examples of such proposals by foreign partners in 1993 for the Tomsk region are shown in Table 8.

The contacts of the Siberian Research Institutes with foreign partners on technology transfer are of great interest as well.

Businessmen from the USA, Germany and England show a high level of activity in this direction. So, in 1993, through the initiative and active participation of the Fund for Democracy and Development (USA) and the OPIC organization (investments to foreign private companies) international conferences were held in Washington and Novosibirsk to discuss the problems of technology transfer from Russia to the USA and of investment in new technological developments in Siberia.

A conference on technology transfer in which new technological developments from Siberian institutes were discussed, was held at New York Polytechnic University in April 1994.

TABLE 8. Technologies Represented by Foreign Partners in the Tomsk Region

Enterprise	Technology	Country
Tomsk poultry factory	Technology and equipment for poultry meat processing	Germany
Joint-stock company "Tomsk oil-chemical group of enterprises"	Technology and equipment for methanol, polypropylene production	Firm "Toye Engineering" (England)
	Technology improvement of methanol synthesis and production "EP-300"	Firm "Mont Edison" (Italy)
Joint-stock company "Tomsk mills"	Technology and equipment for bread baking	Sweden
Joint-stock company "Samus river base"	Technology and equipment for repair of small tonnage boats	Finland
Joint-stock company of opened type "Tomsk oil"	Technology for oil output increase by the oil-bearing bed burst method	Firm "Frankmaster" (England)
	Production technology of trade oil-processing plant	USA
Achinsk oil-processing plant	Technology for catalytic cracking of middle and heavy oil fractions	France
Tomsk radio plant	Screwdriver technology for color TV sets assembly	South Korea

Proposals of Siberian institutes concerning new technological developments suitable for transfer or elaborated jointly with foreign firms are shown in Table 9.

Conclusion

The industry and the Research Institutes of the Siberian region of Russia represent a unique basis for technology transfer because:

a) Siberian industry by its character is focused on resource-mining and requires improvement both in the area of extraction and in the area of raw material reprocessing. There is also a great need for technology of environmental and resource protection;

TABLE 9. Proposals of Siberian Institutes for Technology Transfer

Institute	Technologies
Tomsk Polytechnic University	Radiation technologies for new materials: ceramics, high-temperature superconductors, polymers. Ecologically pure economical vacuum-beam technologies of production of composite plastics as roll facing materials and covers. New ecologically safe technologies and control devices for the environment. Neutron devices of undestructing control and identification of the hidden backing of explosives. Electro-pulse technologies: the use of high-voltage changes for rock destruction, treatment of solid non-conducting materials and waste utilization.
Institute of heavy-current electronics	Technologies of electronic ion and plasma beams. Production technology of non-linear crystals for laser optics of ultraviolet range and jewelry industry. Modification technology of surface solid bodies by ion beams.
Institute of high voltages	Production technology of ultra-dispersed spherical powders of metals, alloys and combinations in the metastable state based on the electric explosion.
Institute of strength physics and materials	Technology for powders and dense materials production in shock waves.

b) The Siberian research-technical potential today offers a great number of projects in the field of new technologies and is ready to transfer these technologies to the industrial enterprises of Siberia or to joint Siberian - foreign ventures;

c) Siberian higher education establishments have the potential for training specialists in the field of technology transfer and specialists for the development of new technological projects.

References

1. Amosenok, E.P. and Bazhenov, V.A., Military industry of the region, *Economy and Organization of Industrial Production* **9**, 17-29.

2. Bovin A., Guseinov R. and Kashchenko, N. (1992) Siberian economy: state and prospectives, Siberia, *Policy, Economy, Management* **1**, 39-54.

3. Chernomyrdin, V. (1993) Russian reforms and Siberia, *International Life* **4**, 8-12.

4. Dobretsov, N.L. (1993) Development of scientific technical potential in Siberia (experience, effects, prospectives), Basic Materials for Discussion at the All-Russian Conference on Siberian Economic Development, Novosibirsk, **8-11 June**, 63-79.

5. Ershov, Y.S. (1993) Latest economic history, *Economy and Organization of Industrial Production* **9**, 3-29.

6. Geftler, M. (1990) Reflections about fortunes of Siberia, *Fatherland* **11**, 58-61.

7. Industry (1994) Business chart 94 - Russia/western Siberia, *Industry* **3**.

8. International Life (1993) Population of Siberia. Facts, *International Life* **4**, 154-156.

9. International Life (1992) Siberian oil in policy and economy of Russia and world, *International Life* **10**, 14-29.

10. Progress (1993) Cities and towns of Siberia and Far East, in F.M. Borodkin (ed) *Concise Economical-Geographical Reference Book*, Progress.

11. Repub. Inform. Publ. Centre (1993) Russian Federation, republic, territory and regions of the western Siberian economic district in 1992, *Repub. Inform. Publ. Centre*.

12. Repub. Inform. Pub. Centre (1993) Russian Federation in figures in 1993, *Repub. Inform. Pub. Centre*.

13. Volvok, V. (ed) (1993) Economy of the country by the end of 1993: economic review, *Economist* **12**, 3-11.

7. SOME ASPECTS OF TECHNOLOGY TRANSFER BETWEEN RUSSIA AND WESTERN COUNTRIES

SERGEI A. ARZHAKOV
Polymer Department, Faculty of Chemistry
Lomonosov Moscow State University
Moscow, Russia

1. Introduction

The post-war years were characterized by an intensive development of scientific and technological cooperation among the developed countries. Technology transfer was involved in such a cooperation. According to the definition given by the United Nations Organization in 1974, technology transfer implies transfer of a set of knowledge and know-how, which allows production of goods or services, including the experience necessary for technology introduction.

2. Technology Transfer in Russia in the Face of Economic Hard Times

In recent years, Russia became involved in the process of technology transfer. The high level of Russian research and development (R&D), compared with many other countries, goes without saying. That level was ensured by the activities of well-qualified and competent scientific and engineering staff, working at two different types of organizations: institutes of the Russian Academy of Sciences and industrial institutes of various ministries and departments.

The scientific production of institutes of the Russian Academy of Sciences is characterized by a world class level of fundamental research in all areas: mathematics, physics, chemistry, biology, etc. In many cases, the scientific results obtained can be effectively used for the development of new advanced technologies.

G. Bugliarello et al. (eds.), East-West Technology Transfer, 99-106.

The activities of the industrial institutes of various ministries and departments are focused on the solution of applied problems. However, in some cases, their research programs directed towards the development of new technologies necessitate the solution of fundamental and purely theoretical problems. Usually this work is carried out via contracts with institutes of the Russian Academy of Sciences and institutes of higher education.

The economic revolution in Russia has brought about a substantial reorganization of R&D activities. Even though the Russian government is well aware of the high level of science and technology in Russia and the value of its scientific priority, at the present it cannot afford sufficient financial support and investments. Thus, the intellectual resources of this country have a hard time. To preserve the skilled scientific staff, most institutes try to solve their financial problems by themselves using their main resources, that is, inventions and advanced technologies as well as the knowledge and competence of their staffs.

To improve this situation, the Russian government is working out a new policy. In this connection, some new forms of cooperation with developed industrial countries have been worked out:

- Research is performed by scientific staffs in Russia via contracts with foreign firms. This system, however, does not quite satisfy the Russian side, for, in this case, the cost of knowledge transfer can cover only the wages and salaries of the people involved.
- Some Russian scientists have been invited to go abroad and work for Western universities and firms. For Russia, such a policy implies nothing else but a "brain drain" associated with a deep feeling of public dissatisfaction. The policy of many industrial countries to take advantage of the current miserable situation in Russia has no future, and from the viewpoint of justice and general security seems to be rather shortsighted.
- Research activities in Russia are supported by various funds, such as the Soros Fund. However, one can hardly be particularly enthusiastic about it because of some of the peculiar terms specified by this Fund. Let us also mention the financial support from the technological center founded by the U.S.A., Japan and Western European countries for scientists involved in research on nuclear physics, to prevent both their departure and the transfer of information to third world countries.

3. Suggested Solutions: Technology Transfer

We believe that the best way of preserving the high scientific and technical potential in Russia involves self-financing of Russian science via technology transfer. Even though this is rather difficult, it offers unique and far-reaching advantages for the development of fruitful and mutually advantageous cooperation between Russia and its foreign partners. At present , many world-level technologies worked out in Russia may be transferred to other countries.

In many aspects, the current situation in Russia is similar to that of post-war Germany with respect to technology transfer. Germany was as open to such cooperation as today's Russia. At that time, the strategy of transfer of technologies, know-how and finished products gave a new and strong impetus to technological development in countries involved in such cooperation, and allowed them to overtake their competitors.

Those countries which manage to establish business relations with Russian organizations may gain a marked profit from using the technologies worked out by a set of R&D and engineering institutes in Russia. As to the realization of these unique advantages, the Western countries, with their singular experience in technology examination and adaptation, can become large importers of Russian technologies. They have the necessary scientific infrastructure and an excellent system of technology diffusion. For Russia, this policy will help to save many skilled personnel. Furthermore, this approach can satisfy the urgent need of Russia for hard currency, which is necessary for conversion of a well-developed military industry into a civilian one. In this connection, the transfer of many advanced technologies developed in Russia can provide an important source of financing.

4. Combating the Problem of "Brain Drain" and Loss of Technology

In other words, to overcome this difficult situation, Russia is faced with the necessity to prevent spending its scientific and technical potential, and the disintegration of its scientific groups. At the same time, it is common knowledge that many Western countries are heavy users of foreign technologies, and their principal efforts in this area are concentrated on technology adaptation. For Russia, scientific and technical cooperation is beneficial for the following reasons:

- At present, Russia has many world-class technologies but little experience in licensing, patenting and technology transfer.

- Adequate organization of technology transfer will improve the current situation and allow Russia to take its due place in the world market as a large technology supplier.
- Such an approach will allow Russia to enter the modern information-based economy.
- This policy will allow Russia to take advantage of contacts with Western technologies by concentrating on technological development.

5. Advantages for Western Partners

For the Western partners, the development of technological cooperation with Russia also seems rather beneficial, offering a number of unique advantages. The Western partners will be able to:

- have access to advanced Russian technologies, which may serve as a catalyst for their own technological progress;
- develop new systems of technological search, to study commercialization in Russia, and to consider the activities of specialized agencies and mediators - engineering, patent agencies, legal services, management bodies, bookkeeping, etc;
- insure the continuity of Western policy toward Russia of economic and industrial development, with priorities in scientific and economic assistance;
- eliminate a serious lag of some enterprises, facilitate economic development, and reorient military industries both in Russia and Western countries;
- strengthen international cooperation between Russia and Western countries, thus insuring peace and security in the world.

6. Technological and Scientific Cooperation Difficulties

Technology transfer is a very complicated venture. Scientific and technical cooperation between Russia and other countries is deeply affected by a number of serious problems, such as language and cultural barriers, and a marked difference in management systems, laws, and regulations.

In connection with this, it would be useful to have a general description of the technology transfer process and to outline the principal related difficulties.

Cooperation in the field of technology transfer should be primarily oriented toward satisfying current demands for technologies. Hence, the interested parties should have updated information on the supply-demand balance based on well-developed systems of data collection and information exchange.

Elaboration of a strategy for technology transfer should take into account the following factors:

- the problems of communication;
- differences in legal and management culture. For example, the Russian institutes have rather limited possibilities to learn about international trade relations. Any assistance to Russia in this field would be very helpful;
- the absence of adequate legislation for protection of intellectual property and rights in Russia.

7. Advantages for Both the West and Russia of Economic and Technological Cooperation

Technology transfer between Russia and Western countries began several years ago. However, so far such cooperation has solved only a few particular problems. No effort has been made to develop a universal management system for technology transfer. As a result, many Western firms are not in a hurry to invest their money and Russian organizations are still overcautious in supplying the necessary information.

These negative factors have a strong influence on the effective development of integrated activities between Russian and Western partners. However, even these negative experiences seem to be rather useful. They will allow both partners to concentrate their efforts on developing new principles of mutually advantageous cooperation. To make such cooperation more realistic and concrete, the exchange of competent specialists would seem to be necessary.

The initial stage of such cooperation necessitates a thorough analysis of the urgent demands associated with the involvement of scientific and technical personnel in technology transfer between Russia and Western countries.

It is high time that these activities begin. At present, the relations between Russia and Western countries are taking a dramatic turn. Both partners show mutual interest and willingness to cooperate.

A fundamental restructuring of the Russian economy is practically unexplored. The economies of the Western countries are in a period of stagnation.

The happy solution of today's urgent problems, will have a strong influence on our life in the XXI century.

The lack of adaptability to current conditions has resulted in the appearance of alarming symptoms in the economies of both Russia and of Western countries. However, if the beginning of economic cooperation seems rather encouraging, cooperation in the field of science and technology suffers from a lack of proper planning. The rules of the game are rapidly changing. The traditional economy is replaced by so-called "information" economy and the principal source of national wealth is competitiveness based on technological innovation.

Under conditions of financial instability of many enterprises and research institutes in Russia, the time factor is most essential in regard to "brain drain." Many talented and skilled specialists would prefer to stay in Russia, if it were not for the current economic difficulties and instability. To ensure stable exchange of technology and know-how, the problem of "brain drain" is most urgent. To insure the survival of world-class institutes, laboratories, and scientific groups, the problems related to keeping and using experienced scientific and technical personnel in Russia are very important.

Taking into account the time factor, one should find ways to achieve positive results in the short run, since such first steps may serve as a solid basis for further long-term cooperation.

The initial stage of cooperation in technology transfer is related to an elaboration of a mechanism that would meet the interests of both sides.

To initiate technology transfer, we must set priorities and recognize the groups of technologies which are of primary importance to world industries. This will allow the partners first to recognize and then to satisfy urgent market demands, thus promoting mutually advantageous cooperation.

Elaboration of the mechanism for technology transfer should also take into account the possible effect, on related industries, of the successful development of leading industries. For example, some materials may be widely used in different fields such as aeronautics, transportation, power supply industry, processing of raw materials, and food. Materials is a key branch of technology, which will determine, to a large extent, the industrial development in the XXI century, and may serve as a solid base for long-term cooperation between Russia and Western countries. However, as a first step in such a long-term cooperation, we must identify those directions of technology transfer which will allow quick receipts of hard currency or investment in the Russian economy.

Even though, at present, our main efforts are focused on cooperation with Western countries, this strategy will allow both Russia and Western partners to satisfy the market demands of the third world.

8. Developing Organizational Structures between Russia and the West

The development of an organizational structure responsible for technological cooperation and technology transfer should be planned with respect to the considerations above. A structure should be created to provide not only a well-organized exchange of updated information but also enhanced possibilities for entering into contracts and trade agreements. Such a structure should be based on integrated activities of both Russian and Western experts. We believe that this is the only way to facilitate technology transfer and create an atmosphere of mutual trust.

The development of such a structure should include the following goals:

- studying urgent problems related to absorption of scientific and technical personnel for partnerships via technology transfer mechanisms;
- studying principal areas of cooperation between leading organizations;
- choosing the right moment for trade negotiations and agreements;
- providing effective access to information about Russian technologies.

The organization should be flexible, so as to meet current demands and to be modified according to the current conditions; its heart should be an active and flexible group of people, whose activities are concentrated on establishing new relations between the interested sides and performing operations on a contract basis. A necessary condition is that this organization be non-commercial and non-profit. Hence, the effective development of technology transfer must be planned well by many specialists in the fields of technology, legislation, and financial management.

As a model, the structure may be represented by some joint organization, for example, an International Technology Transfer Center. The organization should concentrate the efforts of well-qualified staff with valuable experience in dealing with both Russian and Western partners. The personnel involved should also have broad knowledge in the field of technology transfer, protection of intellectual rights, commercial legislation, specific features of Western business as well as on the sources of venture capital, social financing, etc.

The creation of such an international center may serve as a catalyst for the development of mutually advantageous relations between Russia and Western countries. Without such organization, the establishment of business contracts will be rather ineffective and take a long time and much money. Various contributions and possible commercial receipts would soon allow this center to be an independent and self-financing organization. The budget of the center can be derived from receipts from its various activities. However, the initial stage related to collection of technologies and development of an organizational structure should be financed from the state budget.

In conclusion, the problems outlined are rather difficult and have no immediate solution. We must resort to some unorthodox approaches. Both Russia and Western countries possess sufficient capital and human resources, which can ensure the stability of such cooperation. The key point is to work out a general approach which allows a simultaneous solution of all urgent problems. Some reliable and interesting information on cooperation between Russia and other countries was obtained by an active group headed by Mayor Dore of Montreal. It seems advisable to invoke their experience.

At present, we need to look to the future. This will allow the world community to enter the XXI century in a condition of partnership, not confrontation.

8. TECHNOLOGY TRANSFER PROBLEMS FOR THE REPUBLIC OF KAZAKHSTAN

DIAS DAUKEEV
Deputy Minister of Science and New Technologies
Almaty, Kazakhstan Republic

1. Introduction

The transfer of advanced technologies must be an important component of the successful economic development of the Republic of Kazakhstan, to enable it to take advantage of its own and foreign achievements in science, engineering and technology.

Technology transfer is a final stage in a long chain of scientific investigations and research (Figure 1) and any problem at any stage can affect its intensity and effectiveness.

In a case of successful development of all the necessary scientific, technological and organizational foundations, the necessary conditions exist for transferring quickly the most advanced technologies. However, this is still not a guarantee of successful technology transfer, because it depends on a number of circumstances: industry and agriculture interest in new technology assimilation, and the implementation of the procedures (Figure 2) to transfer the most advanced, economically effective and environmentally sound technologies.

Of course, foreign technologies can be purchased or advanced technology can be transferred from military to civil applications as well, sometimes with revisions (Figure 1).

G. Bugliarello et al. (eds.), East-West Technology Transfer, 107-118.

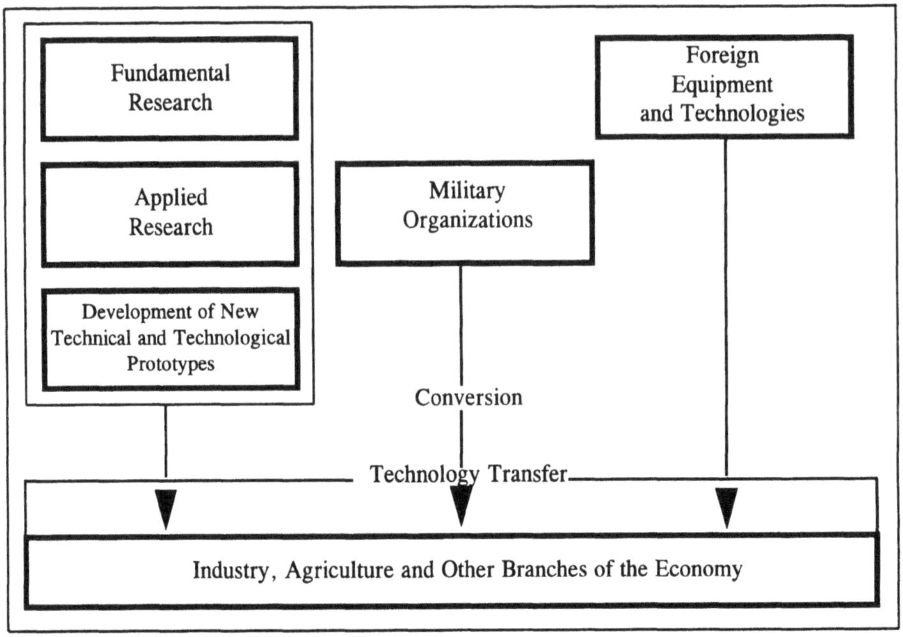

Figure 1. The Steps from Fundamental Research to Applications

2. Assets and Characteristics of Kasakhstan Economy and Science and Technology

To understand clearly the problems related to these types of technology transfer, and their application in Kazakhstan, it is necessary to consider the peculiarities of economic, research and technology development in Kazakhstan (the three stages shown in Figure 1) before and after the disintegration of the former USSR.

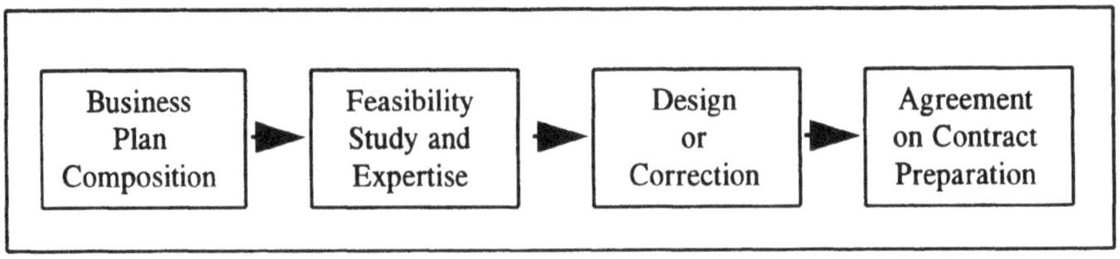

Figure 2. From Plan to Contract

Kazakhstan is richly endowed with industrial raw materials. These include deposits of oil, coal, iron ore, chromite, manganese, copper and other nonferrous metals - all of which occur in sufficient quantities to permit net exports to other former republics. Its net imports of gas and electricity are more than offset by exports of coal and oil. The Republic is also a major producer of a few manufactured goods - such as rolled metal, mineral fertilizer, selected construction materials, bulldozers, tractors, and agricultural machinery.

For the most part, however, Kazakhstan depends on outside supplies of a wide array of industrial materials and manufactured goods - such as chemicals, petrochemicals, most types of machinery, forestry products, soft goods and processed goods. That is why the economy of Kazakhstan declined after the disintegration of the USSR by roughly 15% in 1992 and 29% in 1993, in comparison with the level in 1990.

As for science and technology, there are approximately 280 scientific establishments including 60 Higher Educational Institutes. The potential of the Republic's scientific human resources is thus rather high.

3. Scientific Potential of the Republic of Kazakhstan

The National Academy of Sciences comprises 46 scientific institutions, including 38 Research Institutes. It has a staff of 1,645 Ph.Ds and 419 Doctors of Science and a total of 3,785 scientific workers.

The Kazakh Academy of Agriculture Sciences comprises 32 scientific institutions including 16 Research Institutes. It has a staff of 650 Ph.Ds and Doctors of Science and a total of 3,300 scientific workers.

The Ministry of Education comprises 34 universities and educational institutes, 2 research institutes and a number of research laboratories. It has a staff of 390 Ph.Ds, 23 Doctors of Science and a total of 2,200 staff members.

There are many research and design institutes in different branches of the national economy, including 97 from the former USSR. It is well-known that the basis of the scientific and technical progress in the USSR stemmed mainly from the requirements of the military-industrial complex, which actually decided not only the strategic fields of scientific research, but also the geography of such research. Essentially, the interest in Kazakhstan and its science did not spread further than considering Kazakhstan as a raw materials producer. This included high-tech production either in or out of the territory. Since Kazakhstan's science and technological potential was never exploited, its science was developed in a rather occasional and evolutionary manner.

Kazakhstan differs from other republics in that, due to the plans of the military establishment, it became a huge testing ground of weapons, which were developed always without Kazakhstan scientific and engineering personnel. Therefore, this potential did not meet the requirements of Kazakhstan but was used for USSR interests only.

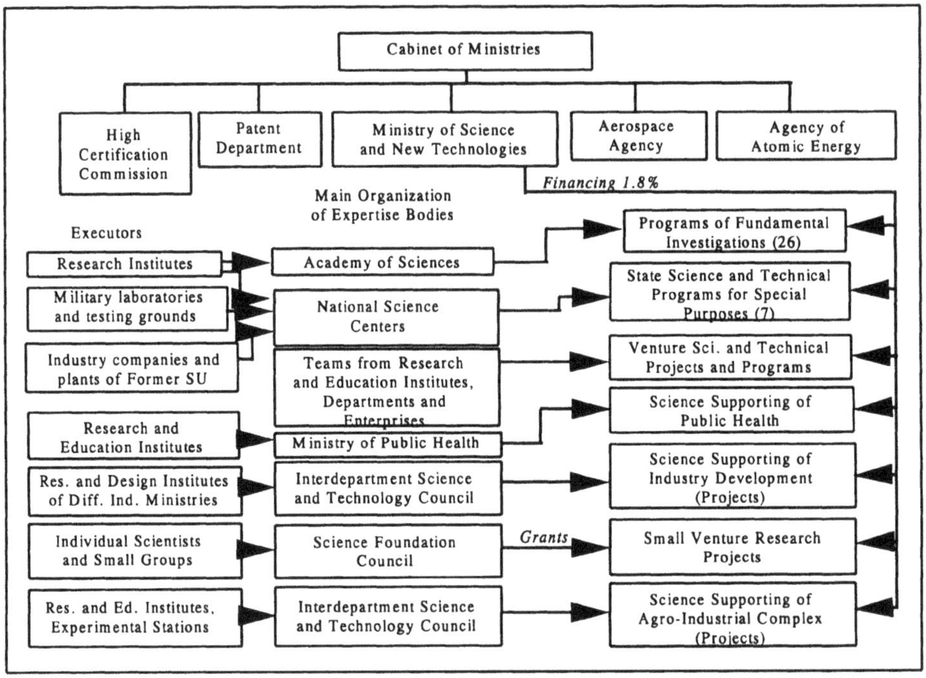

Figure 3. Present Management and Financing of Science in the Republic of Kasakhstan

4. Scientific Difficulties Connected with the Disintegration of the USSR

Before the disintegration of the USSR:

1. There was no autonomous science management system in the republic.
2. Many scientific and technical establishments, testing grounds (especially military) and enterprises with high technologies were directly under ministries and departments of the USSR.

TABLE 1. List of State Special Science and Technical Programs

Program's Title	Main Organization
1. Nuclear Power Development in Kazakhastan	National Nuclear Center
2. Modern Telecom System Development	National Center on Electronics and Telecommunications
3. Applications of Gene Engineering and biotechnologies in agriculture and medicine	National Centre on Biotechnology
4. Complex Utilization of Mineral Raw Materials based on resources-preserving, highly-effective technologies in mining metallurgy	National Center for Complex Utilization of Mineral Resources
5. Development of State System of Scientific and Technical Information	Kazakh State Institute of Scientific and Technical Information
6. Development of Global Ecological and Natural Resources Monitoring	....
7. Informatization in different fields of economics	....

After the disintegration, all these establishments became the property of independent Kazakhstan. In order to manage this diverse complex, we were obliged to form our own management system with new principles of financing (see Figure 3).

We refused to finance establishments and began to finance instead scientific and technical programs and projects. For the unification of different scientific establishments, including the ones from the former USSR, several new National Science Centers were set up, corresponding with priority programs (see Table 1).

The difficulties in the scientific and technical development of Kazakhstan can be divided into two groups: a) difficulties connected with disintegration of the USSR and b) the difficulties connected with breaking of economic, scientific and technical links with partners from the USSR. These are mainly financial and economic difficulties.

According to US specialists, it is necessary to understand the difficulties connected with destroying the centralized state system of science and engineering information collection, ordering, storing, searching, and disseminating different published and unpublished documents. That important system was capable of performing the task of launching the first Soviet satellite.

As a consequence of the collapse of the USSR, the information links between the republics were broken and information sources were divided and mainly owned by Russia. Thus Kazakhstan was left without a substantial part of the necessary science and engineering information. Also, as a result of decentralization of the old management system, the unique specialized information funds in many ministries and councils in Kazakhstan were destroyed. Recently, because of the state deficit, the reduction of our natural science publications, and insufficient hard currency, the income from sciences and engineering literature decreased in 1992 to 40% of what it was in 1990. This is a serious problem. To solve the information crisis a State Special Program, "Development of a State System for Science Engineering Information in Kazakhstan," is being established.

Of course it is also necessary to develop interactions and new rules to enable Kasakhstan scientists to use the information resources from CIS and foreign countries.

5. Political and Other Difficulties

1. The policy of sovereignty of the USSR sometimes did not allow the joint usage of large and unique facilities, testing grounds, or the settling of accounts with each other. It leads to the destruction of the facilities and infrastructure in the scientific towns where they are situated.

2. Lack of democracy and a shortage of market structures and management by state monopolies, in most cases, did not allow for free election or quick elaboration and implementation of new ideas.

3. The number of research workers, both academic staff and technicians, is now about 15 thousand less than just two years ago. High quality specialists go mainly to commercial organizations. Salary, research opportunities and their implementation and practical application, as well as a loss of scientific work's prestige, are given as reasons for leaving.

4. The problems of attracting young people to research activities have become deeper, and fewer post graduate students are being produced.

5. The system of finance is imperfect and ineffective.

6. The supply of materials and equipment is low and equipment is worn out.

7. There is a lack of basic scientific and high tech branches such as accurate and computer-controlled machinery production, and electronic, electrical engineering and scientific equipment.

8. There is a network of both open and secret R & D and design-engineering organizations of the former USSR. They should be re-established and added to a system of scientific activity in Kasakhstan in order to respond to the urgent tasks of our country.

9. There is bad management and poor technical supply of researchers, who have to spend a lot of time and effort doing non-dedicated work. Of course, the prototypes of new equipment and new technologies cannot be produced without scientific-technical development. Surely there are prototypes developed in Kazakhstan. But, firstly, not all of them meet the requirements of sovereign Kazakhstan today, and secondly, many of them have not been transferred to industry and agriculture. This is due to the former command-administrative management system where the obligatory production plan dominated every manufacture. Sometimes quality production was not required by the customers. Manufacturers could not permit themselves, without higher approval, to implement new technologies, since this required money and time. There was no competition which could make industrial companies look for new technologies and support special scientific research. Science had developed according to its own laws and its results did not find practical applications. Research for military aims, which was generously financed, was an exception.

6. Market Economics and Specific Needs

Now, all former USSR countries are turning to market economics, but the true market is not yet established. Moreover, due to the collapse of the USSR, there are deeper problems in the management of the economy. Under these conditions, a broad implementation of new technologies does not occur for a simple reason - the companies cannot find the necessary financing. The main production of many fabricating companies in Kazakhstan does not meet the requirements of the republic. At the same time, very often, the products required in the Republic are not imported, for various reasons.

However, we still hope that economic relationships between CIS countries will be restored and the above mentioned problems will be removed. But, even in that case, technologies, equipment and devices should be renewed to improve the quality of products to meet world standards. The corresponding state policy has to be worked out to do that. First of all, the state companies should be privatized. The State Program of Privatization in Kazakhstan has just slightly touched large State companies. Since it is necessary to support private small companies, a special State Foundation has been established to do so. The State scientific policy should be changed. In addition to the Foundation, it is necessary to create a new management system for scientific-technical progress to establish big R & D centers in priority fields, and to form joint stock companies working in the field of new technologies. This process has been started in Kazakhstan. One such company is the R & D Center "New Technologies." Its structure and main fields of activity are shown in Figure 4.

Another joint stock company is "KazinformTeleCom," whose main activity is the development of telecom networks for information on Kazakhstan economy - including the State system of scientific and technical information. However, the functioning of this kind of associations and companies requires investments, both domestic and foreign. But to obtain investments, especially foreign, it is necessary to present well grounded projects, and to carry out independent research to check technological feasibility, economic benefits, and other aspects, i.e. to fulfill all the procedures of Figure 2.

Today, in Kasakhstan, there is very little experience in these areas; pertinent services are just being established. Therefore, Kazakhstan is very much in need of international aid, particularly in the establishment of such consultancies and expertise on an international level. Creation of joint ventures in this field would be welcomed.

Another problem is that, previously, engineers and researchers in our country did not think about implementation of their own results, and, therefore, their proposals are now too far from the application stage. Consequently, extra work needs to be done to study markets and to revise projects. No services to do so exist. Since budgeted funds for science and research development are limited, reassessment of on going projects and cancellation of projects with no future becomes especially important. But we cannot solve this problem without the help of foreign experts.

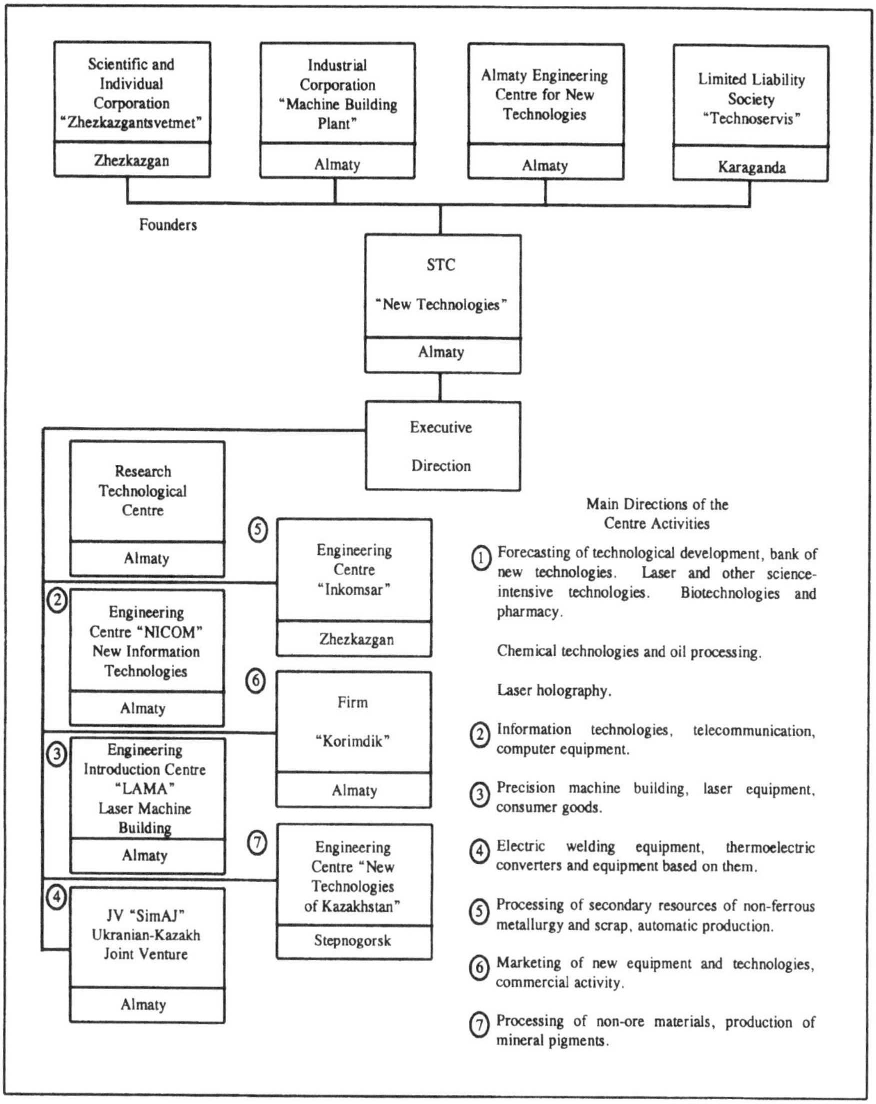

Figure 4. Structure of the Scientific Technical Centre "New Technologies"

7. Problems Related to Peacetime Conversion of Military Enterprises

Finally, let us consider the problems related to the conversion of military enterprises and utilization of their production capacity, technologies, and specialists, for the fabrication of peaceful products.

Theoretically, there are great opportunities because there are many such organizations and testing grounds in Kazakhstan. Large scientific and technical potential and unique equipment are concentrated there. However, this is not simple to do in practice. A lot of military enterprises lost military orders and did not get financing for conversion. Now they have to take a chance and start production of simple (in engineering terms) products. There are some separate conversion plans, but they are only partially carried out due to payment crises, lack of credit or financing or budget limitations.

A single state conversion policy is necessary and has been worked out with the participation of the Ministry of Science and New Technologies. New organization structures were founded to manage this process, and international seminars were held where a technical approach was sought that would profit from the experiences of Russia, Ukraine, the USA, and Euro-Asian states. A solution is seen in a) privatization of defense enterprises; b) foundation of local corporations; c) analysis of new military doctrine needs and corresponding military orders and of the enterprises carrying out those orders; d) winning investments from our State and foreign countries; e) creation of clear legislative regulations and insurance system; f) review of companies' brands and patented technologies.

Some defense enterprises and testing grounds, such as the Semipalatinsk nuclear testing ground and the Sary-Shagan Radio Technical testing grounds, have become part of the above mentioned National Research Centers and take part in the execution of special research programs granted by the State. However, the maintenance of the large infrastructure of those testing grounds and the conversion of their activity require a lot of money - an impossible task without the participation of foreign countries. Kazakhstan is ready for a joint use of those testing grounds, with a partial transfer of rights in their management and in the use of the sites to foreign partners. The rental of the Baikonur Cosmodrom (launching site) to Russia is a good example of one form of cooperation.

In circumstances of limited funds for science and of brain drain, the establishment of diverse international foundations for the support of researchers from CIS countries is especially welcomed, and so is collaboration with scientists from EEC and NATO countries. Unfortunately, due to lack of information about possible partners abroad, poor English skills, and unreliable telecommunications, we cannot exploit those possibilities completely - with the exception of the Soros Foundation, which has opened its office in Almaty and has facilitated our international contacts.

Also, a very important problem because of the disintegration of business links with CIS countries, is that of retaining the ability of existing high tech enterprises which lack materials and spare parts, to sell their products.

8. Conclusions

Many favorable conditions exist in Kazakhstan for successful scientific development and technology transfer.

1. There is a single state scientific and technical management and financing system.

2. National science centers have set priorities involving both research institutions and industrial units, to remove the obstacles to fast implementation of research results:

- a state policy of privatization and maintenance of small business is underway;
- a conversion policy of defense enterprises is being initiated;
- a patent and trademark law has been adopted, which protects inventions, utility models, industrial designs, trademarks and copyrights. Kazakhstan is a member of the Paris Convention, Madrid Agreement, and WIPO and PCT Agreements. All these laws provide protection for technology transfer.

These are essential advantages for those seeking to implement new technologies. Nevertheless, there are many obstacles to technology transfer.

To speed up the process of advanced technologies transfer in the industry and agriculture of the republic of Kazakhstan, besides domestic reforms, NATO aid is very desirable in the following forms:

1. Direct investment in techno projects, above all in telecommunications development, in order to computerize all branches of the economy, to transfer data fast, including those about advanced technologies with connections to international networks. The implementation of such projects would improve the conditions for effective international cooperation.

2. Foundation of joint R & D centers in Kazakhstan, or participation in existing centers. This would promote the introduction of Kasakhstan scientists and specialists to international experiences and Western management skills.

3. Establishment of joint consulting-expertise associations and companies.

4. Organization, education and fellowships for Kazakhstan specialists, to learn management in scientific and technological fields.

5. Establishment of a special foundation to support exchange visits of Kasakhstan scientists, specialists and officers to gain experience in the field of advanced technologies and their transfer.

9. PROBLEMS OF TECHNOLOGICAL RENEWAL IN THE KYRGHYZ REPUBLIC

T. Koichuev
President of the National Academy of Sciences
The Kyrghyz Republic

1. Introduction

One of the most modern factors of sharp economic advancement - technology transfer - is being put somewhat tardily on the agenda in the republics of Central Asia. After the collapse of the USSR and the destruction of its single economic sphere, technology transfer would seem to be an extremely effective means of helping our economy out of its serious condition.

2. Priorities of the Kyrghyz Republic

In the field of new technologies, in accord with the development priorities of the Kyrghyz Republic, the following main directions have been approved: promising processes for turning out agricultural products; new technologies for processing agricultural produce; biotechnology; computers and microelectronic; progressive technologies for the complex exploitation of fuel and power resources; new materials and chemical technology.

Work has been initiated and some progress has been achieved in accord with these priorities. However, putting new foreign technologies into production entails a number of difficulties which will slow the pace and scale of technology transfer.

Firstly, to a predominant extent the technology used in the Kyrghyz Republic was Soviet, inferior in its quality to the more effective Western technology. Thus, switching production to a new technology will require time and the means to dismantle the old technologies and renew them. To do so within a short time, such a large scale renewal if beyond anyone's power; besides, to be carried

G. Bugliarello et al. (eds.), East-West Technology Transfer, 119-122.

out economically, it must be developed in carefully planned stages. Production ought not to be stopped simultaneously on a large scale .

Secondly, lack, not to say today absence, of means (currency) does not only limit but makes it impracticable to introduce new technologies or renew existing technologies and construct fresh capacities with more effective technologies. At present, the exploitation of fresh capacities is practically at zero.

Thirdly, the Republic has limited or no information about Western technologies as well as a lack of sufficient engineering and other personnel who know Western technologies and are able to work with them. We need to train such specialists in the Republic and in training programs in the West for improving the specialists' qualifications.

Fourthly, the weakened scientific, technical and economic ties in the territory of the former Soviet Union limit sharply the exchange of information and "know how" within the framework of the Confederation of Independent States (CIS). Exchange, when it occurs, is principally implemented on an international basis. This implementation is in great difficulty because international contractual relations between the new states in the area of "know how," as well as in economics on the whole and in other fields have not been properly implemented and do not work normally. Improvement of relations in the field of "know how" between states (former republics of the USSR) is also necessary, for not everything in the USSR was bad. To establish real links with Western countries and other "remote" foreign countries for the use of new technologies, it is necessary to develop concrete projects. We can then jointly determine concrete organizational forms for their implementation, to expedite the definition of spheres of competence and scale and stages of development. The important criteria must be as follows: gains in time (acceleration of returns), magnitude of impact, significance of a development for the whole economy, opportunity to increase export potentials and to generate currency returns, ability to reduce the Republic's dependence on the import of a number of goods, and saving currency to satisfy the demand for the goods which the Republic needs badly. Of course, it is important that the new technological projects put forward be profitable for the foreign partners as well.

3. Specific Branches of the Economy Where New Technologies Need to be Introduced in Order to Help Overcome the Current Crisis

There are minor but important technologies in agriculture and agricultural processing that are needed for the development and productivity of large farms and small peasant farms, to enable them to provide the population of the Republic with food products. This eliminates the necessity of importing basic food stuffs from abroad, and saves currency.

There are effective technologies for the extraction and conversion of rare elements and non-ferrous precious metals which may gain important resources for the Republic through export.

There are new technologies for the fuel-and-power complex (production and exploitation) in order to diminish our dependence on the import of resources and to increase our export potential to neighboring states.

There are effective technologies for the Republic's machine-building and light industry, to enable their product to compete in world and regional markets.

There is a need to create a modern information system.

The introduction of new technologies must be pursued actively by economic and legal means at the state level as well as at the managerial level. Of course, the state will need to infuse funds into the existing state enterprises. It must also help new technologies reach the newborn private sector with credits from its own resources and from resources borrowed from foreign investors. This will help private owners to have direct contact with foreign partners. It is important to have laws and agreements which encourage the introduction of new technologies and attract foreign investors.

4. Environmental Problems and Opportunities

The transfer and introduction of new technologies are also connected with insuring ecological safety, to make the environment suitable for human life. In our Republic, the environment is endangered. At the time of the USSR, uranium was extracted and processed in Kyrghyzstan. The waste left after extraction and conversion was not removed, but buried on site. Was it safely buried? This question gives rise to doubts and anxiety for the environment and for peoples' lives. The anxiety continues to grow after the Chernobyl tragedy and the natural disasters which have occurred frequently as of late.

With the help of international organizations and experts, one could organize the oversight of these uranium burial-grounds and, if necessary, using modern technologies, shield the environment and the people from the hazards. We need international help.

It may be asked, why was everyone silent about this uranium menace before? The answer is that everything concerned with uranium was wrapped in deep mystery, and the totalitarian regime could keep the people silent, making them believe in the safety of Soviet uranium storage technology and in the harmlessness of uranium extraction and conversion.

In our Republic today, using the capacities which were engaged in uranium conversion, we could develop a powerful industry for reprocessing the waste left from the extraction of useful minerals. We could also process the waste from other countries, with the aim of repeated extraction of useful components. It is important, however, to ensure environmental harmlessness; for instance, one should never reprocess uranium waste.

Of course, the transfer of new technologies is connected with the problem of conversion of military industry capacities. But in the Kyrghyz Republic, such capacities are few. There is no defense industry, so the problem of conversion practically does not exist.

But there is another problem. Many large-scale machine-building enterprises had an All-Union specialization with the USSR as their market. After the disintegration of the USSR, economic connections were broken, and now there is the problem of either restoration and normalization of former connections, or of changing the specialization of these enterprises. This will require new technologies and the re-education of personnel.

5. Conclusion

These are the problems and opportunities connected with the transfer of new technologies, which will be the most important factor in raising the industrial level in the Kyrghyz Republic. The transfer, in turn, would have a positive social effect: training and re-education of personnel, improvement of their qualifications and greater ecological security. We are interested in a broad transfer, but have limited means for putting it into practice.

The Republic is ready to cooperate with interested parties in this field, using credits, joint ventures and any other devices.

10. UZBEKISTAN AND ITS SCIENTIFIC POTENTIAL FOR THE UTILIZATION OF ITS NATURAL RESOURCES

N.R. YOUSURBEKOV
Commissioner for Science and Technology
The Uzbeki Republic

1. Introduction

After it gained its independence, Uzbekistan had the opportunity to choose a new path toward economic development.

Traditionally, the Republic was an agrarian and raw material adjunct of the central regions of the former USSR. In fact, in spite of its great intellectual potential and rich natural resources, the Republic produced a limited number of finished products - mainly intended for domestic consumption - or semi-products.

In choosing a new economic path, many problems arose, including:

- the introduction and mastering of new production processes,
- the processing of our own raw materials,
- the production of finished products for domestic consumption and for export.

Engineering brain power, designers, technologists and scientists play a great role in the solution of these problems. Their efforts are aimed at the most advantageous and economically expedient ways to discover, develop, create and buy modern technologies and equipment, to reorient the engineering forces toward the mastering of resource preservation and of manufacturing in an economically sound way. There is a need to develop and market products that satisfy world quality standards.

In order to find a solution to these problems, President I. A. Karinov has suggested some transitional steps toward a market economy that include five principles:

1. Priority of the economy over politics,
2. State regulation of the economy and control of the economic tools,

G. Bugliarello et al. (eds.), East-West Technology Transfer, 123-127.

3. Consolidation of discipline and of law and order in the Republic,

4. Creation of effective mechanisms of social protection of the people and strengthening the assistance to the people,

5. Formation of market relations and preservation of political stability while the problems of the transition period are being solved.

2. The Natural Resources of the Republic are Varied and Rich

Uzbekistan possesses agrarian resources valued at 5.1 million ha (4.23 million ha of irrigated soil), which at present meet population demands for agricultural products.

The Republic has considerable power resources: power from generating stations amounts to more than 12 million kilowatts, and total power generation is 47 billion KW/h, of which hydroelectric power stations generate 9 billion KW/h, and thermal stations 36 billion KW/h. The unified power system of Central Asia and South Kazakhstan is also operating. Significant is the wide use of non-traditional energy sources (solar, wind, biomass, hydroelectric power from small rivers).

Additionally, prospecting has shown that the region contains important deposits of gold, silver, polimetals, tungsten, copper, lead with rare and rare earth elements, oil, gas, etc. More than 100 types of mineral raw materials, concentrated in 500 deposits and 480 ore indications have been discovered by scientists and specialists of the Republic. More than 600 industrial enterprises are operational - gas, oil fields, mines, quarries, chemical plants, water intake plants, etc. The commercial reserves that have been prospected not only insure the normal operation of existing enterprises, but also afford opportunities for growth and modernization. Production progress in ore mining has enabled the Republic to mine a whole complex of ores over a range of depth levels.

The Bukhara-Khiva region, and the Surhandarya and the Ferghana valleys, have been identified as most promising oil and gas-bearing regions, where both resources are in large supply. These regions are characterized by complex seismic conditions; the majority of the prospective oil and gas bearing deposits occur at depths of more than 5 - 7 Km. This is why existing geophysical methods of preparing areas for deep drilling do not give consistently reliable results: deep drilling is less effective and special equipment is required for stripping the horizons.

3. Present Prospecting Operations and Difficulties

At present, negotiations are underway with foreign countries (Saudi Arabia, USA, France) on the question of participation in tenders for the extraction and refining of oil from deposits at Mingbulak and Kokdumalak. Research has indicated that in the future oil and gas drilling in this area will need to be increasingly deep: by the year 2000 the depth of the drilling should reach 8-10 Km. This deep drilling will need to be carried out in abnormal conditions of high formation pressure (up to 850-900 atm), through thick salt and gypsum deposits under productive horizons containing high-mineralized water, with hydrogen sulfides and carbonic acid. These conditions lead to possible gas explosions, placing stresses on casing in salt-bearing deposits and leading to corrosion of above and below ground equipment.

Deep borehole drilling will require thicker drilling systems, special drilling casing and tubing, and gusher equipment. We are considering appealing to investors and firms in the Islamic countries which produce such equipment, for help in solving these problems.

4. Planning for Future Mineral Production

Intensive studies of the territory of Uzbekistan give us reason to believe that the easily extracted mineral deposits are exhausted. Therefore, any new deposits of metals, non-metallic raw materials, oil or gas will require development and introduction of new methods of geochemical and electrophysical search and prospecting, and of new methods of break-down, extraction, production and processing.

At present, we are exploring all opportunities for attracting foreign firms - such as the Newmount Corporation (USA) -and investors for work on the exploitation of the gold deposits in our Navoi region. Western banks have extended credit amounting to 70 million dollars for this purpose. Specialists estimate that 6-8 tons of gold will be produced in the Republic per year. The government of Uzbekistan has adopted a program to increase considerably the production of gold and rare metals above the 1992 level by the year 2000.

5. A State Program

A State scientific and technological program for fundamental and applied research is studying the links between formations of gold and silver rare metal polimetal mineralization and the structure of the upper lithosphere in different geological formations, the discovery of mineral formation parameters, and the extraction of non-ferrous rare and precious metals from ores and production wastes. This state program embodies all the components which may increase the funds and economic potential of Uzbekistan. The areas of study include: forecast and search, exploration, technology of production and extraction of useful elements, instrumentation and analysis, and environmental control.

The studies will focus on:

- scientific problems in increasing the noble metals resources
- discovery of the mechanisms of ore formation in Uzbekistan
- traditional schemes for stripping
- sequence of deep horizon mining
- increase of mines' concentration
- development of modern equipment
- utilization of production wastes
- geomechanical safeguarding of work sites

We are interested in cooperating with Islamic and other countries in the production of extrapure metals and other science-intensive technologies. Autonomous power plants which work on low-potential sources are also available.

6. Natural Resources Exploration

Additionally, we are conducting studies in the production of photo-electric batteries from amorphous silicon, and of wind power devices for the purpose, among others, of enabling water to reach distant livestock. These new avenues of research will become increasingly important in the Republic. Almost one tenth of the scientists and specialists, including 50 doctors and 600 doctoral candidates in the sciences, are engaged in the study of the effective use of natural resources, of secondary raw materials, and of industrial waste.

7. In conclusion

The current scientific development in the Republic is characterized by progressive qualitative and quantitative scientific growth, progress in the training of national specialists, improvement of skills, strengthening links between scientific research and the economy, multifaceted complex demands, and technical progress.

In order to compete on the world market, we are trying to raise our technical skills to world levels.

The government of the Republic is paying great attention to the issue of concentration of scientific resources to respond to the problems identified by our science and technology policy.

Of great importance are expansion of contacts with scientists and specialists from other countries, and international cooperative investigations of a broad spectrum of scientific problems, such as the complex use of mineral resources, recoverable energy sources, etc. All of these activities are carried out under the guidance of the Republic of Uzbekistan State Committee for Science and Technology.

To reiterate, we attach great importance to strengthening our cooperation with other countries, and we will promote in every way possible the active exchange of both scientific and technical information.

In conclusion, we want to join the working groups represented at this Advanced Research Workshop for contacts on the rational use of natural resources, on engineering and environmental control, and on training and retraining of specialists.

11. THE EASTERN EUROPEAN LATECOMER FIRM AND TECHNOLOGY TRANSFER: FROM 'MUDDLING THROUGH' TO 'CATCHING UP'

SLAVO RADOSEVIC
SPRU, University of Sussex
United Kingdom

1. Introduction

The ability of Eastern Europe to 'catch up' crucially depends on their enterprises' active approach to technology transfer (TT). Transfer should include mainly intangible assets, such as quality, organization, software and marketing as these are the most deficient assets. The use of TT as mechanism of firm restructuring is central to the 'catching up' process. The lessons learned by the South-East Asian countries about 'catching up' have some relevance for Eastern Europe. However, history never repeats itself in the same way and the external conditions for this process have changed significantly. The new context of the liberalized and globalized economy within which firms must restructure and gain access to technology and markets poses more uncertainties than answers.

This paper aims to discuss the problem of firm restructuring in Eastern Europe and the use of technology transfer as a mechanism to facilitate this process. The main concern of this paper are the main micro and mezzo issues involved in the move from the current stage of firm adjustment, which I describe as 'muddling through,' to the dynamic 'catching up' stage. I will first present the main characteristics of TT in the new conditions and related firm and policy issues. Then I will briefly introduce some stylized characteristics of Eastern European firms in the time of transition. On the basis of this background I will discuss firm-level strategic options, as well as the strategic policy approach, to support the growth of Eastern European firms.

G. Bugliarello et al. (eds.), East-West Technology Transfer, 129-153.

2. Technology Transfer and the Latecomer Firm in a Liberalized and Globalized Economy

The context of TT has changed significantly since the 1970s, when a clear policy pattern was established, based on the following assumptions [28]:

- that unrestricted flow leads to high and rising costs of technology transfer;
- that unrestricted imports of technology inhibit the development of local technological capacity and the learning process;
- that technology can be equally developed in a protected environment;
- that mechanisms for technology transfer do matter and that equity control and ownership play an important role in it;
- that the business of 'pricing' technology determines the international distribution of 'gains from technological advance;'
- that the main problem in technology transfer is not the availability or access to technology but its price.

This approach led to a strong focus on contract bargaining, to protection in the form of restrictive clauses, and to a great concern about the level of payments for licenses and other indirect payments. However, by the mid-1980s it became clear that these assumptions and policy responses had become obsolete and highly irrelevant to the new conditions.

An increasing liberalization and globalization of the world economy and increasing difficulties in ensuring technology imports required new approaches to TT.[1] Changes in the macroeconomic context and in the character of technical change account for much of these influences.[2]

1. Changes in the macroeconomic context are centered around several factors. First, a liberalization wave in international trade has led to a relative stagnation in international production but to an increase in sourcing.[3] Second, an increasing market segmentation has radically changed the logic of growth of some sectors in such a way that the concept of demand is replaced by the concept of client.[4] This shift requires knowledge about users' needs as much as knowledge about the process of production. Third, we see a strong divergence among developing countries (including Eastern Europe) in their capacity to import technology and attract foreign direct investment (FDI). Private capital flows and portfolio equity inflows, which now dominate financial flows, will influence TT in a way we are not yet able to envisage.

2. New technologies are based on a growing knowledge of complexity and intensity, on an increasing role of organizational change and on increasing

technology implementation capability. Most applications today involve systems and networks. The number of sub-technologies in most production systems has increased. All this makes TT an increasingly complex process as systemic gains are more difficult to achieve. In such a context packaging technology becomes increasingly difficult. On the recipient side, it implies that 'unpackaging' as an attempt to master some elements of technology becomes highly irrelevant. Mastering of TT and acquisition now involves more actors and require multiple channels. Effective TT now requires more investments in training and organizational change.

The elements on which I touched upon very briefly under 1 and 2 imply several points.

First, it is not possible to expect technology to be acquired behind protective barriers. In a liberalized environment, the main problem is how to get access to production networks and how to become a partner in the value-added chain of transnational firms.

Second, market segmentation requires much better knowledge of specific users' needs. However, the costs of serving markets (marketing barriers) become too high for many firms (including Eastern European ones).

Third, the complexity and systemic character of technology makes it difficult for industrial firms to master it. In the area of technological development they are now relatively more dependent on other domestic and foreign firms organized as networks. Knowledge and innovation links become as important as 'in-house' capability.

Although these stylizations might seem an exaggeration, they reflect to a high degree a new environment in which the 'catching up' of Eastern European firms is to occur. They reflect a need to formulate firm responses within a context that I would characterize as a 'sourcing paradigm.' By this I mean the context of liberalized economies where virtuous or vicious circles arise from inclusion into or exclusion from value-added chains of global networks. This need to access networks stems from the integration and exclusion mechanisms that are very powerful in a globalized economy.[5]

The main enterprise and policy issues of this new situation are based around the following pillars:

1. Technology transfer is a transfer of firm-specific capabilities.[6] Firm-specific capabilities imply that much of the knowledge transferred is tacit, i.e., difficult to codify, and cannot be encompassed by traded elements of technology. Effective TT depends to a much greater extent on the recipient firms' capabilities and its links with a supplier, which goes beyond contract specifications. The

perception of TT as merely an issue of distribution of technology rents and reduction on pricing issues omits the complexity of technology that cannot be reduced to commodity.

2. The importance of implementation ability, in essence a managerial ability to get things done, has been underestimated. The management gap in technology adoption and implementation is most often the crucial problem. The implementation problem arises from the fact that an effective transfer involves not only technical, but also organizational elements, which are closely interlinked.

3. Technology transfer now occurs more through FDI and informal channels (subcontracting, networking, export), and much less through arm's length licensing. A reliance on only one channel is not possible today since technology is a multidimensional commodity and a particular package might not be available from a single supplier but from a combination of resources. While this has always been the case to a certain extent, the point is that the systemic and non-standardized character of much of today's technology has increased.[7] This implies that a much more differentiated choice of channels must be developed in order to grasp the systemic character of much of information technology based equipment and technology.

The institutional basis for gaining and blocking access to technology has broadened, and is not confined to firms and R&D institutes. It also includes public or quasi-public institutions, groups of firms that collaborate, firms that set up technology acquiring-cum-developing organizations, technology imports that acquire firms in developed countries, and participation in joint collaborative agreements, networks and alliances [2].

4. Simultaneous access to technology and markets is critical in the 'catching up' process. The experience of successful newly industrializing countries (NICs) shows that selective market and technology access can be a powerful motor of technological development. Contrary to the experience of import-substituting economies, the chief mechanisms by which firms achieved export-led technology development was by exploiting a variety of foreign technology and marketing channels. Often these channels served a dual purpose: as a means of product marketing on the one hand and as a mechanism of technology acquisition on the other [18]. The implementation of simultaneous technology and market access is the most important issue in a new international arena of 'free trading blocs' and increasing neomercantilistic policies. It leads to a paradoxical problem in a liberalized environment - that of market and technology exclusion.

At the firm level, the simultaneous access to technology and markets is crucial in overcoming two gaps, those of product development and market development [9]. For this, the timing of entry and speed of technology access is crucial. Only then will the latecomer be able to develop his market presence rapidly so that he can obtain revenues at an earlier stage than other companies [3]. This is the consequence of the constantly moving technology frontier in which the approach based on product life cycle is meaningless. What matters is how to embark on a dynamic capability building process.

THE LATECOMER FIRM -A CENTRAL AGENT OF 'CATCHING UP'

The central element of a new-sourcing-paradigm in TT is the *latecomer firm* and its related network. One of the mechanisms by which successful NICs grew was the learning effort of their local firms combined with the acquisition of foreign technology. A latecomer firm is a firm located outside the loci of world innovation and R&D. Such a firm does not come face to face with demanding buyers in its domestic markets on a large scale and is 'cut off' from leading industrial clusters and important marketing networks.[8] Consequently, a latecomer firm must overcome these 'negative externalities' through a dynamic capability building process.[9] Over the years, big latecomer firms may partly improve their industry infrastructure (university-industry links, technical services, subcontractor networks) to a level beneficial to other firms, too. In this way they create positive externalities in the economy.

Their path of technology acquisition differs from firms in developed countries. It starts with simple tasks, such as labor-intensive assembly, and ends with formalized R&D.

Since the technology gap with technology leaders is big at the beginning, the latecomer firm must make judicious use of foreign technology sourcing as a way to acquire the needed knowledge (by relying on customers to provide specifications and through the use of original equipment manufacturer (OEMs) agreements and FDI). The effectiveness of a firm in combining foreign technology elements with its own experience and knowledge in order to strengthen its internal capabilities is crucial. The ability to complement its own technological effort with technology import is an important management ability that latecomers have developed.

Based on the above discussion the three important issues for Eastern European companies are the following: What are the main stylized characteristics describing the Eastern European latecomer? Which possible channels and options would enable Eastern European latecomers to use TT as a mechanism of 'catching up'? What are policy implications of a new context, which I described as a sourcing paradigm?

3. The Eastern European Latecomer Firm: Some Stylized Characteristics[10]

1. THE EASTERN EUROPEAN LATECOMER MUST COMPENSATE FOR PHYSICAL, KNOWLEDGE AND SYSTEMIC DEFECTS OF THE BUSINESS ENVIRONMENT

Eastern European latecomers must compensate for systemic defects that are comparatively much stronger than in other middle-income economies. These defects come from high uncertainties in the economic environment caused by slow and undefined privatization, high transaction costs due to underdeveloped financial and other markets and macroeconomic imbalances. The industrial structure in which a firm operates is fluid and firms are continuously faced with strategic choices.

The most important structural constraints with which they are faced are financial repression, a lack of long-term capital and high costs of working capital. Inherited social functions, such as provision of welfare services, in some countries, particularly in Russia, significantly reduces room for maneuver.[11] The possibilities for restructuring based on the domestic market are most often minimal due to radical erosion of domestic demand. The only real opportunity for growth and restructuring is in accessing foreign markets. Hence a central question is how a firm can enter a specific segment of the world market.

2. STRATEGIC MYOPIA AND CRISIS MANAGEMENT DOMINATE DECISION-MAKING

Strategic myopia is a pervasive characteristic of the latecomer's decision making. The managers are so occupied with every day business that they have difficulties to comprehend the full scale and scope of changes and the strategic choices before them. 'Transformative management' is squeezed by 'crisis management'. Overwhelming strategic confusion and lack of focus are general characteristics. Most companies do not have sufficient information to compare themselves to their competitors. Many do not even know their domestic competitors.

Myopic perceptions of their internal environment are equally pervasive. These are best reflected in the difficulties of management to appraise the real sources of production inefficiencies.

3. INHERITED COMPARATIVE ADVANTAGES AND EXPORT OF NEGATIVE EXTERNALITIES INTO THE DOMESTIC ENVIRONMENT: BACKBONES OF SURVIVAL STRATEGY

The survival of enterprises is based on soft and informal credits offered to customers and received from suppliers as well as on inherited (accumulated in the past) production and engineering know-how.

Arrears became a very popular source of enterprise finance since nobody could be properly punished for overdue payments where mechanisms of enforcing contracts are weak. In such a situation price competitiveness is sustained by transferring the burden of high costs onto domestic buyers through higher domestic prices. Companies not able to fully switch the cost burden onto the domestic market export by reducing the value of assets. Even companies able to export under the same prices as on the domestic market are induced to charge higher prices on the domestic market to insure themselves against non-payment by domestic customers or high inflation. Also, the real profitability of exports is artificially improved by a sometimes negative interest rate of capital for the preparation of export jobs (preshipment and post-shipment finance).

The Eastern European latecomer goes through three adjustment phases. The first is the transfer of costs of non-competitiveness into an external environment. This is what I call the export of negative externalities into the domestic environment.

The export of negative externalities is combined with the exploitation of past results. Companies exploit their acquired capabilities, which are in accumulated engineering and adaptive development. However, this is an exploitation of past results, which is now done much more cost-effectively. The longevity of these acquired advantages will depend on the development of organizational capabilities necessary to develop new and higher value-added activities.

In the second phase, enterprises implement passive adjustments and start a process of 'muddling through', i.e. searching for ways to adapt to external changes at the lowest costs but in a defensive and rather opportunistic way. In the third phase, enterprises reach the point at which they can conceptualize active adjustment and exploit higher order economies (strategic repositioning, networking). The next stylization therefore deals with the passive and active adjustments.

4. 'MUDDLING THROUGH'—THE MOST COMMON TYPE OF ADJUSTMENT

Although structural constraints and strategic myopia are pervasive, an intensive process of learning in the form of trial and error and organizational restructuring is taking place. We shall distinguish among three types of adjustment: passive, productive and active.[12] The literature gives very contradictory signals regarding the prevalence of one of these types of adjustment.[13] Nevertheless, it is possible, though very tentatively, to conclude the following:

- passive adjustment is the widest in scope and is deep in its effects. The negative externalities effects of this type of adjustment perpetuate and deepen macroeconomic instability and increase uncertainty;
- productive and active adjustments are present to different degrees in different countries and different industries. However, their shallow efforts and scope are common to both. It seems that enterprises are increasingly exploring restructuring possibilities rather than engaging actively in these activities. The significant management gaps and structural constraints with which they are faced imply a 'muddling through' adjustment rather than an attempt to engage in the 'catching up' process.

Enterprises are generally sticking to their old routines, trying to produce in the same way reduced number of products, but essentially maintaining the same range that they were producing before. The difference lies in the significantly reduced number of workers, increased marketing efforts and greater awareness of quality and delivery times as crucial factors for expanding exports. In playing the card of lower labor costs, companies are neglecting the much higher potential of cost reduction hidden in operations, logistics, input consumption and process efficiency.

Current firm adjustments are minor structural shifts within the existing product mix. Changes are taking place in organizational structures (thinning of numerous hierarchical layers), an increased marketing and sales effort and an elimination of the most unprofitable lines. Depending on the institutional context of a country, 'lay-offs' and privatization also belong to this group of mainly passive responses to new circumstances.[14]

More active adjustments would require additional capital, long-term stability, and an intensive process of building markets. Nevertheless, some firms are now in some respects (size, ownership, organization, production experience) capable of further strategic changes.

5. THE TECHNO-ECONOMIC PROFILE OF THE EASTERN EUROPEAN LATECOMER: A SHIFT TOWARDS INTANGIBLE ASSETS

Irrespective of a lack of strategic awareness, a re-configuration of capabilities within firms is taking place. Complementary capabilities, by which I mean finance, marketing and organization as opposed to technology capabilities, are the weakest in the spectrum of firms' capabilities. The lack of competencies in these areas is the consequence of practices from the old system, in which these functions were transferred either to big foreign trade organizations (marketing) or to ministries (finance). The biggest shortage of skills is probably in the area of system integration (product level) and network building (enterprise level).[15] Production know-how is comparatively better developed.[16]

The focus of management is shifting towards intangible activities like marketing, quality, and organization. These elements are not close to their previous experience, which was confined to production engineering and negotiations with other actors within the administrative structures of centrally planned economies. This creates the biggest problem for Eastern European enterprises: human resources and intangible asset management. The lack of awareness of the importance of skilled labor and key specialists is common. On the other hand, used to a clearly prescribed set of tasks, the labor force has difficulties in learning to become 'all-round players'. The empowered position of management, fears of 'lay-offs', and a need to react much faster than before make managers much more susceptible to resorting to hierarchy and direct control than to team work and persuasion.

6. 'TURNAROUND SPECIALISTS': KEY AGENTS OF ENTERPRISE ADJUSTMENTS[17]

In a fluid industrial structure with high environmental uncertainties, routine management is not of much use. Pressures from within (lower management, key specialists, workers) and from outside (privatization, agency, ministry, potential investors, the local community) have created a situation where the usual distinction between strategic, tactical and operational management is breaking down. Many seemingly tactical and operational decisions are implicit strategic decisions.[18] Also, in order to become flexible and cost-competitive, explicit strategic decisions are taken more often, like debt/equity swaps with banks, 'lay-offs', constant reshuffling and downsizing. However, a widespread 'wait and see' syndrome is also evident. These are situations where management is unable to declare many strategic decisions as its own position and room for maneuver is constrained by strong stakeholders (privatization agency, workers, ministries, the local community).

Managers and management teams able to move enterprises in the direction of productive and active adjustments are the scarcest resource. The combination of strategic insight, a tacit understanding of business and the ability to bargain with stakeholders is a set of skills rarely found. These specialists are not necessarily found within an enterprise. Former big trading organizations and banks are now embarking on a wave of acquisitions, thereby creating large conglomerates. The sustainability of these newly created structures will depend on their ability to turn around very diversified business portfolios.[19]

7. SUCCESSFUL 'CATCHING UP' OCCURS MOST OFTEN IN FOREIGN AFFILIATES

The most active adjustment responses come from firms that have been privatized through foreign privatizations [15]. While domestic enterprises lack direction and have significant management and financial gaps, these drawbacks are overcome through foreign affiliates. Re-learning is a task that is sometimes impossible to perform in the same organization. Only foreign management and the insertion of affiliates into an international structure can transform the internal culture and add value to existing production competencies.

These seven stylizations, which very roughly approximate the real situation, indicate the type of difficulties that the Eastern European latecomer encounters. Short adjustment time and the possibility to master state-of-the-art production and management techniques is more likely to happen if domestic enterprises build links with foreign partners. TT that occurs in such a situation can benefit not only affiliates but also linked domestic enterprises. This motivation lies behind the discussion in the next chapter of possible strategic options to access foreign technology and markets.

4. FDI, Technology Transfer and Eastern European Firms: Strategic Options

It seems obvious that strategic ways of gaining access to foreign technology and markets will not come from the advice of analysts but from the trial and errors of Eastern European enterprises. However, it is also true that enterprises are not isolated islands but are also governed by institutional change and policy actions in the environment. From many possible mechanisms of TT we will discuss some of the most important ones: FDI, licenses, subcontracting (as mechanisms of technology import) and vertical market niches (as channels of technology export).

FOREIGN DIRECT INVESTMENT

Eastern European countries see FDI as the first best solution to their accumulated problems. FDI brings a mixed package of marketing, finance, and technology. The important issue is how to maximize technological benefits from FDI.

The possibilities for this maximization are determined by the position of the affiliate within the structure of a trans-national corporation (TNC). In the case of Eastern Europe, all three locational strategies or motivations of foreign investors [13] are present: sourcing natural resources, reducing costs and accessing foreign markets.

Sourcing natural resources dominates the oil and gas industry of Russia and Kazakhstan. Cost reduction dominates FDI in smaller Eastern European economies and is most present in the auto parts and car industry. Access to foreign markets is a driving motivation of strategic investors (global companies) that have a long-term horizon and see the whole of Eastern Europe as one regional market. The main strategic problem of host economies is how to deepen and network the presence of FDI so that it can become a powerful integrator of these economies into the world economy. To illustrate the point, I summarize the possible routes of development of FDI below.[20]

Without clustering local enterprises with foreign investments, liberalization of FDI alone may not lead to technological spillovers. Indeed, countries may embark on a vicious circle where FDI will perpetuate the initial comparative advantages in cheap labor. The mere presence of TNCs is not sufficient to provide the impetus for fast economic growth. It is TT to the local industry that provides the impetus. Training of local personnel in foreign affiliates is not sufficient to constitute transfer of technology.

Type of FDI	*The direction of deepening*		
Resource-based	Extractors →	Processors	
Cost-based	Offshore →	Source factories	
Market driven	Importers →	Focused factories →	World product mandates/Lead factories
R & D driven	R & D subcontracting →	High-tech joint ventures	

Figure 1. Strategic Possibilities for Technology Deepening of FDI in Eastern Europe

ARM'S LENGTH LICENSING

Arm's length licensing is a very unlikely possibility for technology import in Eastern Europe[21]. Financial capacity for technology import will delay this option until the revival of high growth.

SUBCONTRACTING

Subcontracting is a sourcing where a host country's supplies are part of the value chain of a principal's production.[22] Subcontracting implicitly functions as a training school where knowledge inputs are received through production specifications, requirements and supervision while marketing is transferred to the principal. Subcontracting relationships are an appropriate structure when learning economies are significant and technology is network -rather than firm - specific. Thus, to the extent that a subcontractor can accumulate experience by serving several customers' requirements, a new user of that subcontractor's services benefits from the subcontractor's learning without having to repeat the learning process [14]. The subcontracting relationship cannot be understood only in terms of production. Marketing as an integral part of the production process is also transferred.

In a globalized economy, different types and transformations from one sourcing position to another are the key issues of TT[23]. For the Eastern European latecomer it is critical to develop a network of suppliers (subcontractors) and to move from being a cheap producer to a specialty subcontractor position.

THE 'VERTICAL MARKET NICHE'

The 'vertical market niche' option may capitalize more explicitly on learning related to the application of new technologies in the old system. The closed economy and specific restrictions and constraints to which Eastern European producers were exposed have in some areas created new trajectories and capabilities that have a promising future in an open economy. In fact, these are now competitive advantages of which some are already commercial high-tech products. Examples of these capabilities are the specific skills of Soviet software engineers and the several software packages already on the market.[24]

5. Strategic Approach to Support Latecomers' Growth

Embarking on any of the strategic options above may seem entirely the responsibility of the enterprises. Indeed it is so. However, the 'catching up' process of Eastern European latecomers is highly conditioned by the removal of some of the structural constraints with which they are faced and which are beyond their control. Enormous transaction costs, which enterprises are forced to bear when seeking new suppliers and customers, are the result of a low degree of development of information, marketing and knowledge infrastructure. Uncertainty, opportunism and conservatism are enforced by the poor working of financial markets, which do not automatically identify insolvent enterprises. Poor public administrative capabilities cannot develop programs of restructuring jointly with enterprises, which would separate candidates for bankruptcy from the rest of industry. This leads me to two points of importance for Eastern Europe.

First, the traditional framework for government policy based on market failure is not very helpful in the context of the very strong uncertainties, structural restrictions and negative externalities prevailing in Eastern Europe. On the other hand, low administrative capability hides very real dangers of government capture and government failure. The development of public/private interaction mechanisms that go beyond the justification of market failure but at the same time are not costly interventions and thus avoid the dangers of government failure, are of high relevance for Eastern Europe.

Second, TT ceases to be a distinct policy area. In a liberalized environment, TT issues are increasingly becoming industrial policy issues. The technological import problem within thc sourcing paradigm is how to develop and harness local factors of production to a technology upgrading effort led by foreign capital and foreign technology for foreign markets. This is done through distinctly domestic policies, like training and diffusion and the creation of domestic subcontractor networks.

Based on these two points two questions naturally follow: What kind of policy can avoid the constraints of simultaneous market and government failure approaches, and how is this alternative approach applicable to TT? The concept of strategic technology policy is an attempt to conceptually analyze and resolve this problem. It is defined as explicit targeting for the improvement of technological and related capabilities based on the coordination of groups of companies and government.[25] It is strategic in the sense that its formulation and implementation is based on the interaction among firms, or of firms, universities and government.[26] It is in essence a very targeted horizontal industrial policy designed in cooperation with industry. Its horizontal character avoids the challenge of 'picking winners,' which would be anyhow senseless in the currently very fluid conditions, while targeting deficient capabilities avoids the drawback of an horizontal industrial policy, i.e. its slow effects and undefined clientele.

The main areas of application relevant to TT are:

- assistance in the self-organization of industry,[27]
- assistance in the creation of subcontractor networks,
- information systems for TT,
- coordination of FDI,
- government -industry forum for export promotion,
- promotion of industrial and R&D alliances and assistance in accessing foreign alliances,[28]
- public assistance for restructuring sectors and enterprises in trouble.

These measures focus on strengthening the absorptive capacity of a host economy. An implicit assumption is that foreign investors will agree to participate and cooperate in pursuing national training, diffusion and networking objectives. However, this may not be always the case. While complementary policy options are almost nonexistent in the case of small Eastern European countries, in the case of bigger countries, and especially Russia, policy makers might reconsider the use of performance requirements.[29]

It is not possible to reach general conclusions on the effects of performance requirements. Eastern European countries should carefully examine whether the benefits from such policies might exceed their costs. Whether they will contribute to the integration of foreign affiliate production into a host economy or into a TNC network depends on many specific factors. Administrative and negotiating capability and the relative power of partners are more important than normative performance requirements.[29]

Whichever policy option is taken up, it is essential that it be conducive to enterprise growth. The inherited culture of non-cooperation and confrontation between the public administration and the business community should be replaced by a better understanding of a specific industry's problems. Public administration must learn to build a 'playing field' for open competition and, at the same time, to cooperate and assist the self-organization of industry and the support of new markets, especially business services.

IMPLICATIONS FOR PERSONNEL AND LEADERSHIP

In a liberalized economy, Technology Transfer is no longer only a foreign trade area but equally an area of domestic industrial policy. This implies that the usual administrative responsibilities for TT are breaking down. TT can no longer be the responsibility of one or two ministries but must become an inter-ministerial job carried out in close cooperation with industry.

The need to develop a dialogue with industry and support programs for enterprises implies that the distinction between public and business administration in terms of competencies and understanding of very specific industrial problems is breaking down. In a time of very short-term orientation of enterprises, public administrations must assist in developing strategic views within industry as well as by supporting a market of infrastructural services (business and technical) that may facilitate the reduction of environmental uncertainties.

Footnotes

(1) Here I use Dunning (1993), which defines the globalized economy as one in which there is a close interdependence among the leading nations in trade, investment and commercial relations, with few restrictions in trade and foreign direct investment (FDI).

(2) For a longer discussion on these issues, see [28].

(3) By 'international production' we assume transactions within TNCs, while 'sourcing' refers to transactions between independent firms where one firm purchases sub-assemblies, components or processed materials produced by an independent firm located in another country. Contrary to widely held beliefs, the international integration of production is not dominated by transactions within TNCs. The proportion of intra-firm trade in total trade for the US has fluctuated, around 30% for exports and 40% for imports during the 1970s and 1980s. While the absolute level of intra-firm trade has increased sharply in recent decades, intra-firm trade as a proportion of total trade has declined for the US in 1977-82 [23].

(4) For an example of shift from demand to client in the case of mining and metallurgy, see [6].

(5) The point is that the link to a global production system through FDI subcontracting or alliances may also foster a vicious circle of backwardness and stagnation of low value-added activities, perpetuating the initial advantages of a host country in unskilled labor. The ability to avoid this trap of globalized economy and to use of global networks as mechanisms of domestic restructuring is the main challenge of TT under the new conditions.

(6) While this may seem obvious today, the focus in the 1970s was more on the technological rents that come from different pricing and less on the firm as a main repository and agent of technology acquisition. The appreciation of the role of the firm as a key agent of TT is the key difference with the 1970s, when the firm was seen as a passive subject whose activity was to a great extent determined by the TT government policy.

(7) For example, in the CIM (computer integrated manufacturing) area turnkey capabilities do not yet exist, i.e. firms supplying the whole range of products and services required by standard turnkey capabilities [1].

(8) For a similar approach along these lines, see [18].

(9) The approach on which the theory of latecomer firm might be built falls into a broader group of 'competence view' of the firm dynamic organisational capabilities [8]; dynamic capabilities [31]; core competencies [27]; and technological competence [7]. When these contributions are compared with the literature on technology capability they show a convergence in conceptualizing firms in developed and developing countries [10; 33].

(10) This part is based on Radosevic [29], Kuznetsov [21], Estrin et al [15], Hughes (1994), Torok [32] and IIASA [19]. I am fully aware that any attempt to stylize the very chaotic and nontransparent situation of Eastern European firms is a high-risk operation. However, I believe that even at the current, rather modest, level of enterprise research it is possible to develop some generic characteristics of the Eastern European latecomer.

(11) Kuzentsov [21] states that in the enterprises of the Soviet military industrial complex, up to 40% of labor was employed in the social sphere and security units.

(12) Active adjustment are responses like new organization, marketing/sales development, export orientation, cost control, quality development, etc. Productive adjustments are responses like closing production lines, altering product mix, laying off workers, reorganizing production towards cheaper inputs, etc. Passive adjustments are responses like accumulation of debt and arrears, nonpayment of suppliers, accumulation of inventories, etc. [15].

(13) See references on which this chapter is based (footnote 9).

(14) There are very important differences in 'lay-offs' in different countries. Russia, where lay-offs are not implemented as a part of restructuring process, is probably a good example.

(15) The following description from *Business Central Europe* (1993) illustrates this point: Despite the emphasis on manufacturing, the brightest prospects in the domestic sector are those firms which are able to take imported Western hardware from a range of suppliers, network them together, perhaps add their own software applications and install them at a customer site with consultancy and support services, preferably developing their expertise to serve specific vertical market sectors. Such firms are highly sought after by Western suppliers, but they are relatively few and far in between. There are no shortcuts to gaining the necessary skills and perfecting the right supplier relationships.'

(16) Quality control is also one of the underdeveloped capabilities in Eastern European firms. However, it can be considered mainly as organisational weakness and result of poor management, not as a problem caused by the lack of know-how.

(17) For an application of the 'turnaround specialist' as a concept in the Russian context see [21].

(18) Whether to buy from a traditional partner or from a top manager's newly formed company, which serves as a mechanism to liquidate his 'nominal' enterprise, is implicitly a strategic decision ('wild', 'spontaneous' or 'nomenclature' privatization) as well as many other forms of private -public enterprises links.

(19) For a detailed description of Eastern European domestic acquisitions, see *Business Central Europe*, Vol. 2, No.12, June 1994, 'Hungry for New Acquirers' (p.7-9).

(20) Within resource-based FDI, there are two factory types: extractors, which access natural resources essential to the production process, and processors, which process raw materials and turn them into fabricated materials.

Within cost-reducing FDI, offshore factories use cheap local inputs (labor) to produce components or to assemble products for the parent company. Source factories are an advanced stage of offshore plants providing access to low-cost input but also carrying responsibility for the development and production of specific components. They function as a part of the TNC's value chain. Market-driven FDI contains several types of factories: importers (distributors), local servers, focused factories, miniature replicas, world product mandates, lead factories and outposts. Importers provide marketing, sales, services and warehousing facilities. Local servers service local markets and are often driven by local content regulations. Focused factories produce few product lines for both local and foreign markets and are globally rationalized subsidiaries. World product mandates also manufacture for global sale but are responsible for product redesign on their own account, which is not the case with focused factories. Lead factories are equal partners with the parent firm. For an extended review of this taxonomy, see [13].

(21) Unbundling technology through licensing allows greater scope for local enterprises to learn the mechanics of product design through reverse engineering. However, the great majority of licensing is transferred through FDI. Its beneficiaries will therefore be those economies that will be able anyhow to attract FDI. On the other hand, the increasing technological gap makes it unlikely that arm's length licensing will expand significantly in the future [14].

(22) Subcontracting is an informal mechanism of TT on which a number of NICs began export-led growth in the 1960s and 1970s, especially in electronics. It is becoming widespread in Eastern Europe but we still do not have systematic insights into this phenomenon. While in East Asian subcontracting experience is very positive, it is mixed in other developing countries.

(23) In the first phase the subcontractor usually, based on his cost advantages (economy subcontracting), produces simpler components which are assembled into a final product by the main producer (the principal). As a subcontractor develops its production and technological competencies it tends to transform itself into a speciality subcontractor, who makes the principal dependent in the technological sense. Original equipment manufacturer relationships (OEM) can be considered as a higher form of subcontracting (though not necessarily technically), where a subcontractor produces finished products according to the principal's specifications. The last phase is own design and manufacturing (ODM), which is an advanced form of OEM. When enterprises enter into OBM phase (original brand manufacturer) they leave the position of subcontractor. In situations where a subcontractor has mastered all production capabilities it is often difficult to get out of the OEM trap because of high marketing costs.

(24) For example, because of its isolation Soviet computing followed a different path of evolution - one firmly rooted in mathematics - than the West. The results were highly developed skills in programming and algorithms. See [12; 16 and 4].

[25] The concept is theoretically developed by Justman and Teubal [20]. For its application in the case of Eastern Europe, see Radosevic [30].

[26] Strategic technology policy should not be confused with policy for supporting strategic technologies. Strategic here refers to the interactions of various agents who jointly determine policy outcomes. The strategic approach in technology policy is very widely implemented in the EC R&D programs, where the actual program design is shaped through the interaction of firms and the EC. See [25]. In the case of Eastern Europe, its application should be much closer to the market in areas like quality and industrial engineering.

[27] Havas [17] gives an excellent example of self-organization of automotive parts suppliers in Hungary. The establishment of their association was initiated by Magyar Suzuki, a foreign affiliate (!), itself is not a member of the association.

[28] Eastern European countries do not need only the pre-competitive alliances of the type being formed in OECD countries. However, they need pre-competitive alliances that would foster productivity enhancement and technology diffusion. The alliances should be formed by firms and subsidized by the government and centered around a particular functional area (such as production engineering). For a wider discussion on this issue for developing countries, see [24].

[29] There are two basic groups of performance requirements: quantitative and qualitative [26]: Quantitative performance requirements are local-content requirements and local labor content. Local material content are requirements for enterprises to place ceilings on imports or to establish minimum local content for inputs. Local labor content require that a certain amount of local labor be employed or a certain proportion of the work force to be nationals. Qualitative performance tests, of which some were present in the TT regulations during the 1970s, include full disclosure of all technical information, full access to future improvements in the technology, transfer of ability to maintain product quality, and an effective training program The Uruguay Round produced 14 trade-related investment measures (TRIMs), of which most are performance requirements (UNCTAD, 1991). They are not intended as a definitive catalogue, but as illustrations of the types of measures to be considered, which include requirements

(local equity, licensing, transfer of technology, domestic sales, manufacturing, product mandating, trade balancing, local content, export and import substitution requirements), restrictions (remittance, foreign exchange restrictions and manufacturing limitations) and investment incentives.

REFERENCES

1. Alcorta, L. (1992) The Impact of New Technologies on Scale in Manufacturing Industry: Issues and Evidence, UNU/INTECH Working Paper No. 5.

2. Bell, M. and Cassiolato, J. (1993 mimeo) Technology imports and the dynamic competitiveness of Brazilian industry and the need for new approaches to management and policy, a report for the Estudo da Competitividade da Industria Brasiliera, SPRU, March.

3. Bloom, M. (1992) *Technical Change in the Korean Electronics Industry*, OECD: Paris.

4. Bojar, G. (1993) The graphisfot story, Paper presented at International Conference: Information Technology and Business Opportunities in Eastern Europe and the Former Soviet Union, October 13-14, Adam Smith Institute, London.

5. Business Centre Europe (1993) Clash of Titans: computers & office technology: survey, October.

6. Bomsel, O. et al. (1990) Mining and metallurgy investment in the third world: the end of large projects?, Development Centre, OECD, Paris.

7. Cantwell, J. (1991) The theory of technological competence and its application to international production, E McFetridge (ed.) *Foreign Investment, Technology and Economic Growth,* The University of Calgary Press.

8. Chandler, A. D. (1990) *Scale and Scope: The Dynamics of Industrial Capitalism,* Harvard University Press, Cambridge.

9. Choi, Y. (1994 Ph.D work in progress) Evolutionary concurrent techno-management capability of mass system: an engine of rapid technological catch-up in the Korean semiconductor industry, Roskilde University Centre, Roskilde.

10. Cooper, C. (1991) Are innovation studies on industrialised economies relevant to technology policy in developing countries?, UNU/INTECH Working Paper, No. 3.

11. Dunning, H. J. (1993) *Multinational Enterprise and the Global Economy,* Addison Wesley.

12. Dyker D. and Stein, G. (1993 mimeo) Russian software: technology transfer and technological capability.

13. Eden, L. (1991) Multinational responses to trade and technology changes: implications for Canada, in McFetridge (ed.) *Foreign Investment, Technology and Economic Growth,* The University of Calgary Press.

14. Ernst, D. and O'Connor, D. (1990) Technology and global competition: the challenges for newly industrialising economies, Development Centre, OECD, Paris.

15. Estrin, S., Gelb, A. and Sing, I. (1993 mimeo) Restructuring, viability and privatisation: a comparative study of enterprise adjustment in transition, London Business School, London.

16. Financial Times (1993) Russians show their mathematical might, November 18.

17. Havas, A. (1994 mimeo) The re-emergence of the car parts industry in Hungary, IKU, Innovation Research Centre, Budapest.

18. Hobday, M. (1994) Export-led technology development in the four dragons: the case of electronics, *Development and Change* **25-2**.

19. IIASA (1993) *Enterprise Behaviour and Privatisation of the Large Enterprises in the Russian Federation,* ETI Project, Working Paper-93-70, November, Laxenburg.

20. Justman, M. and Teubal, M. (1992) Strategic technology policy for new industrial infrastructure: creating capabilities and building new markets, *An Industrial Development Policy Group Publication, Discussion Paper* No. 25, The Jerusalem Institute for Israel Studies, Jerusalem.

21. Kuznetsov, E. (1993) How can economy adjust to simultaneous market and government failure? Lessons from the Soviet Union, contemporary Russia and countries of late-late industrialisation, *Communist Economies & Economic Transformation* **5-4**.

22. Kuznetsov, Y. (1994) Conditional comparative advantages: development of Russian firm-level organisational capabilities to enhance manufacturing exports, Paper prepared for the May 5-7 IIASA Workshop *International Trade Issues of the Russian Federation*, Laxenburg.

23. Levy, D. and Dunning, J.H. (1993), International products and sourcing: trends and issues, *STI Review 13, OECD,* Paris.

24. Mody, A. (1988) Staying in the loop. International alliances for sharing technology, World Bank Discussion Paper, No. 61, The World Bank, Washington.

25. Molina, A. (1993) Insights into the successful generation of a large-scale European initiative: from misalignment to programmatic alignment in the build up of sociotechnical constituencies, Paper presented at May UK PICT National Conference, Kenilworth.

26. Moran, H. T. (1992) The impact of TRIMs on trade and development, *Transnational Corporations* **1-1**, 5545.

27. Prahalad, C. K. and Hammel, G. (1990) The core competence of the corporation, *Harvard Business Review* **May/June**.

28. Radosevic, Slavo (1994 mimeo) Technology transfer policy revisited, UNU INTECH, Maastricht.

29. Radosevic, Slavo (1994) The generic problems of competitiveness at company level in the former socialist economies: the case of Croatia, *Europe - Asia Studies* **46-3**,489-503.

30. Radosevic, Slavo (1994) Strategic technology policy for Eastern Europe, *Economic Systems* **1994**.

31. Teece, D.J. Pisano, G. and Shuen, A. (1990 mimeo) Firm capabilities. Resources and the concept of strategy, University of California, Berkeley.

32. Torok, A. (1991) Market orientation of Hungarian enterprises - EC integration, Paper prepared in the framework of the ACE Programme of the EC, Research Institute of Industrial Economics, Budapest.

33. UNCTAD (1993) Fostering technological dynamism: evolution of thought on technology capacity building and competitiveness: review and analysis of literature (draft), UNCTAD, Geneva.

12. EUROPEAN UNION RELATIONS WITH CENTRAL AND EASTERN EUROPE AND WITH THE COMMONWEALTH OF INDEPENDENT STATES: THE EXAMPLE OF CENTRAL ASIA

MANFREDO MACIOTI
International Consultant
Brussels, Belgium

1. Introduction

The concept of a European Union (EU) gradually evolved over forty-odd years since the time when six Western European States established in 1951 the European Community for Coal and Steel (ECSC). The objective of the subsequent European Economic Community (1957/8) was to create a common market in which goods, services, capital and people moved freely. Its principal external responsibility was the running of a unified trade policy. A third Community, the European Atomic Energy Community (Euratom) was equally established in 1957/8. Over the years, the EU has grown from a commercial and economic power to become a quasi-political force as well. The original six members of today's EU started coordinating their national foreign policies from 1970 onwards in what became known as European Political Cooperation (EPC). Following the adoption of the Single Act (1987), the EU took another significant step toward a greater world role with the launching (Maastricht Treaty of 1992) of a Common Foreign and Security Policy (CFSP).

The EU has a membership of twelve Western European States: up to four new Members may decide to join in 1995. The EU is more than an intergovernmental organization but less than a sovereign State. Responsibilities on external issues are shared between the EU and its Member States. The model offered by the EU is so far unique in the world. Despite its shortcomings and its limited ability to intervene in some crisis situations (like the war in the former Yugosla-

G. Bugliarello et al. (eds.), East-West Technology Transfer, 155-164.

via), the EU has become an example for various other countries in Europe (EFTA), Latin America (CACM) and Asia (ASEAN).

One fundamental principal lies behind the EU policies towards the outside world: enlightened self-interest. The EU's own economic well-being depends on a liberal, multilateral world economic order, as well as on the welfare of its partners.

In response to the far-reaching events of the past four years in Central and Eastern Europe and the Former Soviet Union (FSU), the EU has developed a variety of new cooperative instruments. Among them, a new generation of "Europe" agreements with its Eastern neighbors and new types of cooperation with the Independent Republics of the FSU (e.g. the Partnership and Cooperation Agreements recently concluded between the EU, Kazakhstan, Kyrgyzstan, Russia and Ukraine). Both Russia and Ukraine have been offered a very close partnership in the political and economic areas, and the EU looks forward to working closely with them.

The goal is the regeneration of these countries into the global political and economic system. In the case of the FSU, this is a task for the whole world community, while the common future that Brussels offers Europe is a Union of States bound closely together, based on the three pillars of economic growth, democracy and the assurance of stability. For historical, geographic, economic and political reasons, the EU will bear in the future, as it has done in the past, the greatest part of the burden. On the other hand, the whole world must share - Japan and the US in particular having as much to contribute and to gain in economic and strategic terms, as does the EU.

2. Central and Eastern Europe

We shall consider under the label the majority of the Eastern neighbors of the EU, viz. Poland, Hungary, Czech republic, Slovak Republic, Romania, Bulgaria, Albania, Slovenia, Fyrom, Lithuania, Latvia and Estonia.

The Central instrument of the EU to provide financial and technical support to the process of economic support and social reform in Central and eastern Europe is the Phare program (originally instituted in December 1989 with the objective of providing aid to Poland and Hungary). The Phare budget has increased from 500mECU in 1990 to 785mECU in 1991, to over 1,000mECU in both 1992 and 1993. The priority sectors for EU assistance are as follows:

- private sector development, restructuration and privatization

- agriculture and rural development
- social development, labor and health
- infrastructure (energy, transport, telecommunications)
- integrated regional development programs
- banking and the financial sector
- environment and nuclear safety
- education, training, research and development
- administration reform (including statistics, customs, etc.)
- humanitarian aid

Generally speaking, EU assistance is given as non-reimbursable grants, emphasis being placed on sector programs (rather than individual projects). Grants are given for technical assistance, preliminary studies, action plans or outside expertise and policy advice, professional training, start-up capital or the purchase of essential equipment and supplies.

Besides bilateral programs, Phare develops a number of regional programs in Central Europe, examples of which are the "Regional Industrial Property Programme" (RIPP), the "Regional Telecommunications Programme", the "Regional Transport Programme", or the "Regional nuclear Safety Improvement Programme".

Funded by Phare, but implemented as autonomous EU programs, are the ACE and TEMPUS programs. ACE aims at cooperation between economists and managers in Western and Eastern Europe, TEMPUS promotes interaction between the higher education and industry sectors in the two halves of Europe. TEMPUS has been renewed in 1993 for a second four-year period (TEMPUS-II) starting with the academic year 1994-95.

The EU has granted loans to a number of countries of Central and Eastern Europe to help them restructure their steel industries. The European Investment Bank (EIB) has provided important loans (1.7bECU over the years 1989-93) for investment projects in the region. Priority is given to projects in transport, telecommunications, energy, industry and a total of 3bECU is expected to be loaned by the EIB between 1994 and 1996. The EU also grants loans in support of balance of payments (these are complementary to IMF and World bank loans). So far, ten such loans have been approved for a total amount of 2.5bECU.

In 1992, the EU first launched scientific and technological cooperation programs with the countries of Central and eastern Europe (Copernicus). In 1992, the EU budget provided 55mECU to finance some 3,200 projects. In 1993, the EU allocated another 25mECU to support East/West research projects. Starting in 1993, the EU has opened a number of specific research programs under its own Framework Programme to research organizations and enterprises in central and Eastern Europe. These research programs are "Environment", "Non-Nuclear Energy", "Nuclear Fission Safety", "Biomedicine and Health" and "Human Capital and Mobility"; the EU has decided to provide funding in 1994 (29mECU) so that organizations in central and eastern Europe (as well as the FSU) can participate in EU projects. A further call for proposals was launched in January/ February 1994 inviting the participation of Central and Eastern European countries in cooperative research programs with the EU in the two areas of industrial technologies (information and communications; manufacturing and materials; measurement and testing) and life sciences (agro-and food industries; biotechnology). A budget of 57mECU is earmarked for this action.

The EU has made some funds available for furthering the participation of scientists from Eastern Europe in COST projects.

Another important international partner for financial investment in the Eastern Region is the European Bank for Reconstruction and Development (EBRD). All OECD countries (G-24) are members as well as the countries from Central and Eastern Europe and the FSU. The EU, plus its Member States, are a majority shareholder of the EBRD; the EU further cooperates with the EBRD through Phare. EBRD loans are primarily meant for financing private investment projects.

The Commission of the EU coordinates the assistance offered to the countries of Central and eastern Europe by all the G-24 (coordination being particularly developed in priority areas like balance of payments support, food aid and technical assistance in specific sectors).

"Europe" agreements establishing true association have been signed by the EU with six Republics in the Eastern Region (Poland and Hungary: agreements in force since February 1994; Czech republic; Slovakia; Bulgaria; Romania). These agreements deal *inter alia* with political dialogue, free trade, approximation of legislation, "national" treatment of enterprises, and economic, financial and cultural cooperation.

3. Commonwealth of Independent States

The EU has an interest in economic growth, movement towards a full market economy, social stability and democracy in the Independent republics of the FSU. The EU is interested in closer trade and economic relations. The EU is obviously interested in access to markets, to raw materials, to energy sources. In the Partnership and Cooperation Agreements which are now being concluded, the EU and the new IS (Independent States) are laying down the framework for growth of trade and investment links. The Partnership and Cooperation Agreement with Kazakhstan (initialed in May 1994) may offer a model. The general principles of the Agreement state that democratic values, respect for human rights and principles of a market economy are essential elements of the Partnership established by the Agreement. The Agreement covers, in particular: political dialogue; trade in goods; business and investment; payments and capital; intellectual and industrial property; economic cooperation in many areas (standards, mining, science and technology, education and training, energy, environment, transport, space, telecommunications, etc.)

The EU's main means for helping the region is TACIS: Technical Assistance for the Commonwealth of Independent States. This is an initiative launched in 1991 for fostering the transfer of know-how and technology to the FSU(as well as, more recently, Mongolia). The aim is to support the partner countries' initiatives to develop societies based on democracy and market economies. In its first four years of operation (1991-1994), TACIS has made available 1.87bECU to launch more than 2,000 projects. TACIS provides know-how from a wide range of public and private organizations, which allows for western experience to be combined with local knowledge and skills. The know-how is delivered by advising on the reform of the legal and regulatory frameworks and by setting up various forms of partnerships, networks, twinnings and pilot projects.

The main priorities for TACIS funding include restructuring of state enterprises and private sector development; building an effective food production, processing and distribution system; developing energy; transport and telecommunications infrastructures; nuclear safety; environment; public administration reform; social services and education.

TACIS funding has increased from 400mECU in 1991 to 460mECU in 1993 and 1994; of these funds, Russia has received the greatest amount (496mECU in 1991-93), followed by the Ukraine (119mECU) and Kazakhstan (40mECU).

In addition to national programs, the ECU funds can be used for interstate (or regional) activities in areas where there are advantages to be derived from dealing with problems on a joint basis (regional activities received funding of 395mECU over the years 1991-93).

Current TACIS financing is governed by the Indicative Programmes for the years 1993-95. As an example, we might consider the focal sectors for TACIS cooperation with each of the Central Asian Republics (including Azerbaijan).

AZERBAIJAN

The focal sector is energy; the 1993-95 TACIS programme will focus on policy advice on the management of local institutions and local corporations; improvement of distribution facilities for both industrial and domestic consumption; restructuring of the petrochemical and oil equipment industries. Pre-investment technical assistance will be provided for rehabilitation of the existing pipeline network; technical assistance will also be provided in the filed of energy-saving, efficiency and environmental improvement.

KAZAKHSTAN

The focal sector is enterprise restructuring and development; TACIS assistance will be aimed primarily at implementing the Mass Privatization Programme at local and enterprise level. A small and medium enterprise strategy will tap the know-how of counterpart associations in Western Europe. TACIS will also promote activities to assess and develop an action plan for reform in the financial sector.

KYRGYZSTAN

The focal sector is food production, processing and distribution; TACIS assistance will aim at improving the production capability of the sector, and improving the distribution and marketing activities related to agricultural production and inputs. Special assistance will be provided to encourage the development of oil crop production, to support the organizations of private farmers and to promote the nationalization of livestock production.

TURKMENISTAN

The focal sector is food production, processing and distribution; TACIS will support activities aimed at improving the overall production volume and quality of food and non-food products. A close link will be encouraged between production, agro-processing and distribution.

UZBEKISTAN

The focal sector is human resources development; TACIS cooperation will aim at improving the capability of existing public and private institutions involved in education in fields and topics related to the management and training of a market oriented economy, with particular emphasis on retaining of medium and high level administrators and managers. TACIS action also aims at strengthening the effectiveness of public sector staff involved in policy preparation and employment.

TADJIKISTAN

The TACIS programme is currently suspended for political and security reasons. Tadjikistan receives humanitarian aid (including emergency and food aid) from the EU (e.g. 2.9mECU for a winter programme for people displaced as a result of the civil war.)

The EU and the EIB (European Investment Bank) have actually made available a variety of emergency assistance and loans to the CIS since 1991. Overall, these include:

- a 250mECU grant (1990-91) of food and medical supplies
- a 200mECU food aid for Russia in 1991-92
- ECHO (the European Humanitarian Office) has provided about 58mECU in humanitarian assistance in 1991-93, mainly to Tadjikistan, Armenia, Georgia and Azerbaijan (and for the medical treatment of Chernobyl victims)
- a 1,250mECU EIB loan (1991-92) to the CIS to purchase food and medical supplies
- 1 500mECU credit guarantee to Russia in 1992 for the purchase of food

Total assistance from the EU and its Member States to the CIS up to the end of 1993 represents some 60% of world assistance. The EU is largely concentrating its efforts on technical assistance and humanitarian grants.

In November 1993, the TEMPUS programme was opened to a number of CIS Republics, including Kazakhstan, Kyrgyzstan and Uzbekistan (Russia and the Ukraine being eligible as well).

In the all-important area of nuclear safety, Euratom loans can be made available to an Eastern State. Thus, at the recent Corfu Summit (24-25 June

1994), a Euratom loan of 400mECU was offered to the Ukraine to underpin the reform process in the field of nuclear safety.

Two other science-oriented initiatives are worth a mention. In March 1994, the International Science and Technology Centre (ISTC) in Moscow held the first of two meetings of its Governing Board. Four Partners, (Russia, the US, the EU and Japan) have set up the ISTC to give Russian and other CIS weapons scientists and engineers the opportunity to redirect their talents to peaceful activities, responsive to civil needs, and to promote the integration onto the international scientific and technological community. The budget of the ISTC will be approximately $65 m. for an initial period of two years (the EU contributing 20mECU from the TACIS programme, the USA $25m. and Japan $17m.). New Partners have joined ISTC, among which is Kazakhstan. The other initiative (launched by the EU in 1993) is INTAS (the International Association for the Promotion of Cooperation with Scientists of the FSU). INTAS approved about 560 scientific projects in 1993, to be financed by Western Europe for a total of 25mECU. In 1994, INTAS invited interested scientists and research teams in Western Europe and the CIS to submit proposals for joint research or networking projects. Some 4700 proposals were received in response to this call and their evaluation is under way at the time of writing (June 1994). A budget of 21mECU is available.

Another important area for West-East cooperation is energy. Fifty countries altogether (including the EU, the CIS and the US) have signed the European Energy Charter and are busy finalizing the Charter's Treaty and Protocols. These will, in turn, establish the legal basis crucial for East-West cooperation on energy, covering issues such as investment protection, non-discrimination, transit and open trading conditions, environment needs, taxation, access to capital, technology transfer, intellectual property and the like. Thanks to this Charter, western companies should become more interested in energy investment in the East.

4. Summing Up

The commitment of the West to the integration of eastern Europe and the CIS into the mainstream of the world market and for helping the transition to democracy is considerable. So is the effort mounted by the Eastern partners to help themselves. The EU (including its Member States) takes a major share in this international effort. A key element of the EU programme is technical assistance, i.e. the transfer of know-how and technology. But transfer of technology should not be considered only as a one-way street. Technology is too important for the progress of human society and the world economy to be a monopolistic commodity. We in Western Europe believe we can learn from the well developed indigenous capabilities of the East as much as the East can learn from us. To take once more the example of central Asia, just one item of wealth available in the six republics - the knowledge of local biodiversity, in terms of flora, fauna and their cultivars - could constitute a fruitful objective for East-West exchanges of know-how.

5. Transfer of Technology

The mechanisms for international technology transfer may be divided into several categories such as:

- communication of information (conferences, seminars, technical reports, blueprints, educational programmes, movement of personnel, etc.);
- trade (merchandise goods as well as patents, licensing and royalty arrangements);
- cooperative research (e.g. standards development, participation in research networks, joint R&D operations);
- direct investment (including wholly-owned subsidiaries, transplant factories, mergers and acquisitions).

It is clear that the EU and its Member States, as well as our Eastern partners, can help transfer technology through ad-hoc cooperative instruments (such as GSP for trade, TACIS and Phare for technical assistance and TEMPUS for education). But the pivotal role in transferring technical knowledge and best practices is played by private operators through subcontracting and direct investment in production, sales and distribution. In turn, for western investment to be tempted eastward, the legal and regulatory provisions and mechanisms of the host country - in particular industrial property protection - must be clearly formulated and attractive to the investor. This is true for the large transitional corporation and even more for the small and medium enterprise (which often tends to be highly competent in technology, management and marketing, and very flexible in adapting its knowledge to local conditions).

It is precisely with an eye to the importance of industrial property rights that we, in Western Europe, have followed with interest the relevant legislation being set up by the CIS in recent years. Thus, for example, Kazakhstan has, between June 1992 and February 1993:

a) declared that the WIPO Convention as well as the Convention of Paris, the Madrid Arrangement and the PCT Treaty are applicable to Kazakhstan;

b) enforced a patent law and a law on trademarks; and,

c) set up a national Patent Office.

Encouraging signs are also multiplying in Kyrgyzstan, Tadjikistan and Uzbekistan. The author is convinced that this is an important prerequisite for an effective exchange of technologies between West and East.

13. FINNISH EXPERIENCES IN TECHNOLOGY TRANSFER

Technology Programs

JUHANI KUUSI
Director, Technology Development Centre TEKES
Helsinki, Finland

1. Introduction

Various types of technology programs within which enterprises - large and small - form a kind of alliances are widely regarded as important instruments in increasing competitiveness of the industry in the country via technology transfer and development.

In the final report of the OECD extensive Technology/Economy Program TEP [1] it is noted that "Today, successful policies for competitiveness will be those primarily aimed at supporting the aspects of intangible investment infrastructures and collective governance which are outside the purview of individual firms and at facilitating the formation of linkages, networks and interactive mechanisms."

In most industrialized countries a kind of technology program system was developed and launched during the eighties. So also in Finland. At the international level the European Community framework programs represent major efforts in this regard.

2. The Finnish Framework

Industrialization came to Finland later than to other European countries. As recently as 1960, the forest industry still accounted for 69 % of exports. By 1993, this proportion had fallen to 36 %, but the forest sector is still the most important source of foreign exchange income. The metal, electrical and electronics, and

G. Bugliarello et al. (eds.), East-West Technology Transfer, 165-173.

chemical industries have come to occupy increasingly significant positions in Finland's export trade. Growth of Finnish high technology exports was among the fastest in the OECD in the 1980s. In 1993, high technology accounted for approximately 15 % of exports.

Pulp, paper and engineering products are the traditional mainstays of Finnish industry. Finland is a world leader in the construction of paper machinery and in integrating process machinery and systems. These sophisticated areas have in turn stimulated the development of new high-tech industries. A wide range of telecommunication equipment including mobile telephones and environmental monitoring instruments are just some of the products manufactured by Finland's rapidly growing high-tech industries today. The chemical and the pharmaceutical industries are two other technologically advanced and increasingly international sectors.

3. Active Technology Policies From 1980s

To boost the competitiveness and structural change of the industry was a main focus of the Finnish science and technology policy at the beginning of the eighties.

Total research expenditure in Finland has increased substantially in recent years, in accordance with the science and technology policy plans. While in 1982 it accounted for 1.2 % of GNP, the figure for 1992 was already 2.2 %.

It is to be noted that the share of the private sector - industry - of the national R&D expenditures has been during most of the years over 60 %, which represents a very high level internationally.

The following goals govern Finnish technology and industrial policies:

- ensuring the competitiveness of important branches of basic industry such as wood-processing and metals and engineering
- creating new industries for developing sectors of technology
- generating reliable, economical energy and seeing that it is used efficiently.

There may seem to be a discrepancy between the first two goals, but often in Finland this is not the case. The only way we can secure the competitiveness of our basic industry is by introducing the latest achievements in developing technological sectors (micro electronics, new materials, biotechnology) rapidly and efficiently. This, in turn, is possible only if we have R&D and industrial activity of our own in these new areas of technology. Thus the Finnish goal is a fruitful marriage between high technology and basic industries.

4. Technology Programs: Bringing Researchers and Industry Together

Technology programs carried out jointly by research centers, universities and industry have a key role in brokering marriages between high technology and industries. Within horizontal programs proper technologies may be developed and transferred between various industrial sectors and between industry and research community. Programs shall be planned according to the needs and the stage of development of the partners. Thus, programmers for SMIs have often much lower technological ambitions than those of more advanced larger enterprises. Taking this properly into account is a demanding task for a marriage broker.

In the following the technology based programs for advanced larger enterprises and programs for SMIs and experiences gathered will be described.

4.1. HEAVILY TECHNOLOGY BASED PROGRAMS

Planning of the programs is carried out together with industry, research institutes and universities. Most research takes place in research institutes and universities. Representatives of industry often play an important role in supervisory groups leading the work. Industry also pays between 5 and 50 % of the costs of the program. Concerted involvement by industry in the programs seeks to ensure that they serve the needs of the country's industry, and that benefits from the results are fast and effective.

The Technology Development Centre TEKES is responsible for coordination of program planning and for the principal financing.

TEKES is an agency established in 1983 by the Finnish Ministry of Trade and Industry to coordinate and finance applied technical and industrial R&D. TEKES is financed by the Finnish Government and operates in close collaboration with universities, research institutes and all sectors of industry.

During its eleven years of operation TEKES has started over 30 technology based programs of which 10 were under way in 1994, according to Table 1.

More detailed information on the structure and the type of content of the programs can be seen from Figures 1 and 2 describing the Industrial Chemistry Technology Programme and the Pharmaceutical Technology Programme.

TABLE 1. Technology-based National Programs
1994

			Total budget, million FIM	ECU
Biodegradable polymers	(1992-96)	8 companies	100	16
Synthesis technology	(1992-96)	7 companies	70	11
Process technology	(1991-95)	22 companies	90	15
New generation paper technology	(1992-95)	13 companies	90	15
Mechanical wood processing	(1992-96)	16 companies	70	11
Wood based panels	(1992-96)	11 companies	45	7
Quality in construction industries	(1991-94)	100 companies	21	3
Building renovation	(1992-96)	11 companies	38	6
Rock engineering and construction 2000	(1991-95)	50 companies	23	4
Machine vision	(1992-96)	55 companies	100	16
Industrial applications of engineering materials	(1993-97)	40 companies	65	10
Total		333 companies involved	712	114

TEKES

The programs have yielded much valuable experience and many useful results. In addition to positive technological results, the interaction and concrete cooperation between industry, research institutes, and universities have increased. An evaluation carried out on all finished and partly on ongoing programs, partly by outside experts, strongly recommended continuation of basically the present approach.

International contacts have been intensively utilized in arranging the evaluation of the programs. Each program is evaluated at termination, some at mid-program or even after the planning phase.

As a whole, the technology program at the pre-competitive level has worked well in the implementation of the national technology policy. It has also served as a useful base for international technology cooperation and technology transfer. However, the technology program should be continually refined according to foreseeable needs. Presently more emphasis is focused on near-market aspects. The development of a firm technological base at pre-competitive

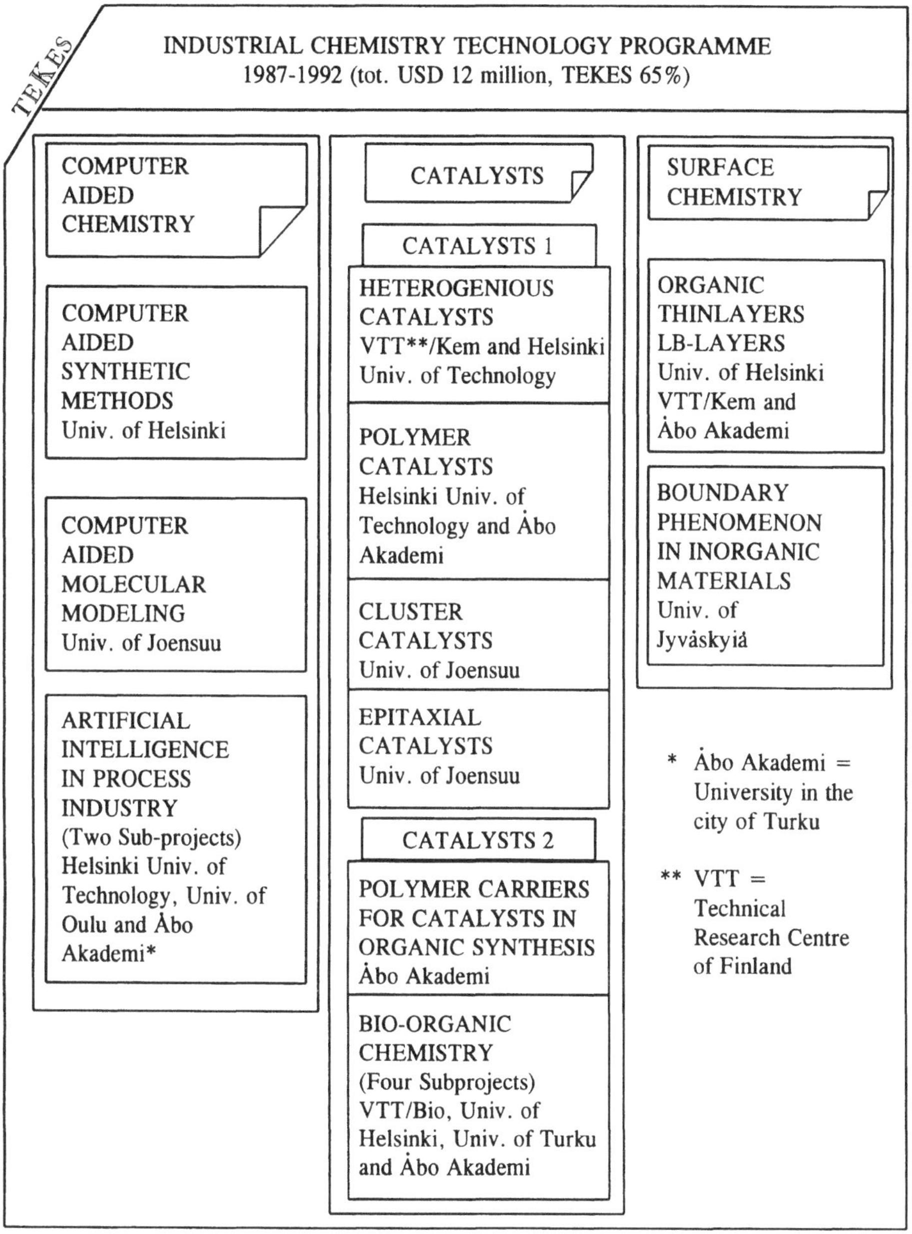

Figure 1. Industrial Chemistry Technology Program

levels to be utilized by innovative enterprises will, however, remain as a main goal of the program activities.

4.2. TECHNOLOGY PROGRAMS FOR SMEs

SMEs Technology Programs or applied technology implementation promoting programs have been launched for SMEs' needs [2]. In these, several smaller companies are clustered together and often have a larger company as a partner.

These smaller clearly targeted projects are focusing on transferring and applying existing technologies and on the utilization of networking. This kind of small company program activity has been built up during 1990-91. Until now

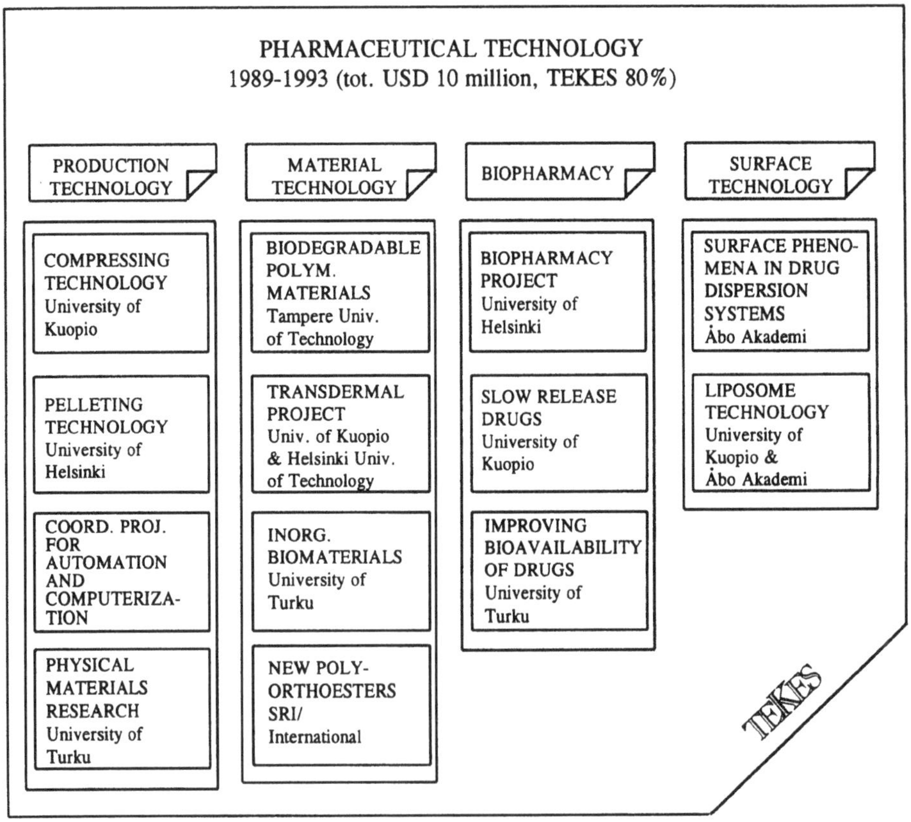

Figure 2. Pharmaceutical Technology

some 50 groupings have started their joint programs. In each of them there are some 9 to 90 companies. The total number of companies exceeds 200 and new groupings are created continuously. The financial volume of these SME programs is some 20 million USD (1991-1993), which is partly financed by TEKES.

An initiative to build up a new technology-based company group comes often directly from companies, but very often TEKES consultants and experts help companies as process consultants to build up a successful programme structure. Thus, at the early phase of a program the role of supporting personnel might be relatively strong, but only in early planning phase. When launching the actual joint development program, it is utmost important that companies themselves take the leading role in the process: in each specific participating company as well as in joint processes.

All programs are focused on a certain technology area; additionally most of the programs are geographically concentrated in some area of the country where companies are close to each other. On the other hand, the value adding partners are not always geographically very close to each other: this kind of grouping creates a better basis for wider national or international collaboration. Table 2 shows fifteen examples of SME programs.

TABLE 2. Examples of SME Programs

	Technology	City	Number of Companies
1	Software Entrepreneurs	Helsinki	20
2	CIM-Implementation	Kajaani	5
3	Production Logistics in Kitchen Furniture	Kuopio	5
4	Object Oriented Software	Lappeenranta	6
5	Precision Mechanics	Jyväskylä	6
6	Fiber Plastics Structures	Mikkeli	5
7	Product and Process Planning of Electronics	Oulu	10
8	Optoelectronics	Oulu	5
9	Surfacing Technology	Tampere	25
10	Digital Signal Processing	Tampere	10
11	Biomaterials in Tissue	Turku	8
12	Hydrostatical Forming	Helsinki	3
13	Automation - Case Studies	Pori	5
14	Simulation Network	Seinäjoki	5
15	Integrated Furniture Elements	Rovaniemi	8

All these 15 examples - out of some 50 ongoing programs - are company driven collaborative programs, which have been promoted and supported by TEKES. The participating enterprises are mainly smaller companies and in some cases they have collaboration with larger companies. In other cases the larger company is the connecting link, by offering technological problems or applications.

A company group can be built on a horizontal basis, where companies are interested in similar technological potentials and, even if they sometimes are competitors, they can utilize some common areas. More often, the joint project can be created on a vertical basis, where participating companies build commercial chains complementing each other in business. Transferring, developing and implementing technologies in the latter type of collaboration is especially fruitful in the utilization of results of joint efforts.

In every type of precompetitive or competitive collaborative work it is most important that companies plan and agree to the framework and rules in their collaboration and utilization of the results. TEKES offers help by advising and providing participants with checklists and model agreements.

Up to now the experiences gathered from the programs have been positive. The ongoing evaluation of the results attained will give more quantitative data for further development of this mechanism.

5. Conclusions

The various types of technology programs have proven to be useful instruments in transferring technology between research institutes and industry and also between industrial partners.

Essential for success is that programs be carefully planned to meet the needs and capabilities of the partners. It is also important that the interaction of the deeply committed partners be intensive and continuous, so that information about the results flows continuously between them.

References

1. Heurlin, M. (1993) *Developing and Acquiring Technology - Experiences in Assisting SMEs, Six Countries Programme on Innovation,* Dublin.

2. OECD (1992), *Technology/Economy Programme TEP*, *Final Report*, OECD, Paris.

14. TECHNOLOGY TRANSFER: A VIEW FROM A MARKET ECONOMY

W. A. de JONG
Ruygenhoek Advies B.V.
The Hague, The Netherlands

1. Introduction

No member country of the OECD other than The Netherlands combines a relatively large export with extensive foreign industrial investments. Therefore, the Dutch science and technology policy of the past 25 years has had the objective of stimulating industry to generate new business at home and abroad, and at ensuring that the country remains an attractive place for foreign investment. In line with the above, much room was and is being given to the private sector to develop, apply and transfer technology, both into and out of the Netherlands. The government confines itself to the provision of high quality education at all levels, a strong science and technology infrastructure of universities, research organizations, institutes and regional Innovation Centres to assist companies in attracting technology from abroad and from national sources. In addition, various programs for supporting R&D are being executed and financial support is being given for the development phase of new products and processes and for the improvement of various aspects of management, mainly for small and medium-sized enterprises (SMEs). Tax incentives were recently added to stimulate in-house R&D.

In short, a technology policy in the form of a set of generic instruments was created. Direct support to individual companies has declined considerably, in contrast to some other EU countries. In addition, privatization of previously government-owned companies is progressing satisfactorily.

In this context, a public structure for supervising the promotion and the monitoring of technology transfer was not set up, the more so because of the small size of the country and the ease of communication within the Netherlands.

G. Bugliarello et al. (eds.), East-West Technology Transfer, 175-189.

Many companies are perfectly able to manage their technology assets and some of them are using the relatively independent contract research institutes (CROs) as means for technology generation and transfer. Dutch universities are free to offer their services to national as well as foreign clients. Nevertheless, improvement of the technology transfer from CROs and universities to the private sector has been and is still being sought. The only restrictions imposed on the transfer of technology are those based on international agreements, e.g. EU regulations, UN-supported boycotts and rules concerning sensitive knowledge and know-how in the defense field.

Therefore, the main problems to be taken care of are the generation or adaptation of technology suitable for use in the private sector and the (finding of partners for) transfer of this technology. The CROs are primarily responsible for developing a strategy to make available the right kind of expertise, marketing actions aimed at obtaining a clear picture of the demand for technology and informing potential clients of the technology portfolio offered by them. Another important mechanism that is useful in this context is the formation of Innovation centres sponsored by the Ministry of Economic Affairs.

In view of the above, this paper will be restricted to a description of the role of the scientific infrastructure in transferring technology. Some information will also be given on the Innovation Centres which assist industry and business in adapting new or existing technology to their needs, both foreign and national, and absorbing this technology into their business. Other mechanisms will not be considered, such as (strategic) alliances between companies for the development of new science and technology, the provision of suitable technology to co-makers by manufacturers of complex products, etc.

2. Interaction Between Industry and the Scientific Infrastructure

2.1 APPROACH

Any discussion about the transfer of technology from the scientific infrastructure should start from the needs of the recipients of the technology , in this case industry and business. For contract research, companies enter into a client/supplier relationship with research performers, usually contract research organizations (CROs), i.e., institutes, technical centres, conglomerates of institutes or companies active in generating, transforming, adapting and transferring technologies or, more generally, scientific and technological information. The clients specify their wishes, pay in full and obtain the industrial property rights.

Most of the work done by universities for the benefit of industry can be classified as "contract research," in which a company providing research grants is given the right to inspect and take out patents or study the results or use them internally for follow-up developments. The university retains the right to publish in the open literature after a suitable waiting period, e.g. 1-2 years. An added advantage for industry is that in this way young science and engineering graduates acquire experience in fields of science of interest to companies. This is in line with the main task of universities, *viz.* education and performing longer-time basic or strategic research. However, the universities should remain independent as far as research programming is concerned.

General rules for setting up interactions between various types of clients and the scientific infrastructure cannot be given since the motives of clients for taking part in the generation or transfer of technology may differ appreciably. For the purpose of this discussion, the following archetypes of clients are distinguished:

1. *Large companies* with substantial in-house R&D facilities (LCs)
2. *Pathfinder companies*, small and medium-sized companies (SMEs) in an advanced technology area
3. *Active follower SMEs* following technological developments closely but usually not initiating them
4. *Late follower SMEs* following developments at a distance

2.2. TYPES OF CLIENT

2.2.1. *Large Companies*

Large companies often have extensive in-house R&D capacity which contributes substantially to the management of their technology assets by generating new technology in the company's core business area where confidentiality is most needed. Part of the research may be farmed out to CROs, organizations skilled in working in the well-defined type of project structure applied in industry. CROs also supply expertise located outside the core business area of clients, which is often preferred to the setting up of a new in-company expertise, for cost reasons and because relying in part on external know-how may speed up the development of new processes or products. The preferred role of universities often is to supply part of the background knowledge.

Absorption of new technology developed wholly or partly by others usually does not present problems when sufficient know-how is available in the donor CRO supporting the company, although the "not invented here" syndrome may complicate matters. The tendency to farm out part of the work on a client/supplier basis increases as the need for multi-disciplinary work is greater and the time to market must be shorter.

2.2.2. *Pathfinder SMEs*

This type of company usually operates in a limited technology area and possesses advanced and specialized know-how in this area alone, often in the form of results obtained in their own R&D function. Since they depend critically on this narrow area for growth and survival , their need for secrecy is usually very high; moreover, these SMEs often require outside expertise in adjacent areas. They are ideal partners for CROs, the more so because their time horizon can be rather far away, but it is essential that the fear of leakage of information be overcome. Weak points may be market information and orientation, but safeguarding industrial property rights is well understood and practiced. Pathfinders may also join forces with university groups provided that these can operate in a project team and are leakproof. Like LCs, pathfinder SMEs insist on being the leading partner in a project team.

2.2.3. *Active Follower SMEs*

Active followers usually combine a time horizon for the medium term (from 2 to 4 years) with a limited R&D capacity. Therefore, they need external help from partners of high R&D calibre in formulating a research or development program, preferably a CRO and sometimes a university. This type of SME is less likely to initiate generic research projects in a very advanced field; collaborative research[1] with one or more other SMEs and a CRO is more suitable. Work for active follower SMEs is usually rather close to the market. Adequate support is needed in securing industrial property rights.

2.2.4. *Late Follower SMEs*

The SMEs of this group have a short time horizon, are less R&D conscious and usually have a negligible R&D capacity of their own. They can benefit substan-

[1]*Collaborative research* is work carried out by 2 or more SMEs by their in house R&D capacity, which may or may not be done together with CROs. The results are combined and used jointly by the participating SMEs. This type of research can be quite close to the market.

tially from collective[2] or cooperative research[3] initiated by industrial branch organizations or CROs and defined in close contact with a group of SMEs interested in the subject. On a national scale, such projects have proved to promote innovation in various industrial sectors by introducing new or existing generic technologies. For many late follower SMEs this is the first direct contact with technological research and some of them are encouraged to proceed to other types of R&D if the results are satisfactory. CROs use collective research programs to attract new clients.

2.3. THE TECHNOLOGY MARKET

Taken together, the Dutch CROs cover a very broad market containing clients of all four types discussed previously. The Dutch technology-oriented institutes (GTIs) serve well-defined markets of sufficient size to warrant a separate institute, as is shown in the Table on the next page. Most of the available capacity is located in TNO, the Netherlands Organization for Applied Research, a single larger corporate entity consisting of 16 institutes under a joint top management structure. Unlike the GTIs, TNO institutes interact very closely, which is an advantage because the extensive body of expertise can thus be made available to every client, obviating the need to disperse auxiliary departments or service units over the organization, thus avoiding the setting up of sub-critical units. Combinations of several TNO institutes are particularly advantageous in work on large projects in which multi-disciplinary R&D is needed. Another virtue of this structure is that smaller segments for which a separate institute is not feasible economically can thus be supplied with the full range of the available expertise.

Apart from contract work for companies in The Netherlands, much work is done for government departments and agencies. A good example is provided by the Delft Hydraulics Institute with a home market containing an appreciable fraction of work for government departments such as Public Works and the Agency responsible for design, construction and maintenance of the physical infrastructure canals, rivers, harbors and the costal defenses against the sea. In addition, much work is done for companies active in this field.

[2]*Collective research* is defined as research performed by a Collective, i.e., a structure which is formed and funded by SMEs in the same branch of industry with the similar activities. This type of work reinforces the technological base of the SMEs of the Collective and usually does not yield marketable products.

[3]*Co-operative research* is research in which 2 or more SMEs form a fund from which contract research on problems which they have in common is paid; the work is often performed by CROs under contract. The distance from the market is less than for work on the technological base but greater than for collaborative R&D.

Table 1. Size and Expertise of CROs in The Netherlands

Institute	Staff 1992	Budget 1992 MUSS	Available expertise or markets covered
Delft Geotechnical Institute	289	19	Soil mechanics. Geotechnical Engineering Environmental Engineering, Environmental Geochemistry. Market includes some aspects of Offshore Engineering
Delft Hydraulics Institute		no recent data	Estuaries and seas, water resources and the environment, hydro-surveys, industrial hydrodynamics and dredging technology, harbors, coasts and offshore technology, rivers and navigation
Energy Research Centre	953	82	Nuclear energy, fossil fuels, non-conventional and renewable energy sources, environmental research connected to energy conversion, energy policy studies
Marine Research Centre	225	18.5	Hydrodynamic research in connection with ship design and offshore constructions, software engineering, instrumentation for marine use, e.g., determination of position, training simulators
National Aeronautics and Space Laboratory	817	66	Aeronautics and Space research
Netherlands Organization for Applied Scientific Research TNO	4900	387	Main areas: Building and Construction (8%), Industrial Technology (27.5%), Nutrition and Food (11.5%), Environment and Energy (14.5%), and Policy Research (3.5%) (percentages in % of the available research capacity)

Moreover, the institutes listed in the Table also operate extensively in international markets. An example is the maritime institute MARIN which derived about 85% of its total 1992 revenue from international contracts, about half of which came from foreign sources. For the industrial sector of TNO the corresponding figures are: 70-75% of the total 1992 budget was earned from contracts, about 25% of the contract coming from foreign clients.

3. Management Changes

3.1. CHANGES IN MARKET ORIENTATION

To increase the market orientation of a CRO to the level indicated above, the first priority should be to introduce new ways of managing the "Program and Marketing" (P/M) function at all levels in the organization. In the case of TNO the formation of an effective and efficient P/M department took a period of turnaround management of more than ten years. The end result, an increase of the percentage of the total budget earned from contracts to more than twice the 1980 level, justifies the large efforts invested. Since 1980, when this change began, the funding from government sources for financing strategic R&D declined correspondingly and both these trends are continuing to this very day. Some of the methods employed are outlined below.

3.2. THE PROGRAM/MARKET FUNCTION

3.2.1. *Strategy Development - Science and Technology Policy*
One of the main objectives of the science and technology policy of the Dutch government is to allocate the inevitably scarce resources to fields which will most likely be or continue to be of major importance to the economy, while enriching and reinforcing the country's identity in a cultural and social sense.

During the past few years satisfactory progress is being made with the development of an overall strategy in various fields covering contributions from all sciences - natural sciences, technology, humanities and social sciences. A pronounced bottom/up component has been introduced into the process of strategy development by employing teams consisting of scientists and engineers as well as users.

The main aims of the technology strategy are:

- to emphasize fields of major present or future importance for the national economy
- to improve the market orientation of the science and technology infrastructure
- to create the organizational environment needed to implement the strategy
- to improve transfer mechanisms to industry and business and create new ones.

The organization of the S&T infrastructure is characterized by the "hands off" policy followed by the government, leading to a large degree of independence of universities, institutes and particularly CROs. The development of national strategies in various fields does not imply that the government prescribes which of the institute(s) should implement the strategy. This is understandable in the light of the strong market orientation: in the end, the demand for new technology is the deciding factor. The institutions are encouraged to use the results of the strategic teams in developing their own strategy. The government is advised on more general aspects of S&T policy by a standing committee, the Advisory Council for Science and Technology Policy reporting to two ministers (Science and Education and Economic Affairs) who introduce the reports in a subcommittee of Cabinet ministers.

Strategy development by CROs. When the above national strategy efforts were initiated, the Dutch CROs had been active in formulating strategies of their own for about 10 years. This was done to build up a technology portfolio, i.e., capabilities in fields in which demand was likely to occur and for which high quality expertise should be acquired to satisfy the demand. This requires a certain amount of strategic research, which is not intended to produce "finished" products, processes, software, etc. but to accumulate the necessary experience and know-how in the technology fields for which markets can be found. The reason for this is that qualitatively good results of development work done in CROs may not be fully in line with the needs of clients, with the consequence that the data are difficult to sell for a price that recovers the invested funds and also leaves a small profit. The ground rules in contract research are that *clients* should specify their wishes and that the R&D work should be programmed jointly with them and subsequently approved by them. In other words: market pull should be as strong as possible and technology push no higher than is needed to introduce new technology elements.

Development of a strategy is therefore a must, taking changes in demand as well as technological developments into account. The process begins near the shop floor and is carried out by sections or departments of sufficient size having detailed knowledge of their market. Existing relations with clients and in the scientific environment of the unit should be the sources of the information needed to analyze their strengths and weaknesses and to trace opportunities and challenges.

The results are integrated into a strategy for the entire organization in a process controlled by top management in which priorities and posteriorities are set so as to put the resources available to the institute or organization to the best possible use. The resulting strategy acts as a policy guide for the next 5-10 years and is used as the basis for more concrete planning for the medium term (2-4 years) and for short term operational plans needed to draw up the next budget. On the basis of the strategy the exploratory and strategic research can be programmed and decisions regarding the acquisition (make or buy) taken. TNO is required by law to develop a strategy every four years; the resulting strategy document must be discussed with the government , the supplier of the funds for the strategic R&D. Formal approval by the government is not required but the result is transferred to Parliament together with the comments of the Cabinet. The rationale behind this procedure is that the consequences of a deficient strategy will have to be borne by the organization; additional funding to solve problems stemming from inadequate strategic decisions will not be forthcoming. This procedure is one of the consequences of placing the Dutch CROs at arms length from the government and making them responsible for the continuity of technical generation and transfer in their mission area. Similarly, the Board of Management of the TNO organization is responsible for reaching the strategic and operational objectives of the organization. This policy has contributed to the increase in market orientation of the Dutch CROs.

3.2.2. *Marketing*

Among the actions to be taken for marketing and selling technology successfully are the following:

- Teach researchers to deal with every type of client (*cf.* 2.2., above). This is particularly necessary for work for active and late follower SMEs, with whom one should talk in *their* language, not in difficult sciencespeak. Good courses to educate CRO scientists and engineers on this topic were unavailable until the early 1980s, causing TNO to develop the marketing and other research management courses in-house.

Several years later these courses were made available to a wider public by transferring them to a management consulting firm. However, not every researcher should be turned loose on clients because many excellent scientists and engineers cannot sell technology and will never learn to do so, mainly because they do not have any commercial talent, are overly convinced of the quality of their own expertise and have difficulties in listening carefully to clients, which is a prime requirement.

- Make effective marketing and selling of R&D and consulting for clients valued items of performance evaluation of employees and consider this as an important ingredient in determining salary levels.
- Adopt marketing practices such as periodic but not overly frequent discussions with clients to assess their needs and do not try to talk clients into accepting projects; rather, try to find out what their real needs are. Every marketeer should offer the expertise of the entire institute or organization, not just that of his own department.
- Make sure that a prospective client who wishes to determine whether the institute contains the expertise he needs knows how to find it. This is particularly necessary for a large and multifunctional TNO organization. TNO has established a central staff unit capable of guiding clients to the right researcher with the aid of a (confidential) database of the available expertise. It acts quickly, trying to reply within the hour, if possible, and in more difficult cases within 24 hours.
- Help clients who need help in defining their problem. Many SMEs are unable to state them sufficiently clearly as a basis for action. If necessary, assist clients in finding funds from external sources.
- Making use of available mechanisms for collective, collaborative or cooperative research for groups of SMEs and assist the leaders among the group to draw up project proposals in a way which is understandable to their colleagues. Promote follow-up contracts with individual members of these groups, to help a company to adapt the results of previous group projects to its specific needs. CROs consider this type of project as a good source of individual contracts with new clients.
- Enlist the help of others serving the same clients, such as banks, accountancy firms, organization experts and technology brokers by arranging joint presentations.
- Above all: make sure that the work offered is of high quality but avoid "quality give-away" by proper pricing. Good technology costs money.

3.3. OTHER IMPORTANT MANAGEMENT FUNCTIONS

3.3.1. *Administrative organization*

It is quite impossible to process thousands of projects varying in size from a few hundred dollars to more than 10 million, often involving several institutes, without recourse to extensive administrative systems. These include the usual project management and financial systems from which the performance per project can be read shortly after a week has ended and the performance of the entire institute can be assessed regularly. In the case of marketing, a database containing all projects and clients is a must, not only to know the amount of work in stock for every budgetary unit but also to analyze changes and shifts in market demand. Similarly, it is advantageous to know which projects have been worked on by a certain researcher or small research unit over a period of *e.g.* 5 years to provide a continuous survey of the available expertise. More generally, personnel information systems are indispensable. The systems should enable top management to establish the position of the organization at any moment to permit rapid policy changes if the need arises.

3.3.2. *The Personnel Function*

A good personnel policy determines to a large extent the vitality of a CRO for the longer term. First of all, sufficient flexibility is needed to ensure that the correct mix of expertise and ages is available. A way in which this can be achieved is by creating a flow system consisting of:

- *Flow-in,* i.e. the hiring of more young graduates and technicians than will be needed in the long run. Evaluate their performance regularly and decide after 5-7 years which of the good performers should be retained and assist the others in finding new jobs in industry, the service sector, government and education. This also serves to build up a network of prospective clients.
- *Flow-out:* not only help good but redundant people to find employment elsewhere but also remove less satisfactory performers. If this is not done demotivation of good researchers and engineers may be an unwanted result.
- *Flow through:* frequently move people, particularly of the middle and higher management levels, to other research units and from staff line and back. This is essential for preparing potential future managers for higher responsibilities and also creates more understanding between line and staff departments.

Another major component of personnel policy is to introduce an institute-or organization-wide system of training. This applies mostly to subjects such as project management and promotion of creativity, leadership issues, marketing methods, personnel management and senior management. Since every researcher is expected to keep himself informed about developments in his own field of science, scientific courses are usually limited to people who are given the task of developing a new field of expertise.

3.3.3. *Internal Communication*
A complex CRO can only function in the market-oriented way described above if the internal communication is very open and effective. Horizontal interaction between employees in different institutes and vertical communications between the different management levels are equally important, since this is a prerequisite for mobilizing multidisciplinary groups for large projects of contract or strategic research. This capability is one of the principal reasons for the existence of large CROs covering a very broad science and technology market. A good internal communication system is also essential to provide the institution with an identity, which is one of the ingredients of improving an organization's image in the market.

4. Other Channels for Technology Transfer

4.1. UNIVERSITIES

One of the strengths of universities is that they can put basic knowledge at the disposal of industry for the benefit of companies with a competent R&D department. This applies particularly to the three Universities of Technology in The Netherlands which have maintained long-standing and close relations with their industrial environment. During the past 5-10 years interactions between academia and industry have increased, mainly because the universities wish to add new funds to their declining budgets provided by the government. However, with the exception of the Universities of Technology, the disciplinary organization of faculties does not constitute the best basis for applied industrial research - let alone development - for which multidisciplinary teams are often needed. Moreover, many universities lack the capability of working to the tight schedules required for industrial R&D and are having trouble in meeting deadlines. This is offset to a certain extent by the fact that universities may posses fundamental knowledge needed to arrive at new breakthroughs.

One of the means to provide the best of two worlds is to set up joint ventures - research groups or new institutes - in promising fields requiring the simultaneous development and transfer of science and technology in promising new market areas.

Such joint ventures exist in several European countries; in The Netherlands the management of the contract research part is usually done by TNO and the exploratory or strategic research is contributed mostly by the university. Combinations of this kind are only feasible if industry is sufficiently interested. A joint venture may also be profitable for technologies in rapid development where build-up of new capacity is needed before contracts can be acquired. A detailed risk analysis should be carried out before decisions are taken. However, the difficulties of merging the two cultures - academic and business-like - should not be underestimated.

4.2. INNOVATION CENTERS

Although much of the technology applied in industry is acquired by in-house R&D, licensing, take-overs of other firms, strategic industrial alliances and joint work with CROs and/or universities, there is also a need for other mechanisms of technology transfer. Companies, particularly SMEs, may need help to locate and evaluate technology which they plan to absorb.

For this reason the Dutch government replaced the Industrial Service Agency of the ministry of Economic Affairs located centrally in The Hague by 18 Innovation Centres in various regions of the country. Each centre is independent of the civil service, governed by a board consisting of industrialists and financed by the government. It employs an average of 7-8 consultants who advise companies on technological problems and matters of industrial management in general. The main advantage of the regional location is that the centres are situated close to the companies they serve. The independence of the centres has proved to be a major asset: it reinforces the feeling that industry has the lead in the consulting activities and that there is a minimum of red tape and government interference.

A central unit in The Hague distributes experience and information among the regional Centres and takes care of personnel and financial administration. It is not a head office able to dictate local policies. A second central unit is providing assistance regarding industrial property rights and assists in patenting.

The average number of contacts per Centre was around 1000 in 1993 and the total number for the entire system between 15000 and 17000. A recent evaluation shows the present system to work reasonably well; it is much preferred over its predecessor. However, constant attention is invariably necessary with market-oriented structures to ensure that performance remains up to standard.

5. Discussion

It should be emphasized here that every structure for technology transfer should fit well in its environment. The conditions applying to The Netherlands may not necessarily apply elsewhere. A few examples are given below.

One of the main points to be taken into account is the nature, geographical location, state of development and quality of R&D capabilities in companies. The way in which industry operates and is organized is about as important for good results as the structure of the scientific infrastructure since the factors determine to a large extent the size and structure of the S&T market.

Another significant factor is the relative status of scientists working in CROs and universities and those working in industry. In a number of countries the percentage of professors and scientists of CROs or Academies of Science is regarded as high as compared with industry employees. It is of crucial importance to attract high quality scientists and engineers into industry since otherwise the communication between clients and researchers becomes quite difficult. In The Netherlands the formation of small R&D nuclei in SMEs has been one of the technology policy objectives for many years. In those cases where highly qualified engineers were put at the disposal of small companies worthwhile results have been obtained. However, progress in this field has been rather slow.

Moreover, there is usually much room for improvement of the management structure of some SMEs. While entrepreneurs may be very successful in the early years of a company active in a profitable market niche, problems may arise when new markets have to be entered where the main demand is for more sophisticated products than the company produces. In such cases, partly government-funded management training facilities may be helpful. Other attractive means for assistance are support in developing new products and adapting the management structure to accommodate the new products, inclusive of the processes needed for their manufacture. CROs may satisfy the demand for this activity.

6. Conclusion

The description of the Dutch way of generating new technology and transferring it from the scientific infrastructure to users shows that market orientation combined with scientific and technological excellence are the main factors determining the success of the science and technology policy. Other management functions should be set up in such a way that the transfer process is reinforced.

Every management system will require constant updating, periodic updating of the strategy and timely and adequate changes in structure and way of operation of the technological institutions if the need arises. Management of the science and technology infrastructure should be a perfect example of the management of change.

15. SWEDISH PERSONNEL AND LEADERSHIP EXPERIENCES IN TECHNOLOGY TRANSFER

HANS G. FORSBERG
President, Royal Swedish Academy of Engineering Sciences
Sweden

1. Introduction

Before I start to deal with the Swedish experience in this particular field, I would very much like to place us in the right historical and economic perspective.

As I see it, the entire history of modern man is about three successive phases of development and dissemination of technology. The first one appeared around 12,000 years ago in this part of the world with the use of metals to construct tools. Those tools increased drastically the productivity in agriculture, enabled our forefathers to build roads and cities and made it possible for a part of the population of a tribe to devote their life to anything other than producing the material needs for themselves and their families and develop - what we with one modern word would call "culture."

But the spreading of knowledge was slow - it took years copying it from one village to another and many centuries for the first appearance of bronze created by a metallurgical mistake in the Far East to reach the "Golden crescent."

The second phase - the so-called "industrial revolution" - started 200 years ago in western Europe. But it took decades before the steam engine would be accepted as a real useful tool in mining and manufacturing to replace human beings and animals.

The third one, the electronic revolution, appeared during and after the second world war, mainly in America. Within weeks or months knowledge achieved could be made available to everyone who was permitted access to it - alas, a lot of it were military secrets. But the development in information technology in the last decade and the political changes over the last 5 years have made it feasible to transfer knowledge and technology within seconds all over the globe.

G. Bugliarello et al. (eds.), East-West Technology Transfer, 191-200.

Let me now go over to Sweden. The political reason why I am participating in this workshop is probably due to the fact that Sweden for special reasons stayed neutral in both world wars of this century and also, after the second world war, decided to stay outside political and military alliances.

When the Middle East and European cultures were born and even during the classical period 2,000 years ago, Sweden did not exist. What is now agricultural and urban land was covered by water. The land was depressed after the glaciation which withdrew only 12,000 years ago. The land still rises out of the water at the rate of up to 1 meter per century. Hence, we have no domestic concern with the possible consequences of the greenhouse effect raising the level of the oceans.

As a united kingdom Sweden appears in the history book less than one thousand years ago. But already before then there was trade between our ancestors. Artifacts from the Middle East culture are found in tombs from the bronze and early iron ages and Greek and Roman records tell of trade of fur, tar, iron ore, copper and silver, not to mention solders and slaves.

In the year 1288 for the first time there is mention of a company, STORA, as operator of a coppermine. That company has existed continuously for more than 700 years and ranks number 200 among the corporations of the world. But the mine had already been operated for many centuries before that.

With imported know-how we started mining of other minerals like silver and iron ores. Tar, timber and charcoal were bartered for more precious manufactured goods and we provided a lot of soldiers for the European wars in progress in the 17th and 18th centuries.

Sweden remained, however, a poor country for a long time. In 1799 the Scottish economist Thomas Robert Malthus, author of *An Essay on the Principle of Population*, described Sweden as "the most barren and worst supplied country in Europe." During the 19th century a third of Sweden's population were forced to leave our country for America to avoid starvation.

The so-called industrial revolution which conquered Europe in the 19th century was late in reaching Sweden. Really fast development started as late as the turn of the last century. Ores, steel and cellulose products still play an important role in our production and export. Swedish industry today is, however, highly diversified.

2. Swedish Industry Today

The expansion of industry made possible an economic and social development which in the 1960s gave Sweden the leading position in international standard-of-living indices. We have in recent years lost that position but we still rank among the top ten.

Historical trends have created a somewhat unusual industrial structure in Sweden. Let me mention that among the 500 biggest industrial companies in the world today, 16 are Swedish. For a country of 8 million people, this is a high figure. Only the United States, Japan, France, Great Britain and Germany have a higher number! And many of those Swedish companies trace their origin to the end of the last century. I will just read you some of the names: ASEA (now the 'A' in ABB), AGA, Alfa Laval, Atlas Copco, Ericsson, Nobel, Saab-Scania, SKF, Trelleborg. Some are younger, for example Astra and Pharmacia, the two pharmaceutical houses of Sweden, Tetra Pak, founded in the 1940s, which has now merged with Alfa Laval to form Tetra Laval, and Gambro, to mention just a few.

How was this possible? Seventy-five years ago half the population of Sweden were farmers. How could Swedish society be transformed from a rural community to a highly industrialized one?

After all, many of the obstacles which prevented Sweden from profiting earlier from the industrial revolution still exist, don't they?

First of all, one obvious reason is the fact that Sweden has not been involved in a war since the early 1800s.

Another reason was that already at the turn of last century, everyone in Sweden could read and write. There was a sound pre-industrial tradition of mining and craftsmanship. But there also existed a tradition in science and engineering. Engineering education in some form or other had started as early as in the 18th century, and the first technical university was created in 1877. And the Swedish market was not very attractive to foreign entrepreneurs as there were only a few of us, scattered over a large area and we had a peculiar language. On the other hand, Swedish engineers travelled widely in Europe and picked up information freely.

It should also be mentioned that we did fill some gaps. The successful industrial revolution seems to have taken a short pause by then, as many people were satisfied with the course of events. In fact, the head of the American patent organization suggested in 1899 that his office be closed down because everything that was worth patenting was already known.

Another reason might actually lie with those characteristics which at first sight might seem to be a disadvantage. For example, the fact that the Swedish market is so small has forced our industry to look abroad to expand their markets very early on. Once in a foreign market these companies have had to challenge international competition.

3. Some Problems

However, I cannot deny that Sweden has serious problems right now.

Swedish big companies tend to become transnational and expand faster outside Sweden, where they are close to the markets, than within Sweden. The mergers of ASEA Brown Boveri and the recent one of AKZO and Nobel are obvious examples. The failed merger of Volvo and Renault was not due to national considerations, but to shareholders' opinions that the deal was too meagre.

The international business slump has also hit Sweden extremely hard in the last two years. We were used to an unemployment rate of between 1 and 2 percent. Now we are living with rates of between 7 and 12 percent, depending on how we define unemployment. The comeback will be slow and arduous. Our industrial leaders and politicians have a heavy responsibility to take decisions which might not be popular in the short run, but which are necessary in the long term.

The technical level of the leading Swedish companies is second to none, but they are truly transnational and do not any longer see Sweden as a privileged area for sharing of technology. They are participating in such schemes in many other countries where it may be part of a government policy to have foreign companies engaged in such activities as a price for establishing themselves. This is not the case domestically.

Our situation has certainly several similarities to what has been described earlier in this conference. A part of the economy is very healthy - the small and intermediate companies are, however, struggling with survival and development and the country has a considerable unemployment which can be fought only through the expansion of small and intermediate companies - either as subcontractors to the transnational ones or with their own product based upon their own research or licensing.

4. Applying Technology Transfer: The Swedish Model Compared to Other Countries

My learned friends sometimes point out to me that the meaning of technology transfer is frequently misused. They point out that knowledge has great value, because it carries power. Knowledge about technology is especially valuable. The benefit of technology has long been appreciated by society, and we have developed mechanism both to protect its owners and to ensure that its benefits are widely available. This contradiction should be theoretically sold by using two different terms: *technology transfer* and *technology diffusion*.

Technology transfer is the controlled release of information to a selection of privileged people or organizations, whereas diffusion implies a general, almost random, release to society at large. Until recently transfer was largely an industrial activity, based on knowledge acquired through private funds, with control encouraged and made effective by legislation on patents, trade marks, and copyrights. The knowledge was owned by those who had paid for its evolution.

Diffusion, in contrast, was mainly an academic endeavor, accomplished via publication and conferences. The diffused knowledge was obtained through public funds, and dissemination was intended for the public benefit. The practice was encouraged, and promotion was reserved for those who carried it out assiduously. No question of ownership arose.

The conventions of transfer and diffusion have not developed by accident. One would question the management of a company that opened its doors and reports to competitors. Less obvious, but no less crucial, is the need for wide communication of scientific achievements, for confirmation by peers, and to facilitate further advances. Technology transfer implies restrictive access, foreign to our traditional view of a university. Large companies place a high value on exclusivity, an obstacle to diffusion.

Technology diffusion is not always effective. The obstacle cannot be a lack of R&D results. It is more likely that those who would benefit from the results are not aware of them, or do not appreciate their significance.

The companies in greatest need lack personnel with the scientific training necessary to interpret and exploit the information, a situation which will grow worse in the years to come - and mobility among research workers is low. Academics may not feel the necessity to describe their work in terms that are readily understood by non-specialists. Language difficulties make the problem even greater.

The problem is not equally pronounced in all parts of the world dealing with high technology. In the U.S. there is traditionally a very close relationship between universities and industry, and their high degree of mobility eases information dissemination. In Japan unofficial talks take place, because here internal competition is not about technology but about products. Japan has no long history of encouraging university research relevant to industrial products. Instead they seek knowledge from overseas universities, and their contacts grow steadily.

A question which has been asked many times is what has been the effect of very large governmental programs in areas such as defense or space research. In the late 60s there was a very heated discussion in Europe about "le défi Américain," the American challenge, and the gap of technology which was supposed to exist between the United States and the rest of the OECD countries. It was the very high figure for research and development in certain high technology areas paid for by the United States government which created a fear of a drawback.

Eventually, after many international conferences, consensus was reached that high research costs - particularly when financed by taxpayers - do not necessarily spell success, neither for the company, nor for the country. Instead it is the competence of the system in which the research is performed and the money spent, that will decide the results. It is now clear to all economists that it is the efficiency of the market economy as such, which judges if input in research and development makes for success. High governmental spending may be necessary to reach political goals: to create an efficient defense system, to put man on the moon, to build up a certain infrastructure, but further use of the development to achieve success and economic development can only be secured if that money spent in companies, which also have access to a modern market where competitive forces meet.

Certainly some American companies benefited enormously from governmental spending. The light water reactors developed for submarines became the main tool for development of the civilian nuclear power systems. IBM benefited from the evolution of enormous computational devices developed to provide information how to bring a spaceship safely back to earth.

This also created the very heated discussion about potential "spin-offs" from the governmental spending. Various programs were launched, for instance in the United States, but with limited success. Once again, it was found that the most efficient method is where the same company could use the knowledge achieved to develop and market products for other uses. But it had almost as a rule to create special entities or subsidiaries. The military and civilian marketing methods are completely different.

There is no public or governmental policy in Sweden with regard either to technology transfer or to technology diffusion. It just takes place. It should also be pointed out, that almost two thirds of all research and development efforts in Sweden take place within private companies, paid by company's own income. Government's most important role is to provide society with well educated people, scientists, engineers, etc. There are very few governmental research institutes, so governmentally sponsored research takes place either at university or in around 20 research establishments, where a number of companies and the government have agreements to support jointly pre-competitive research either oriented to one particular industry, such as metallurgy or pulp and paper, or technology wise, such as corrosion research or surface research.

In Sweden governmental support to defense research is small in comparison with other countries. However, it is fairly obvious that SAAB would never had been able to develop and market internationally commuter aircrafts, if it had not had 40 years of experience of governmental paid military aircraft development. Ericsson has probably benefited very much in its development of mobile telephone system from experience collected in the military signal field.

The only real experience we have of technology transfer in the meaning I defined earlier was in the development phase of the most recent fighter, the Griffin.

We organized around 10 seminars where the main participants in the project presented to an audience of small companies and university research units all the materials technology, most of the computer development and production technology, such as gluing the plane together. Some of the technology came not only from the Swedish companies but was part of the international sub-contractors program. These seminars were well received, but I am not able to quote any example of a small and intermediate company where this information was crucial for its further development efforts. What was, however, useful was that a number of new links were created between the big companies and a couple of potential sub-contractors.

What has been done, and could probably be applied elsewhere is to create a market by asking companies with established technological competence to use it for another field where there is a general public need. I can refer here to efforts to use qualified defense technology to approach problems such as environmental deterioration and possible care. We have tried it, and also experienced many failures. For instance, the 24 regional units who carry the responsibility for the hospitals in Sweden, and may sometimes want each to be the leading one in the application of a new technology. And worse - there are almost 300 local communities, each having the responsibility for the local air and water quality management.

5. Swedish Technology Diffusion

I will instead focus, for the rest of this paper, on the Swedish experience in the field of technology diffusion. I will use three examples; the science attache system, the spin-off companies from universities and the role of the precompetitive research establishments I already mentioned.

Sweden is, as I pointed out, a country with between 8 and 9 million inhabitants. We estimate that we produce in Sweden something of the order of 1 percent of the world total efforts in research and development. But our industry needs access to very much more. From the 1940s on there was established a Swedish science and technical attaché to the Swedish embassy in Washington, D.C., whose task it was to follow and report home progress reported in publications and conferences in the U.S. This proved very useful, and over the last 50 years this system has been extended and we have now reporters that send home scientific and technical information from four places in the U.S., from Japan, from Bonn, Brussels, London, Milan and Paris. We also had offices in Beijing, Delhi and Moscow. The basic costs for this system are covered by the Swedish government; with the present economic situation caused us to concentrate our efforts, we had to close down the three offices I just mentioned.

The basic reports are freely available to big and small companies and research institutes. The attaché system also accepts commissions from individual or groups of companies to write special reports where the information is limited to the customers for around 6 months up to one year.

This system has worked very well and will continue.

It has also another value. Top man in each office is an experienced scientist or engineer, but he supervises between 5 and 10 younger ones, who for a limited period, normally 18 months, do most of the job. When they return to Sweden, they have got an extremely useful piece of education, which makes them very attractive on the labor market.

As I already noted, most of the basic and a lot of applied research takes place in the university. But university institutions are not well established to develop products. Government and private funds have been very generous in providing funds and facilities for spin-off companies. There are for the time being around 700 such companies, mainly in high technology research parks around the central universities.

The basic problem is of course that an entrepreneur is another kind of animal than a scientist. Even if economy and management is taught within the curriculum of the technical universities, the teachers have limited practical experience. And in a way entrepreneurship cannot be taught; it has to be experienced.

Many of the 700 companies are successful, but small. And these companies have a hard time to expand. Some are not even interested in expansion.

It is easier to motivate and manage a small group of 10 to 20 persons. When expanding beyond that, the founder has to devote interest to personnel issues, to company and public relations. This is no fun to a real exploratory mind.

We have realized that there are not easy solutions to these problems. Inventors and entrepreneurs always complain about the lack of money. Yes, venture capital is scarce and high interest on borrowed capital can kill any new company very quickly. But analyzing the operations of those small companies, which have gone bankrupt, we soon realize that it was most often not the lack of money that killed the company.

It was the lack of analysis and understanding of the situation and - and this is the most essential point - any company is enormously dependent upon its customers. It is absolutely necessary from the beginning to work with customers and find out what the real needs are, not of a vague marketplace, but one real customer!

Unless a small company has good customer relations and tries to understand the customer's real problems and how much he is prepared to pay for a good solution, the inventor or entrepreneur will never be able to charge the right price and build up reserves he needs for bad times.

A company has also to evaluate which quality a potential customer would appreciate - and estimate the size of the market. In this context quality means the characteristics of a product or service which a customer is prepared to pay for. "Quality" is not constituted by narrow tolerances or clean surfaces but properties which give the product an added value for the customer over alternatives available. To polish the surface of a steam roller does not provide quality - it only increases cost.

Too much secrecy may also be a bad thing. It is necessary for small companies to have good and experienced people in the board of directors or as paid consultants. And it is also necessary to show up at trade conferences and exhibitions. Many inventors are afraid of being robbed by competitors, but in our experience this rarely happens. Even copying takes much longer time than people think, though we are planning to set up a government fund for assistance to support small companies in disputes with international giants or other patent infringers.

My third example of Swedish experience are the semi-governmental research establishments. Many of these have half a century of experience. Their main task is to do precompetitive studies and research for leading Swedish companies.

But smaller companies can also participate and will learn from participating in projects of various kinds. They can also send a personnel for continuous training. They have also proven to be excellent first job situations for newly educated engineers and scientists. After a few years in such a laboratory they will have the opportunity of getting a very good career in real industry and take with them knowledge.

6. Conclusion

This leads me to my conclusion. The spreading of knowledge, through technology transfer or technology diffusion, is not provided by books or electronic mail. It is carried by persons who know how to use all the traditional and modern forms of communications. Education and training are the only road to improve a company's or a country's competitiveness.

16. TECHNOLOGY TRANSFER - SOME GENERAL REMARKS AND NOTES ON TURKEY

NAMIK K. PAK
Vice-President, TÜBİTAK
Ankara, Turkey

1. Technology and its Transfer - General Remarks

Technology is defined as any tool or technique, any product or process, any physical equipment or method of doing or making by which human capability is extended. It may be in an "embodied" form, namely, in machinery and equipment, and in human beings, or in a "disembodied" form, namely, in industrial properties, in know-how, patents, trade marks, technical data, technical services, etc.

Technology is continuously generated through inventions and innovations, and then assimilated, diffused, further develop, enhanced, bought and sold, by a variety of means. Invention means solution to a specific problem, and may be related to a product or a process, whereas, innovation is the application of new technique, which increases performance at lower costs; innovation may also make possible things that could not be done before.

Summing up, we may define knowledge base as a system composed of entrepreneurial, organizational, managerial and innovational components, as well as more concrete elements, such as blue prints, patents, machinery, etc. It is linked but distinct from science in being exclusively demand driven.

The pace of technological progress is ever increasing. For instance, in the 20th century, we have witnessed more inventions and innovations, and technological changes than the whole previous history of mankind. It is now clear that there is a very strong correlation between the industrialization and economic development, and technology is the key element in the industrialization process. Indeed, the growth of the many economies of the contemporary world is related primarily to the rate and the quality of the technical progress in their countries.

G. Bugliarello et al. (eds.), East-West Technology Transfer, 201-210.

Clearly, it is this technological capability that the developing countries would need to harness as an instrument of growth and socio-economic development.

Technological knowledge is normally acquired either via independent research and development within a country, or via transfer from elsewhere. With the mounting complexity and cost of development of modern technologies, with the accelerating pace of inventions and innovations, monopolized by a limited number of advanced countries, the transfer mode is left as almost the only viable option of acquiring technology for the developing world for the ultimate aim of industrialization. It is to be noted however, that the technological dependence can be both the cause and effect of general dependency relations. Because, if not handled properly, an enclave economy, dependent on advanced countries for inputs, market, management, finance and technology, may be created, thus establishing a vicious circle in which a weak technology system reinforces dependence, and dependence perpetuates weakness.

Technology transfer differs from the dissemination of scientific knowledge. Namely, it is more concerned with the utilization of end products or processes, than with the incorporation of new conceptual schemes into the general framework of technologists' field of activity.

In simplistic terms, technology transfer is the process by which technology is moved for the purpose of application towards end-products. Transfer can take place from laboratory to application or from one sector to another, either domestically or across national boundaries from one country to another.

Technology is transferred in the forms of: a) Foreign direct investment (FDI), b) Licensing, c) Joint ventures, d) Management, marketing and technical service contracts, e) Turn-key contracts, etc. Usually, overlapping occurs among these categories. For instance, FDI is frequently combined with licensing agreements between a parent company and its affiliate. Similarly, joint ventures between trans-national corporations and local enterprises often include licensing agreements, and management, marketing and technical service contracts.

FDI may involve either the acquisition of an existing enterprise or the organization of an entirely new enterprise. The technology is provided as part of a complete package, which may include capital goods, industrial property rights in the form of patents, trade marks, and brand names, secret unpatented process know-how specific to the investing firm, and the investing firm's accumulated experience and skills in organization, management and marketing. A licensing agreement is a legal contract under which the licenser confers certain rights upon the licensee for a certain duration.

Under suitable market conditions, the traditional technology transfer process involves several steps which form a cycle: 1) Assessment of the techno-economic needs, 2) Assessment of available technologies and selection of the appropriate technology, 3) Assimilation, adaptation and diffusion of the acquired technology, 4) Attainment of excellence, which enables the user to improve production techniques plus diversification of product range, 5) Search for newer technologies - and the cycle starts all over again.

After setting the classical features of the technology transfer mechanism, let us turn our attention to some critical points which might be crucial in assessing the success or failures in different countries [1].

First of all, the transferred technology should be a new technology. Clearly transferring an old and outdated technology, especially without state protection, can never lead to a competitive advantage. In this case, there is no hope of passing to the creative stage and attaining a technology development capability.

Although licensing is the most widely used form of technology transfer, it is not the most beneficial form of the transfer, particularly if the recipient country is a developing country, because suppliers usually agree to license their technology when it is in line with their own strategic interests. This often means they only license when a particular market is closed to other forms of exploitation or when their direct interests in exploiting it themselves are small. Licensers usually try to avoid creating future competition. Indeed, many firms in Turkey, for instance, which have acquired their technology through license agreements have recently gone through this experience. Once they have entered the international markets, the licenser firms were not very responsive to their demands for new product licenses.

For the developing countries, one can distinguish two main mechanisms of technology transfer. There are "direct transfers" which involve transactions with machine suppliers, engineering consultants, and other agents in industrialized countries; and the "indirect transfers," which are done by way of license agreements with innovative firms in industrialized countries which have successfully appropriated relevant segments of the production technology. Indirect transfers may or may not involve foreign direct investments.

Direct transfer recipients are supplier dominated, whereas the recipients of indirect transfers operate in production-intensive or scale intensive sectors. Direct transfers center around the import of innovative equipment from capital goods suppliers, though they may require support from other suppliers of technological skills, like engineering design and consultancy firms or plant contractors. However, regardless of the complexity surrounding this form of the transfer, none of the agents involved have interest in delaying the "filling of the technology gap process" in the recipient. Suppliers of innovative machinery will be specifically concerned to sell it regardless of the location of their customers. So these countries that are aware of their real needs and have sufficient technological knowledge and infrastructure, will have a higher probability of closing their technology gap by using the direct transfer mode than those using the indirect mode under licensing agreements.

This could be one of the reasons behind the gap between the industrialization levels of Turkey and those of the Newly Industrialized Countries (NICs) of the Pacific, even though the attempts started almost about the same time. Turkey has heavily subscribed to the indirect mode under license agreements; whereas the NICs used the direct method more extensively.

The above arguments are equally valid for the other traditional forms of technology transfers, FDI to quote but one.

2. New Perspectives on Technology Transfer

Under the new political and economical situation, a post-1989 syndrome, the so-called technology perspective of the 60s and 70s has lost the ground to a new one. The old perspective was "the market, especially when the capital markets are operated efficiently, the international capital moves to the markets of the developing countries naturally, where profit rates are somewhat higher than those of the developed ones." When the capital moves, especially in the form of FDI, it brings technology (embodied and/or disembodied types) together, The crucial factors for the success of this mechanism were suitable markets, liberal trade and exchange regimes.

Nearly for a generation, that is for 30-40 years, market economies (developed or less-developed alike) operated under this perspective. The conditions or the constraints stemmed from the Cold War, consolidated the above mentioned perspective, because in a bipolar world, both systems had their technology leaders which produced technology and diffused it nearby.

The two systems had similar technology powerhouses of pioneering technologies, i.e., nuclear delivery systems, rocket fuels, metallurgy, aviation, etc. Some important ingredients of the success of the Soviet technology system were believed to be legal or "illegal" technology transfers from the West. For this reason, a COCOM mechanisms was established to prevent this sort of transfer of technology from the Western countries. But there was a point which could not be ignored. Since the Soviets could transfer, absorb and improve some of those imported critical high-techs, then their technological infrastructure, i.e., scientific and technical manpower and research facilities, must have been highly developed and extensive.

During the cold war era, the focus was on military-strategic technologies, especially for the Soviets. They did not care much about the consumer technologies which facilitate everyday life, in comparison with the West. At the same time, Western firms which have strong technological bases were not interested in investing in centrally planned economies, with few exceptions. The former Soviet Union, and other socialist states were interested however, in investing in the developing countries via bilateral agreements which provided technical aids and direct investment. Turkey, for instance, has benefited from Soviet technical and economic aid for textile factories in 1930; Ìskenderun Iron-Steel Mills and Seydisehir Aluminium Smelting Plant in the 1970s, etc.

One of the main characteristics of the post-cold war period of the late 80s, is the abandoning of the military-strategic focus of technological progress; thus COCOM had to disappear. Consumer technologies (civilian or marketable technologies) have gained the upper hand. If the CP countries and East European countries could organize themselves according to market principles, a capital and/or technology flow would have been imminent. But this technological monsoon somehow never occurred, to the great disappointment of all interested parties.

Instead, a new and important paradox came forth. The former Soviet Union had had one of the best and largest scientific manpower stock and research infrastructure. Most likely as a policy decision, they were not interested in producing and marketing "simple" consumer goods. On the other hand, many developing economies which have enough market incentives and other "free market conditions" could not attain the stage of technology production after a generation of technology transfer efforts either. This paradox began to weaken the old technology transfer theory in which the "market forces" were the decisive factor.

To understand the meaning of this seeming paradox, one should look at the success cases like the Pacific Tigers [2]. South Korea or Taiwan have been taking the technology transfer process as a strategic parameter, namely, putting heavy emphasis on the development of a strong S&T structure, not leaving it to the realm of firms alone which could be termed as strategic, planning or guiding the firms' actions with considerable state intervention.

This approach brings two kinds of "appropriateness" criteria different from the well known "appropriate technology" arguments of the 1970s, which was based on neo-classical "factor endowment" theory; namely, the economies should choose their technologies according to their abundance of production factors, labor-intensive techniques for developing countries; capital-intensive ones for developed economies.

One of the new "appropriateness" is the use of appropriate techniques which makes a technology transferring firm profitable in the short or medium run under not-so-perfect market conditions, somehow protected by tariffs, but not providing the country with a technology creating capability. This is the case in Turkey, which produces all kinds of goods and services of varying qualities, but not the technology, since she does not have to compete abroad for most of its manufactured goods which are easily absorbed by domestic markets.

The second type of "appropriateness" is, economy-wise, one which involves some generic technologies that, in the long run, enable the economy to absorb and improve the transferred technologies with some state support and guidance. This is the case of the Pacific countries; Japan has done it in the 50s and 60s, Korea, Taiwan and Singapore have done it in the 70s and 80s.

What are the lessons we can extract from the paradox? Market mechanisms alone are not enough for an efficient technology transfer and creating technology development capabilities, whereas a mature scientific and technological infrastructure, without market incentives, has a better chance of attaining this ultimate goal.

To support this new viewpoint, it is also worth mentioning the new developments in innovative systems: (1) science (research) and technology (development) are getting more integrated, giving way to the transfer of products or production processes from university laboratories to industry directly; (2) product cycles are getting shorter, and; 3) inventions or further R&D activities are getting much more complex and/or science-based. For this reason, "reverse engineering" is losing weight or being confined to small and unimportant areas of the traditional manufacturing sector.

3. The Turkish Experience

Turkey has not completed her industrialization process, yet she has not given up her desire to become industrialized either [3]. With this ultimate aim she has made several attempts during different periods, and her ability to produce and export some industrial goods is the result of these attempts. Textiles, confection, leather, food and glass are the main goods exported as consumer goods, whereas refrigerators and consumer electronics are among the durable consumer goods that are imported.

In general, it is not wrong to say that technology in Turkey is based on technology transfer. However, the R&D activities are far from sufficient. To give an idea, I would like to present some figures about R&D indicators of Turkey [4]. For example, GERD is about 0.50%, the share of the private sector in R&D expenditures is about 18% and the full-time equivalent researchers per 10,000 work-force are less than 10%.

From these indicators, it is easily seen that the Turkish industry is heavily dependent on technology transfer. In addition to this, the indicators also denote that the level of R&D is not high enough even for "right" technology transfer. Also, this low level or lack of local R&D activity and the low demand for scientific and research personnel hinders the development of indigenous engineering and design capabilities necessary for the creation of technology and the effective adaptation and absorption of foreign technology.

Although the present technological situation in Turkey has been seemingly heavily marked by technology transfer, there is not sufficient data available on technology transfer to make a precise assessment. Thus, the patent, license, know-how and management agreements made through the Foreign Investment Encouragement Law 6224 can be accepted as the main legal base for technology transfer. The approved license agreements between 1980-1992, by sector, are presented in Table 1.

TABLE 1. Turkey. Number of License Agreements by Sectors (1980-1992)

Sector	Years														
	80	81	82	83	84	85	86	87	88	89	90	91	92	Total	(%)
Manufacturing	10	21	25	54	59	29	68	81	68	56	62	46	42	621	87.8
Agriculture	--	--	--	1	4	4	3	2	3	3	2	2	1	25	3.5
Mining	--	--	--	--	--	--	--	1	--	--	--	2	2	5	0.7
Service	--	--	--	--	6	--	5	10	5	15	6	6	3	56	8.0
Total	10	21	25	55	69	33	76	94	76	74	70	56	48	707	100.0

As can be seen from the table, almost 88% of the license agreements signed between 1980 and 1992 are in the manufacturing sector. The license agreements in the service sector are an indicator of the promotion of this sector - tourism and banking being the main subsectors. About 44% of the license agreements made between 1980 and 1992 were with West Germany (187) and the USA (120). The United Kingdom, France, Italy and Switzerland follow with a total combined share of 30%. So these six countries were responsible for 74% of the total licenses bought between 1980 and 1992. The overall burden of technology transfer to Turkey between 1980 and 1992 was about 770 million US dollars, 60% of which was for technical assistance. The distribution of the licenses in the manufacturing sector according to different production modalities also reflect the dependence on technology transfer.

4. Concluding Remarks

Technology, being one of the prime instruments of development, plays a decisive role whether the need is for more food, better education, improved health care, increases industrial output or more efficient transportation and communications. Technology is not neutral, it incorporates, reflects and perpetuates value systems and its transfer thus implies their transfer.

Because technology not only shapes a nation's development options but also affects economic and social structures, it is not surprising that technology is of concern to both rich and poor countries. Inevitably, it has become one of the major areas of negotiation for the establishment of a new international economic order.

The large gap between the technological levels of the developed and the developing countries' industries makes it difficult for the developing countries' products to compete with the others from a quality and cost point of view. To make things worse, the developed world has been investing more in R&D, the developing countries less.

Through modern telecommunication technologies and improved media, people today are more aware of product quality versus cost advantages of high technology products. The desire to acquire these products by the public induce an ever increasing pressure on the local industries and governments which, in turn, may result in lower customs tariff levels and the classical dangers of leaving the enterprises with a serious survival problem in the market.

Therefore, technology transfer from the developed industries is necessary for the developing ones to upgrade their technological level, to reduce lead time, get new and better quality products through the development stage more quickly, and to catch up by creating their own technology development capability through major R&D staff and facilities. The selection of the right technology, and its adaptation to local industry conditions and the needs of the target market are critical.

Technology is critical to development because it is a resource and the creator of new resources, is a powerful instrument of social control and affects decision-making to achieve social change.

Acknowledgment

I would like to thank H. Atamer and E. Turkan for valuable suggestions and discussions.

References

1. Cooper, A. (1991) Are innovation studies on industrialized economies relevant to technology policy in developing countries?, UNU/INT, Working Paper, No. 3.

2. Goker, A. (1991) Competitive Advantage or Technological Capability of Turkish Industry, in Competitive Advantage and Strategies in Turkish Industry, *The Chamber of Mechanical Engineers Publications, No: 160*, Ankara, pp. 118-149.

3. Kim, L. and Dahlmann, C.J. (1992) Technology policy for industrialization: an integrative framework and Korea's experience, *Research Policy* **21**, 437-452.

4. OECD (1994) National science and technology policy review of Turkey (draft), TÜBİTAK, Ankara.

17. ASPECTS OF TECHNOLOGY TRANSFER: U.S. POLICY AND PRACTICE

JOHN H. MOORE
Director, International Institute
George Mason University
Arlington, VA, USA

1. Introduction

Technology transfer has long been a important policy issue in the United States. During the Cold War, the focus was on preventing the transfer of military significant technologies. With the end of the Cold War, however, the main issues have shifted from the military to the commercial. This, in turn, has two sides: concern about the unwanted transfer of commercially valuable technology to global competitors and the desire to more effectively utilize technology developed within the U.S. by government-funded programs. This paper addresses the latter of these two points.

The concern about the utilization of research results stems from two factors. First, it is widely believed that American firms are losing technological ground to their foreign rivals, despite the large investments of American firms in R&D. The second factor is the great magnitude of federal spending on R&D. U.S. Government expenditures for R&D reached $68 billion in 1993, or about 42% of all U.S. R&D expenditures. Of this total, $11.4 billion was spent in universities and colleges, $8.7 billion in Federally Funded Research and Development Centers (FFRDCs), and $16.6 billion in intramural federal laboratories [13]. The bulk of the remainder was spent in industry thus amounted to $36.7 billion - 54% of total Federal funds and 23% of total U.S. expenditures on R&D.

Many science and technology experts have argued that the results of these R&D investments have not been effectively used, particularly for commercial purposes. These arguments have gained considerable acceptance and extensive legislation has been adopted as a result.

G. Bugliarello et al. (eds.), East-West Technology Transfer, 211-236.

But technology transfer is broader than these legislated federal programs. It occurs in a setting that has characteristic institutional and cultural features. These, of course, vary from one country to another. The effectiveness of technology transfer depends on the particular setting; U.S. experience as well as economic analysis provides a basis for understanding what mechanisms and institutions contribute to effective technology transfer.

2. Technology Transfer and Innovation

In discussing technology transfer, it is important to understand the nature of the innovative process [6]. Innovation begins with the perception by the innovator of a potential market for a new or improved product.[1] But to develop the new product requires finding solutions to many problems, some of which are technical. The innovator will seek solutions to these problems in the most cost-effective way. This may involve conducting research, consulting with experts, utilizing existing literature, or other means. All such approaches to problem solving may be interpreted as involving technology transfer.

This description is limited since it seems to pertain merely to a one-time innovation. But in the competitive world market, survival requires continuous innovation. Thus the innovative process is also characterized by the existence of many feedback loops. As an innovation is developed, the innovator is constantly assessing the market, making alterations as required and continuing the process of modifying products and ideas as the market reading indicates.

In such a continuous, on-going innovative process, successful technology transfer is not a set of one-time forays into the external pool of knowledge, but requires a complex program. This program may include more or less permanent relationships with sources of knowledge (consultants, universities, outside laboratories), an internal R&D organization that provides both new information for problem-solving and the basis for absorbing knowledge obtained externally, and a capacity for searching for and finding needed information, as well as individualized inquiries on special topics.

The key to the innovative process is that it consists of problem-solving in a market-driven process. Thus technology transfer will occur when potential users find it in their interest to utilize new or existing results. This indicates that technology transfer programs should have strong links between potential users and the producers of new knowledge. This seems to be the direction in which most new U.S. technology transfer programs are headed. This strong linkage also characterized the first major technology transfer program in the U.S.: that of agricultural research.

Thus, an active relationship between researchers and potential users is one key ingredient in successful technology transfer programs. But the large literature on this subject reveals a number of other characteristics that are important to technology transfer.

First, it is widely agreed that there must be an indigenous technological capacity in the society in which technology transfer is to occur [5, 14, 17]. Elements of this capacity include high levels of technical ability and skill, a strong science and technology system, and an effective infrastructure for acquiring and using research results. This last includes a mechanism for rapid diffusion of technological capabilities; in the U.S., this is attributed to, among other things, mechanisms for the direct transmission of knowledge from producers to users (especially in university-industry relationships), the high mobility of technical personnel, low barriers to entry of new firms, and strong pressures to be first in entering new markets [5].

The last items suggest that technology transfer is more than a purely technical matter. Managerial skills and organizational skills are also important. Managers must be able to interweave technical and market factors in the innovation process, to make cost-effective decisions solving innovative problems, and so forth. Organizations must be designed to facilitate this process. In particular, it is important that the technical and commercial parts of a firm be closely related if not actually integrated.

Seen broadly, technology transfer consists of the diffusion of new technologically-relevant knowledge. The nature of the innovative process also has implications for the organization of programs intended for such diffusion: if the process is market-driven, and if technology transfer (diffusion) takes place as part of the problem-solving operation, then a successful program for technology transfer should be decentralized and responsive to market demands. As one expert has noted, decentralization has several virtues in this regard [5]. It engages more actors and therefore a larger set of potential users; the U.S. program in agricultural technology has this characteristic.

Incentive systems also play key role in effective innovation and, therefore, in effective technology transfer. Incentive systems are based on rights to property; this is usually (and rightly) taken to mean the legal setting for intellectual property rights, but should also be seen as including rights of individuals within the organizations that are involved in the innovative process and that are producing the knowledge that is used by the innovators. Thus a sound legal system of intellectual property rights is crucial. In addition, however, agreements between innovators and sources of knowledge must provide adequate incentives, Providing such incentives has been the motivation for extensive recent legislation in the U.S.

Of course, both institutional and human factors are important for effective technology transfer. This investment in human capital is central. The latter has both stock and flow characteristics [5]. A sufficient stock of trained and capable scientists and engineers is required to serve as receptors for new knowledge; their roles include knowing where to look for the knowledge needed during the innovative process, recognizing useful knowledge, and putting it to use. But, like any capital stock, the human capital stock depreciates and, particularly important in a time of rapidly changing technology, becomes obsolescent. Therefore, it is in constant need of replacement and upgrading; it requires continuous investment.

To summarize, successful technology transfer requires first of all an underlying infrastructure. This infrastructure includes the human resources needed for the utilization of new knowledge and the institutional framework (intellectual property, incentive structures, organization, etc.) that is conducive to technology transfer. Recognition of the market-based nature of innovation and the demand for technology leads to implications regarding the structure of programs intended to facilitate technology transfer. In the next section, recent developments in U.S. technology transfer programs are summarized and discussed from this point of view.

3. Technology Transfer in the U.S.: Legislation[2]

The Stevenson-Wydler Act, originally passed in 1980, is a keystone in the architecture of federal technology transfer programs. The Act originally attempted to stimulate the dissemination of information from federal laboratories, mostly by requiring federal laboratories to take an active role in technical cooperation. However, later in the decade, pressures for improvement in the use of research results produced with federal funds became intense. As a result, two amendments were passed that add considerably to its importance: the Federal Technology Transfer Act of 1986 and the National Competitiveness Act of 1989. These amendments acts created Cooperative Research and Development Agreements (CRADAs), making it possible for industrial firms to conduct joint research programs with FFRDCs. The first of the two pertained to government laboratories that are operated by the government itself; the second, arguably the more important, had to do with government laboratories that are operated by non-government contractors (universities and industrial firms). Importantly, the laws provide for appropriate licensing arrangements and royalty sharing.[3]

Another early piece of legislation of considerable importance, especially for university-based research, was the Bayh-Dole Act of 1980. This act made it possible for universities, non-profit organizations, and small businesses to obtain title to inventions developed through research supported by the federal government. In so doing, it was intended to stimulate the commercialization of government sponsored research carried out in these organizations. One apparent result is the rapid growth of university offices charged with licensing and helping to develop commercial applications of such inventions.

Two other pieces of legislation should be mentioned. The first is the Small Business Innovation Research Act of 1982. This Act mandated that government agencies that support R&D with budgets exceeding a certain cutoff level devote a fraction of their budgets to cooperative projects involving small businesses. This has resulted in programs in all of the large government R&D funding agencies. The programs frequently involve cooperation between a small business and a university, thus stimulating the transfer of technology from universities with federal funding.

Finally, the Omnibus Trade and Competitiveness Act of 1988 established centers for transferring federally developed manufacturing technology and Industrial Extension Services within the states. These provisions are the basis for an extensive increase in programs for technology transfer in the Department of Commerce.

4. Technology Transfer and the Federal Laboratories

4.1. COOPERATIVE RESEARCH AND DEVELOPMENT AGREEMENTS (CRADAS)

The amendments provided a basis for industrial firms to obtain legal title to intellectual property resulting from cooperative research agreements with federal laboratories. They also created incentives for the laboratories by giving them rights to royalties resulting from inventions made in such agreements. Thus the legal basis for cooperation was created.

Especially since 1989, when contractor-operated laboratories became eligible for CRADAs, the number of agreements has increased dramatically. Exclusive of NASA, the total increased from 271 in 1989 to 460 in 1990 to 731 in 1991. NASA agreements added another 250 or so by that time. By spring 1993, the total had further grown to more than 1,500.[4] This suggests that private sector contractors have had an advantage in promoting cooperative agreements. In this regard, it is of some interest to note that CRADAs in the Department of Agriculture, whose laboratories are predominantly government-operated, increased steadily, with no particular sharp increase after 1989. The Department's long experience with technology transfer and its close relations with the agricultural industry may explain this. Much the same can be said of NASA's cooperative R&D agreements.

The increase in CRADAs reflects more than merely the enabling legislation of the amendments to the Stevenson-Wydler Act. It also reflects a shift in policy on the part of industrial R&D directors. In fact, between 1988 and 1992, there was a substantial increase in industrial interest in all forms of cooperation with federal laboratories [14]. Industrial interest in cooperation has grown as industrial R&D budgets have become strained and research directors have come to realize that the federal laboratories represent a source of useful information. This seems to coincide with a broad shift in industrial attitudes in the direction of seeking knowledge and expertise outside their own laboratories. Firms increasingly recognize that the research problems they face cannot be solved with their own resources and therefore seek help elsewhere; this kind of cooperation is obviously demand driven.

The impact of federal efforts to disseminate new knowledge produced in government laboratories can be seen in other statistics as well. The number of invention disclosures[5] rose from around 2,600 in 1987 to about 4,200 in 1991, and the number of patent applications increased from 848 to over 1,900 in the same period. The number of licenses granted also rose significantly, although the absolute number was small: 261 in 1991, up from 128 in 1987 [13]. The large difference between patents filed and licenses granted must reflect a lack of interest on the part of industry in much of what is invented in the federal laboratories, again an indication of the importance of demand factors in technology transfer from the federal laboratories.

4.2. THE NATIONAL TECHNOLOGY TRANSFER NETWORK[6]

The National technology Transfer Network includes the National Technology Transfer Center (NTTC), located in West Virginia, and six Regional Technology Transfer Centers (RTTCs), distributed around the nation. The NTTC was inaugurated in 1991 and the six RTTCs were launched in January 1992. The system is administrated by NASA but is intended to assist and enhance technology transfer efforts of all federal agencies. It is intended to be market-driven, and is to provide a number of services to industrial and business users.

The NTTC provides a gateway to Federal R&D and technological resources by various means, including a toll-free telephone number for access to databases, a bulletin board with notices of technology transfer meetings, a system for searching federal laboratory databases, and a telephone directory of technology transfer individuals, resources, and agencies. It serves as a technology database and clearinghouse to assist U.S. industries in forming technology transfer linkages with federal agencies and their laboratories and state and local governments. It provides training and education services to firms and state and local governments to improve their knowledge of technology transfer and to help develop linkages for technology transfer.

These centralized functions are supplemented and complemented by the particular services of the RTTCs. In general, the RTTCs are supposed to provide a set of services to industrial "clients." These include:

- Information services: computerized searches of Federal technology databases and other technology sources, performed on request
- Technology services: technology sourcing and evaluation, assessments of technology requirements, engineering reports, etc.
- Commercialization services: technology brokering (through promoting technology partnerships, for example), business analyses, venture capital sourcing, intellectual property licensing

In addition to these general functions, RTTCs are developing their own programs for technology transfer. The Mid-Atlantic Technology Applications Center in Pittsburgh has developed a desktop computer program, Federal Laboratories Database, that contains information on almost 2,000 federally funded R&D laboratories and facilities. This program is available to industrial land business users at no charge. The Far West RTTC is negotiating with 25 leading venture capital firms to serve as their technology counsel. In this arrangement, the RTTC would match the market-driven needs of the venture capital firms' clients with technologies from various federal sources.

The National Technology Transfer Network is in its early stages of development, and little can be said at this point about its net value. Very little quantitative information is available for that purpose. NASA reports that through December 31, 1993, NTTC had served more than two thousand users. Most of these (68%) were small or medium sized businesses. NASA also reports that the NTTC gateway is handling 200-300 industrial inquires per month [16]. However, no data are available that would shed light on the economic value of applications that might have resulted from the effort.

4.3. THE NATIONAL TECHNOLOGY INFORMATION SERVICE

The National Technology Information Service has existed for many years as an arm of the Department of Commerce, dedicated to making information about new and possibly relevant technologies available to potential users. Originally dealing in printed materials made available on a cost basis (NTIS is self-supporting from sales revenues), it is now moving to electronic media. In addition, it is developing an electronic locator system, called FedWorld, in an effort to improve access to all forms of technology documentation.

The NTIS represents a gateway to the immense amounts of information generated in government-sponsored research work, including published reports, information about work in progress, electronic data files and computer software. The principal problem associated with its use is that of locating useful information in the vast amounts possessed by NTIS. FedWorld may help in this respect.

4.4. THE FEDERAL LABORATORY CONSORTIUM

The Federal Laboratory Consortium (FLC), formally chartered by the Technology Transfer Act of 1986, is another entity intended to enable industrial firms, especially small businesses, to solve technological problems by using the resources of the federal laboratory system. Its formal structure consists of a central office and six regional offices, but its strength is based on network of representatives at 600 federal laboratories throughout the country.

The FLC operates largely on the basis of specific requests from firms seeking solutions to technological problems. The laboratory network is accessed through the regional coordinator, the six regional offices, and the FLC Locator. The last is a clearinghouse that assists in matching user technical requests with the appropriate federal laboratory. Its objective is to put the potential user in contact with the laboratory best suited to the problem at hand. Once the contact is established, the FLC's function is completed. Subsequent cooperation, which may lead to CRADA or other arrangement, is negotiated directly between the industrial user and the laboratory.

The FLC is based on the idea that firms will be able to find answers to their problems in the vast research resources of the laboratories. The premise is that there is at least a potential fit between the firms' problems and the laboratories research programs. This may be so, but, given the very advanced nature of much of the research at federal laboratories, the premise may be questionable. To support its case, the FLC (like most other federal technology transfer programs) lists a number of examples of new products that have resulted from agreements it has facilitated. However, market values of these programs are generally not measured, so the net value of the program (even if an accurate measure of its cost could be obtained) cannot be determined.

5. Selected Agency Technology Transfer Programs

5.1. THE U.S. DEPARTMENT OF AGRICULTURE[7]

The U.S. government agency with the longest record for technology transfer is the Department of Agriculture. In 1914, the Smith-Lever Act created the Cooperative Extension Service, which was originally designed as a partnership of the Department of Agriculture and the uniquely American land-grant universities, which had been authorized by he Morrill Acts on 1862 and 1890. Legislation by the states then added local governments or organized groups at the county level to this partnership.

In the ensuing eight decades, a complex system of relationships has been developed involving professionals in 72 universities and staff in more than 3,000 U.S. counties. The system links researchers and staff in the universities and Department of Agriculture laboratories with users at the local level in more than 3,000 U.S. counties. A key to the system is the two-way linkages between those who work for the Extension Service and those who use it. Especially important are the county-level extension agents, who insure "...that Cooperative Extension remains relevant to local needs and that he priorities set by Extension are those that, in fact, best serve the people" [1].

The Cooperative Extension Service's central mission is and has been the transference of knowledge - i.e., technology transfer - to improve agricultural productively.[8] And agricultural yields have certainly risen during this century. According to expert opinion [1], these productivity increases are the result of a combination of improved management skills, better production inputs, and new technology that is embodied in farming practice.

However, the record for agricultural productivity in the U.S. shows how difficult it is to measure the impact of technology transfer systems. Specifically, yields of the most important grain crops (wheat, corn, and soybeans) began to rise rapidly only around 1940, a quarter century after the formation of the Cooperative Extension Service [18]. The reasons for the pre-1940 quiescence and the substantial increase afterwards are not entirely clear. Agricultural research, through plant breeding, had produced hybrid corn by 1920. From that time production increases were probably delayed until the 1940s by the Depression of the 1930s, the second World War, and the need to educate the farming population to the advantages of the new technologies. In the latter, the universities and the Extension Service played important roles. But the success of the new technologies depended on a variety of factors; the Extension service itself and its technology transfer program constituted only one factor, albeit an important one.

5.2. THE NATIONAL SCIENCE FOUNDATION

American universities play a central role in the generation of new technology, through both research and teaching. Technology transfer is accomplished through the movement of their graduates to industry (according to some, this is the universities' most important function) and through other, more formal programs. In the last twenty years, there has been a great proliferation of such programs, far too many to be covered in a short paper. Rather than attempting an overall survey, a sample of National Science Foundation (NSF) programs is given to illustrate these efforts.

Technology transfer *per se* was not a central element in the NSF mission until recently. Nevertheless, NSF programs dating at least to 1980 have had technology transfer elements and exhibit characteristics that are important to successful transfer.

The first of these programs was the Industry-University Cooperative Research Centers (IUCRC) program, started in 1989. In this program, projects proposed for NSF support are initiated by a university professor who can mobilize industrial support behind an idea for cooperative research. To receive support, the initiator must get solid commitments from industry and the university. Each center develops a research program jointly with its industrial partners, a partnership that is formalized in industrial advisory boards at each center.

These requirements insure genuine industrial interest and clearly incorporate market demand in the undertaking. Industry's interest in practical results and academia's interest in fundamental inquiry must be balanced. For that very reason, the program has had the effect of bringing the academic and industrial research cultures closer together [2]. Once approved, projects are awarded support for five years; after this time, support under the IUCRC program is terminated and the centers must be self-supporting if they are to continue.[9]

Currently, the program supports 53 centers with total funding by the National Science Foundation of $4.8 million, or about $90.000 per year per center. However, total funding is much greater; funds from sources other than NSF, mostly industry, are on the order of $60 million per year. This strong commitment of funds from industry is perhaps the most compelling evidence of the program's effectiveness, although here again quantitative measures are not available [2].

The IUCRC program was the model for the similar State/Industry/University Cooperative research centers (State/IUCRC) program, originated in 1990 through an agreement between NSF and the National Governors' Association. While the IUCRCs focus on genetic, fundamental research that has potential industrial use, the State IUCRCs bring this kind of research closer to the market. There is a distinctive technology transfer element involved, and a special emphasis on small business participation. There are now ten of these new centers located in nine states. Total funding by NSF is $2.7 million.

In the early 1980s, the NSF launched a larger scale program with characteristics similar to the IUCRCs - the Engineering research centers (ERCs). Originally conceived to "...link academic engineering research and education to engineering practice..." [9], the ERCs did not have technology transfer as their primary purpose. However, through their educational programs and close ties to industry, they have nevertheless served that purpose.

As with IUCRCs, the ERCs are cooperative ventures between industry and academia. Each center receives between $1 million and $2 million per year from the NSF, and is required to at least match that in contributions from its industrial partners. Active participation by industry in planning the research program and its execution is required. The Centers must include an educational component along with the research program; the educational programs generally emphasize graduate students, but undergraduate programs have been included. Thus the Centers contribute to technology transfer in two ways: through the research program itself (with active industrial participation crucial) and through the educational programs, which train students who subsequently enter research careers.

The ERC program has been in existence sine 1985; twenty-one centers have been established in several rounds of competition.[10] An evaluation conducted in 1989 by the National Academy of Engineering [9] found strong intellectual links between the university researchers and their industrial partners, evidence of the basis for effective technology transfer. In fact, the report found these linkages were the most important value served by the Centers. It went so far as to warn against extending the notion of technology transfer too far, for example by engaging in prototype development. Thus there is reason to believe the centers have contributed to technology transfer from the universities, although quantitative measures of the extent of such transfer are lacking.

The Engineering Research Centers are only one example of university-based centers that have sprung up across the country in recent years. The NSF itself supports a group of science and technology centers, based in the natural sciences, that have some of the same characteristics. Other agencies support mission oriented centers at universities or centers specifically aimed at technology transfer.

5.3. THE NATIONAL AERONAUTICS AND SPACE ADMINISTRATION

In addition to administering the NTTN, NASA operates its own extensive technology transfer program, and has done so since its inception. Much of the effort is centered in its Technology Transfer Program, managed from NASA headquarters in Washington, D.C. The program operates through regional managers, known as Technology Utilization Officers, at each of NASA's nine field offices, scattered throughout the country.

These managers are responsible for a variety of activities. They are expected to remain current on the research and engineering activities at their centers that may generate transferrable technology. They are responsible for seeing to it that the professional staff identify, report, and document such technologies, and for monitoring NASA contractors to insure they are in compliance with legal requirements for technology disclosure. The officers also serve as liaison with industry and within the professional staff of their centers [10].

This program, unlike the NTTN, is not primarily demand-driven, but it is rather a supply-side effort. It affords a kind of catalog of NASA-developed technologies that may have commercial applications. Whether firms will take these up and apply them depends on their views of market opportunities and the effectiveness of the methods used for identifying needed technologies once market opportunities are perceived.

As the NASA Administrator has remarked [10], technology transfer from the space program has often had a serendipitous character during the last 35 years. The Office of Advanced Concepts and technology has been organized within the agency in a effort to make the process more pro-active. Again, it is too early to evaluate the success of this program. However, NASA points to a long list of innovations as evidence of the value of spillovers from the space program. There is no doubt these represent important technological advances that may be useful in commercial applications. Against their market value (which is largely unquantified and may be non-quantifiable) must be ranged their cost, or at least the cost of the technology transfer program used to seek implementation outside the space program itself. The data needed for this evaluation are not, in general, available,

5.4. THE NATIONAL INSTITUTES OF HEALTH

After the Department of Defense, the Department of Health and Human Services is the largest Federal funder of research development. In 1993, total HHS funding for R&D amounted to $10.4 billion. Of this total, the National Institutes of Health (NIH) provided $9.8 billion, or about 94%. Most of the remainder was spent through the Food and Drug Administration (FDA) and the Centers for Disease Control and Prevention (CDC). Industry provided about the same amount of funds for health R&D [13]. Taken together, these huge investments are undoubtedly the reason for the U.S. worldwide preeminence in biomedical research and the key factor in the success of the U.S. pharmaceutical industry.

The NIH conducts research in its own laboratories (its "intramural" program) and also funds research at U.S. universities and other facilities (the "extramural" program). Indeed, the NIH is the largest federal funder of basic research at universities. Technology is transferred from both intramural and extramural programs.

The intramural technology transfer program consists of two main activities. The first is the CRADA, which NIH organizes in the same way as other federal agencies. These CRADAs are governed by he 1986 Technology Transfer Act. After an initial buildup in 1987 and 1988, the number of new CRADAs has settled down at an average of 30-35 per year. These agreements have produced a modest number of patent licenses (a total of 9 through 1993) [11]. But actual licenses may not be the most important aspect of these agreements. Access to

NIH researchers and their research technologies may be at least as valuable to the industrial collaborators.

The research carried out within NIH laboratories, without industrial partners in CRADAs, produces "hundreds of new inventions" [12] each year. To facilitate commercial use of the of these inventions, the NIH Office of technology Transfer patents these inventions and seeks to license them to industry. The patents are the property of the federal government; the government may then grant any number of types of licenses to industrial users.

Statistics published by the Office of Technology Transfer shed light on the extent of these activities. Since 1987, the NIH has filed about 170 patent applications per year. About one third of these have resulted in licenses issued by the NIH. Royalties earned by NIH on licenses during this period totalled $57 million, more that half of which was due to one license (the HIV antibody test kit) [12]. Clearly, not all of the inventions made in NIH laboratories have seen commercial success, not a surprising result. The royalties obviously understate the actual commercial value of the patents that have resulted in licenses.

The NIH extramural research program constitutes more than three-quarters of its total R&D expenditures. Technology transfer in extramural research is based on the Bayh-Dole Act. As with other government supported research projects, ownership of rights to inventions produced in universities with NIH support normally is left with the university, which may retain the title. If it does not, the NIH may file for a patent, and the inventor may receive royalties on the invention.

Unfortunately, data on the extent of technology transfer made through the extramural program are not presently available. However, it is well known that there are close relationships between NIH-supported university researchers and industry. Once again, the training of highly skilled graduate students, and their recruitment by industry after graduation, may be the most important function of the universities and the most valuable contribution to technology transfer resulting from NIH support of university research,

6. Other Technology Transfer Mechanisms

6.1. UNIVERSITY INTELLECTUAL PROPERTY

The Bayh-Dole Act, which made it possible for universities to retain property rights in inventions made by their faculty under federal research grants, significantly strengthened the incentives for universities to commercialize those inventions. As a result, such efforts have grown significantly. Space does not allow a full review of these efforts, which are widespread. However, a few examples will illustrate the situation.

The first example is a three-way system involving the University of Chicago, the Argonne National Laboratory (a federal laboratory which the university manages), and industry. Recognizing that the laboratory's research has considerable industrial potential and encouraged by the possibility of retaining some of the earnings from commercialization of those results, the University and the laboratory created the ARCH Development Corporation. In six years, ARCH licensed more than 125 inventions, raised more than $20 million in venture capital, and created 13 new firms. Perhaps as a result of its success, the University of California has created a similar organization to focus on its campuses and the three national laboratories it manages.

ARCH and the University of California effort represent partnerships between universities and federal laboratories they manage under contract. Few American universities are in that position; nevertheless, they are interested in profiting from the research conducted by their faculty. They engage in other forms of technology transfer. Most importantly, perhaps, they produce highly trained students who carry advanced technology with them when they leave the university for work in industry. This combination of research and graduate education in the America system of higher education is generally regarded as one of its greatest strengths.

In addition, universities transfer knowledge by faculty lectures and publications, by consulting activities, and by the licensing patents, copyrights, and other intellectual property. And they spin off new companies, often created by faculty members working with venture capital firms to exploit research discoveries. Silicon Valley represents the most famous of these and the Boston area (the famous Route 128 corridor) another. In a 1988 study, MIT identified more than 600 new businesses that had been spun off from its faculty's activities; according to the study's estimates, these firms employed more than 200,000 persons and generated nearly $40 billion in annual revenues [15].

With regard to the formation of new businesses, it is important to emphasize the role of venture capital. The mere existence of a university or a concentration of intellectual talent in an area producing advanced ideas and concepts is not enough. There must be investment capital to support new ventures through their infancies and managerial talent to see them through to maturity. In the United States, venture capital firms have been strong in certain areas (such as

California, Massachusetts, and the Baltimore, Maryland area), and new start-ups have prospered in those areas. In others, where there is also considerable university-based scientific and engineering talent, this resource has not been available, and it has been difficult to establish new firms.

6.2. SMALL BUSINESS PROGRAMS

It is widely[11] believed in the United States that small and medium sized businesses are the most dynamic element of the economy. As a result of that belief, programs directed specifically at promoting the formation of new businesses based on government-sponsored research have been established and are growing.

The older of two programs is the Small Business Innovation Research (SBIR) program. Under the terms of the Small Business Innovation Research Act, every federal agency whose R&D budget exceeds $100 million must devote a specific portion of its R&D funding to this program.[12] Altogether 11 federal agencies meet the budget requirement and thus have SBIR programs.

The basic intent of the program is to stimulate the commercialization of new ideas that originate in the small business community.[13] It was not originally conceived as a technology transfer mechanism. However, in practice, there has been an element of technology transfer, especially in programs involving universities, as university professors serve as consultants to the proposing small businesses and, on occasion, have themselves left their universities to establish, with SBIR support, new businesses based on their university research.

However, the SBIR program may have served to stimulate the creation of another federal program aimed squarely at technology transfer to small businesses. This is the Small Business Technology Transfer program (STTR), established by the Small Business Technology Transfer Act of 1992. As in the SBIR program, a certain fraction of an agency's extramural R&D budget is set aside for small business, but in this case, for cooperative R&D projects between small concerns and nonprofit research organizations (such as universities). The STTR program is now in pilot phase in five federal agencies.

6.3. MANUFACTURING EXTENSION PARTNERSHIPS

In the late 1980s, the National Institute of Standards and Technology (NIST) established seven Manufacturing Technology Centers, located at sites around the country. These centers are intended to provide technical assistance to small and medium-sized firms in manufacturing technologies, techniques, and business practices [3]. In principle, they bear a resemblance to the venerable Cooperative Extension Centers, discussed above.

The Manufacturing Technology Centers are the basis for the development of a national system for manufacturing technology that is one of the centerpieces of the Clinton Administration's technology policy. The new program, called the Manufacturing Extension Partnerships, includes the seven Manufacturing Extension Centers, a State Technology Extension Program, and smaller Manufacturing Outreach Centers. Eventually, according to the plan, the system will include about 100 centers. There are to be linked electronically so information can be freely shared among the centers. The program will be administered by NIST, whose budget is intended to grow very rapidly in the next three to five years to accommodate this and other initiatives.

A central question surrounding this new program is whether the approach that seems to have been successful in agriculture can be transferred to manufacturing. The centers will presumably be stocked with massive amounts of information about manufacturing; can they transfer that knowledge to potential users, mostly small businesses, effectively? Experience in other technology transfer programs suggests that, in the long term, close relationships between producers and users of technology are the key to success. This was the case with the agricultural extension centers, where long term relationships were developed between agricultural extension agents and farmers who were more or less permanently established in their areas. Whether manufacturing will provide opportunities for such long term relationships may be questionable. Moreover, in the case of agriculture, similar technological problems tended to be shared by many farmers. Again, it is not clear this will be the case in manufacturing.

7. Discussion

As the previous discussion indicates, the last decade has seen a very substantial upsurge in efforts to improve the utilization of technology resulting from federally sponsored research. A vast national assemblage of centers, information systems, cooperative agreements, and networks has emerged, and more is on the way. This structure was not the result of a single over-arching plan, but rather of a series of developments more or less independently conceived and implemented. In that sense, it is an evolutionary, almost spontaneous, development - the evolution of a structure that has taken place both within the government and external to it.

The cost of this structure is not known. No good estimates of the costs of creating and managing the hundreds of CRADAs, of the ultimate cost of the MEPs, or of the RTTCs, for example, exist, not is it likely that such estimates will be possible. From a strictly economic point of view, this makes estimating the net value of the structure impossible, even if measures of output were available.

In addition, it must be realized the technology transfer mechanisms that have been described are operating in the context of the American socio-economic system. This complicates, perhaps hopelessly, the task of evaluating the effort. It also complicates the question of applicability of these mechanisms to nations whose societies differ significantly from America's. A few characteristics of American society suffice to make the point.

The first is the educational system and the level of education in the country. U.S. education has both weaknesses (weak secondary education, high dropout rates, inadequate science and mathematics education in pre-college, etc.) and strengths (especially graduate education in science and engineering). The working population, which necessarily is the vehicle through which technology transfer is mediated, is shaped by these characteristics. Research scientists and engineers are well- trained and have the intellectual tools to participate effectively in technology transfer activities. On the other hand, the U.S. does not have a particularly strong cohort of able technicians needed to support technology transfer.

Mobility is another characteristic of Americans that must be taken into account in evaluating technology transfer programs. Since technology transfer is, above all, a matter of personal contact, the movement of people - especially scientists and engineers - from one place to another contributes to technology transfer. Americans are thought to be highly mobile; if this is true of researchers (it is certainly true of students emerging from graduate school), it would contribute to the background infrastructure that partially determines the effectiveness of the more formal technology transfer programs.

Several other factors must betaken into account as well. There is the sheer size of the science and technology system in the U.S.; decades of investment in R&D and education have created a kind of social capital, both physical and human, that forms the basis for both technology development and transfer. The nature of the American economic system and attitudes toward success and failure contribute to relatively easy formation of new firms, founded to exploit new technological ideas. As noted earlier, entry barriers for these firms are also low, and strong competitive pressures work to drive their formation (and weed out the failures).[15]

International factors are increasingly important for domestic technology transfer evaluation as well. Prominent among these is the accelerating importance of global electronic communications, especially the use of the Internet and its related computer networks. By facilitating access to databases throughout the world, these systems contribute technology transfer to the U.S., since they afford lower-cost access to research results from other parts of the world.

Thus evaluation of programs specifically designed to promote technology transfer must somehow account for the particular environment in which they operate - the scientific and technological infrastructure, as it were. For that reason, it is exceedingly difficult to estimate the economic impact of these programs. Most of the available data fall on the input side of the ledger - the number of CRADAs, or of centers, and so forth. On the output side, measures such as the number of inventions licensed or patent applications filed contain little or no information about the actual economic value of a new technology. The spin-offs from university research mentioned earlier, with the data concerning revenues and employment, are a better measure, but are incomplete and relate only to one aspect of technology transfer in the U.S. system.

Besides these data, there is very little hard information that would form the basis for a sound economic analysis. This is not a new problem, of course; it has dogged the assessment of the economic impact of technological change for many years. However, Mansfield's success in estimating the economic return of government-sponsored academic research [8] suggests that careful work can produce useful results.

If little can be said about the aggregate economic impact of the recent technology transfer programs, it is possible, however, to reach tentative conclusions about what is likely to succeed and what is not. University spin-offs, successful CRADAs, and the apparent success of the IUCRC programs and ERCs show the importance of industry initiation of cooperative research programs and close relationships between potential industrial users of new technology and its academic developers.

These experiences also indicate the importance of demand-driven transfer in which users know broadly what they want and look for it in specific locations. This is consistent with the market-driven conception of the innovation process, and suggests that so-called technology-push technology transfer programs are less likely to be effective than those driven by industrial demand.

A number of other recently launched federal programs are also consistent with this view of the process, including CRADAs and the RTTCs. On the other hand, it is not clear that the MEP or the NTIS programs fit this model. On the surface, they appear to represent efforts to bring technological developments to the attention of industrial users. But they do not seem to include the industrial-initiated, long-term cooperative relationships that have been central to the successful efforts of the past. Like Internet, they represent methods of making access to new knowledge less costly than it would be otherwise be. Whether they are themselves cost-effective remains to be seen.

There are other hurdles to be overcome in technology transfer, especially in programs involving the federal laboratories. The laboratories have primarily mission-related purposes, and technology suitable for industrial application may not result from the pursuit of these purposes [4]. Furthermore, there are practical problems connected with the programs, including CRADAs, that have been launched. The problem of federal employee conflict-of-interest rules is a prominent example: the royalty aspect of these agreements immediately raises this issue, and it does not appear to be solved.[16] Conflict of interest problems are also arising in cases of university-industry cooperative agreements, where part of the cost of the research can be said to have been borne by federal government funds.

Furthermore, there is a problem of the Freedom of Information Act, which, it is feared, may require that information transferred in a CRADA from the federal laboratories be open for scrutiny by any firm, including both domestic and foreign competitors of the industrial partner in the agreement, thus diminishing the value of such agreements.

To these legal problems may be added other practical issues. The national laboratories were established and have been run as governmental organizations, on the basis of budgets provided for their missions. As a result, financial incentives have not played a major role in their incentive structures; indeed, there can be outright hostility to such incentives. Furthermore, as defense downsizing and other federal budgetary problems impact on the laboratories, mere survival becomes critical. Technology transfer, unless it is clearly related to that motivation, becomes secondary [7].

In addition, the laboratories, as part of the federal bureaucracy, suffer from being enmeshed in administrative red tape. In a development that is at odds with the problem of lack of financial incentives (but entirely consistent with the problem of survival), some laboratories are trying independently to develop technology which they then seek to commercialize, rather than working with industry from the outset. This creates difficult problems with intellectual property rights as well as running counter to the accepted view that strong industrial interaction is a necessary condition for successful commercial technology development.

Taken together, the technology transfer programs that have been described here, along with the general infrastructure, constitute a major new effort in the U.S. to apply the nation's R&D effort more effectively to commercial ends. Although some of the activities predate the end of the Cold War, that event and its implications for the American defense R&D program are driving part of the program. This should be expected to continue. Whether these efforts will succeed remains to be seen; indeed, as argued here, the very measurement of success is problematic. What has developed represents an amalgam of different approaches, some of which appear more promising than others. It should be the objective of policy-makers and analysts to sort out the successful from the unsuccessful, and to eliminate the latter. Given the tenacity of programs once established, however, it is difficult to be optimistic about the chances for weeding out the failures. Instead, it is likely that these programs will be modified and extended as international competitive pressures grow.

Footnotes

(1) Innovation also may produce new processes, of course. To avoid unnecessary repetition, the text refers generically to products as including both.

(2) This section is based on [20], [4], and supplements as noted.

(3) The Trademark Clarification Act of 1984 gave government-owned, contractor operated laboratories the authority to make decisions regarding licensing of patents, allowed contractors to receive royalties, and allowed laboratories run by universities and non-profit organizations to retain title to inventions under certain conditions. This created part of the legal basis for technology transfer under other legislation.

(4) [4], Appendix B. The estimate for 1993 is from a release from the federal laboratory consortium and presumably includes NASA agreements. Those agreements fall under the provisions of the 1958 Space Act, rather than the Stevenson-Wydler Act [13].

(5) These are papers filed with the U.S. Patent and Trademark Office which disclose an invention pending filing of a patent application. These papers provide evidence of when an invention was conceived (crucial under U.S. patent law), but themselves provide no patent protection [13].

(6) This section is based on [10] and [16].

(7) This section is based in part on [1].

(8) Actually, the reach of the Extension service has expanded steadily through its history. Its mission now extends to strengthening the American family, providing developmental opportunities for youth, and aiding communities in creating good economic, social, and natural environments [1]. This illustrates how an institution created for one specific purpose (which today would be termed technology transfer) serves as a vehicle through which many other political interests can be served.

[9] However, successful centers may still receive NSF support in the form of occasional grants under the so-called Self-Sufficient Partnership for Research program.

[10] Eighteen remain in operation, three having been terminated for various reasons. NSF support is provided for a maximum of eleven years, after which time pre-existing centers may re-apply for support in new competitions. It is expected that the total number of ERCs will rise again to 21 after the 1994 competition.

[11] But not universally. Although a very large number of small business firms are created each year, providing employment for hundreds of thousands of persons, most of these firms fail. In addition, in some fields, the capital requirements for new products are so large and the uncertainty levels so high, that large firms have a powerful advantage and may be the only feasible developers. Microchip manufacturing represents an example. Furthermore, success in holding markets depends heavily on steady, incremental product improvements, rather than revolutionary breakthroughs. Large corporations are best positioned for incremental change, and their R&D programs can be and often are structured for this purpose. Small businesses may base their existence on exploiting breakthroughs; those that succeed may create new industries, but the failure rate is necessarily high.

[12] Until recently, the requirement was 1.25%; it is now being raised over a period of several years to 2.25%.

[13] The program has been criticized for having served more as a vehicle for agencies to pursue pre-established R&D programs, using small business contractors for the purpose, than for truly stimulating new small business endeavors.

[14] Actually, available data pertain mostly to movements of the general population. Relatively little is known about the mobility of scientists and engineers, the key for the transfer of technology. The National Science Foundation, the main source of data about science and engineering in the United States, has not systematically collected or analyzed data about the mobility of researchers. Anecdotal information suggests high mobility of academic scientists and engineers. On the other hand, it is said that industrial engineers often stay with a single employer throughout their professional careers. The mobility of scientists and engineers is an important question for future research.

[15] See [14] for discussion of some of these issues.

[16] The problem was put in a nutshell by Stephen Lazarus: "... the entrepreneurial spirit is chilled by process police seeking to punish conflict of interest and, much more pernicious, potential conflict of interest" [7].

References

1. Aldrich, Jr., D.G. (1983) The cooperative extension service, in the *U.S. House of Representatives Hearing Before the Subcommittee on Department Operations, Research, and Foreign Agriculture, Committee on Agriculture*, **June 30**, U.S. Government Printing Office, Washington, D.C., pp. 48-71.

2. Betz, F. (1994) Basic research and technology transfer, *International J. Technology Management*, Special Issue on Needed Technological Responses to Increasing International Competition.

3. Department of Commerce (1993) *Commerce ACTS*, U.S. Government Printing Office, Washington, D.C.

4. Department of Commerce (1993) *Technology Transfer Under the Stevenson-Wydler Technology Innovation Act: The Second Biennial Report*, Department of Commerce, Washington, D.C.

5. Ergas, H. (1987) Does technology policy matter?, in Guile, B. R. and H. Brooks (eds), *Technology and Global Industry*, National Academy Press, Washington, D.C., pp. 191-245.

6. Kline, S.J., and Rosenberg, N. (1986) An overview of innovation, in Landau, R. and N. Rosenberg (eds.), *The Positive Sun Strategy*, National Academy Press, Washington, D.C.

7. Lazarus, S. (1994) Transforming university/laboratory science into useful commercial products: the intermediating organization, in Teich, A. H., Nelson, S.D. and C. McEbabey (eds.), *Science and technology Policy Yearbook 1993*, American Association for the Advancement of Science, Washington, D.C.

8. Mansfield, E. (1991) Academic research and industrial innovation, *Research Policy*, **February**.

9. National Academy of Engineering (1989) *Assessment of the National Science Foundation's Engineering Research Centers Program*, Washington, D.C.

10. National Aeronautics and Space Administration (1993) *Spinoff 1993*, U.S. Government Printing Office, Washington, D.C.

11. National Institutes of Health, Office of Technology Transfer (No date) Technology development and licensing, Ms.

12. National Institutes of Health, Office of Technology Transfer (1994) Technology transfer activities, Ms.

13. National Science Board (1993) *Science and Engineering Indicators - 1993*, U.S. Government Printing Office, Washington, D.C.

14. Odagiri, H. and Goto, A. (1993) The Japanese system of innovation: past, present, and future, in Nelson, R. R. (ed), *National Innovation Systems*, Oxford University Press, New York.

15. Preston, J. T. (1992) Success factors in technology development, Ms.

16. Root, J. (1994) *National Technology Transfer Network*, Unpublished presentation, April 20, on behalf of the Office of Advanced Concepts and Technology, NASA.

17. Rosenberg, N. (1982) *Inside the Black Box: Technology and Economics*, Cambridge University Press, Cambridge.

18. Waggoner, P. E. (1994) *How Much Land Can Ten Billion People Spare for Nature?* Council for Agricultural Science and Technology, New York.

19. West Publishing Company (1991) *Technology Innovation*, West Publishing Company, St. Paul, Minnesota.

18. BIOMEDICAL ENGINEERING IN THE U.S: FROM BASIC RESEARCH TO COMMERCIAL PRODUCTS AND TECHNOLOGY TRANSFER

PETER G. KATONA
Vice President, The Whitaker Foundation
Washington, DC, USA

1. Introduction

Technology transfer between NATO and Cooperating Partner (CP) countries cannot take place until the two sides understand each other's needs and concerns. This paper thus first describes biomedical engineering in the U.S., concentrating on technology transfer issues within that country. The paper then briefly describes some issues that must be considered when contemplating technology transfer between the U.S. and CP countries.

Biomedical engineering is a relatively new discipline that has defied a rigorous definition. It is often considered to be the "application of engineering tools and principles to solving problems in biology and medicine." It includes such areas as artificial tissues and organs, implantable and external orthopaedic devices, patient monitoring, drug manufacturing, radiological image analysis, and technological aids to the blind. Biomedical engineering also contributes to research for a quantitative understanding of living systems, facilitating the development of new products for health care.

Figure 1 places "biomedical engineering" in the context of other related fields, often referred to as "bioengineering." Biomedical engineering is concerned with the translation of basic knowledge of the physical sciences into devices and systems useful in medical practice. Biotechnology translates basic knowledge in the life sciences into useful products, for example, drugs for medical therapy. This latter translation requires the expertise of chemical and bioprocess engineers. Increasingly, devices and systems are being designed by mimicking

G. Bugliarello et al. (eds.), East-West Technology Transfer, 237-244.

principles governing living systems. Biomedical engineering is thus characterized by strong ties to related disciplines.

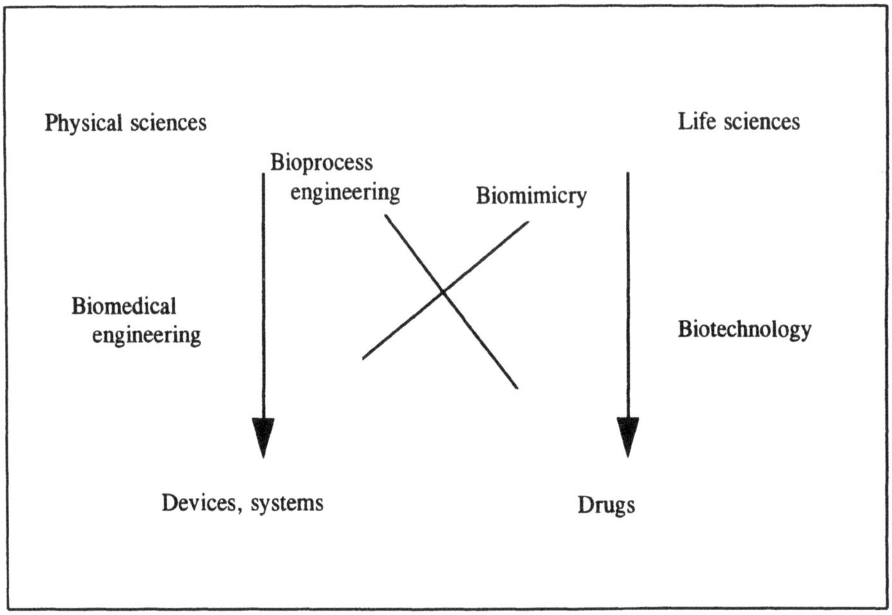

Figure 1. Bioengineering

Although the U.S. health care industry is currently facing severe challenges, it generated a $4 billion trade surplus in 1993. This amount needs to be contrasted with a trade deficit of $75 billion for all goods and services.

The success of the industry can be attributed to three factors. The first is strong basic research that spawns new ideas and concepts for diagnostic and therapeutic devices. The second is a vigorous technology transfer process that translates ideas into marketable products. The third is the availability of highly skilled professionals who can bridge the gap between the engineering and medical professions. These three necessary elements for success are described next.

2. Basic Research in Biomedical Engineering

Most basic research in biomedical engineering is supported by the federal government. The major source of funds is the National Institutes of Health with a total budget of $10 billion. While the NIH has no separate organization specifically devoted to biomedical engineering, it has been estimated that close to $300 million is being spent on projects that include a significant bioengineering component. Most of these are applied research projects where the engineering component is aimed at specific disease oriented problems, but about a quarter of the projects deal with basic technology problems that cut across disease categories.

The National Science Foundation supports basic research in all areas of science with a budget of $3 billion. It has small programs in biomedical engineering and the engineering aspects of biotechnology; total support is approximately $15 million.

Biomedical engineering programs are also supported by a variety of other government agencies, including NASA, the Department of Energy, and the Department of Defense. Most recently, the National Institute of Standards and Technology has expanded its Advanced technology Program that provides research grants to companies. This program aims to promote economic growth through the development and commercialization of promising new technologies. Biotechnology and medical information technology are among the targeted areas.

A major non-government organization funding biomedical engineering is The Whitaker Foundation. This private foundation, established in 1976, is dedicated to enhancing the field of biomedical engineering through a variety of grant programs. The Foundation concentrates on developing educational opportunities and helping young faculty members establish research centers in biomedical engineering. Total annual grant expenditures for biomedical engineering research and education are expected to exceed $30 million in 1994.

The relatively strong investment in basic research by governmental and private organizations builds the foundation for a strong health care devices industry. Basic research results in novel concepts and ideas, which are essential ingredients for new commercial products.

3. Technology Transfer Within the U.S.

The transforming of ideas into products is a long and difficult process. Its difficulty is greatly underestimated by faculty members and inexperienced inventors. Nevertheless, a strong spirit of entrepreneurship and willingness to persevere can overcome the difficulties.

It is generally acknowledged that true innovation in biomedical engineering originates primarily at universities or small companies, rather than at large established companies. It usually starts as a new idea for a product. Since the idea is new, proving its feasibility is the first task. Feasibility proof requires only a demonstration that the concept is a valid one and it can work; it does not consider whether a product can be manufactured and sold at a reasonable price. The proof is generally obtained in the investigator's laboratory as a result of a funded research grant; occasionally the investor may use his or her own resources.

Proof of feasibility does not assure that the device can be made to function effectively in a clinical environment. To demonstrate potential practical utility, a device needs to be constructed that can be demonstrated to function satisfactorily outside the research laboratory. Reducing the concept to practice by building the device typically requires more resources than were available to demonstrate feasibility. Inventors often fail to appreciate the need to build a working device or system before technology transfer can be seriously considered. Obtaining the $20,000 to $50,000 that is typically required to build a working device is a serious difficulty for many inventors.

The hurdle after reducing the invention to practice is to make arrangements for manufacturing and marketing the device. This requires resources that are well beyond the means of the typical inventor who now needs to find capital to finance the commercialization of the invention. The capital may be provided by an industrial partner that is given the license to the device in exchange of payment of royalties once the device is marketed. Alternatively, a company may be established to develop, manufacture, and market the invention. Funding is typically provided by venture capitalists who make an investment of several million dollars in the hope of deriving future profits well in excess of their investment.

Venture capitalists examine the prospects for potential products very carefully. They asses the technology, with special attention given to the uniqueness of the idea and whether the idea can be protected by patents of through trade secrets. They estimate market potential, and examine the strength of the management team. Technically oriented inventors often underestimate the need for putting together a strong management team that meets the approval of venture capitalists. In spite of the scrutiny, the majority of ventures end in failure, and it is the few highly successful products that bring success for many investors.

Raising capital allows the development of a product prototype. The cost of prototype development typically exceeds the already expended cost of research and development many-fold, occasionally requiring the raising of additional capital. Additional capital may also be needed to obtain the data required for regulatory approval of the device.

The primary regulatory agency is the Food and Drug Administration that is charged with ensuring that medical products brought to the market are safe and effective. The process of approval is lengthy and expensive, requiring extensive clinical testing of new devices. The future of many young companies are determined by whether they can obtain FDA approval within a sufficiently short time. Regulatory delays mean the "burning" of investment funds while the company derives no income from sales of the device.

There are relatively few inventions that navigate the long journey from concept to successful commercialization; the failure rate is well over 90%. Commercialization of high technology medical equipment has become especially difficult because of uncertainties surrounding health care reform. While health care reform may provide opportunities for companies that manufacture devices that deliver low-cost care; there is concern that the market for expensive equipment may become restricted.

4. Biomedical Engineering Education

A key element for the invention and commercialization of novel devices for health care are professionals who understand both engineering and the needs of medicine and biology. Biomedical engineering has recently emerged as a profession that fills this need.

The first programs in biomedical engineering were developed in the latter part of the 1960s, leading to doctoral and mater's degrees in biomedical engineering. In the 1970s, programs were established that led to designated undergraduate degrees. Currently, there are over 40 universities offering graduate degrees in biomedical engineering, and 21 that offer accredited undergraduate degrees. The organization of programs differ greatly: there are several that are based in major stand-alone departments, while others are administered by committees that cut across traditional engineering and life-science departments.

The areas of emphasis of biomedical engineering departments are changing. In the early programs, the strongest linkages were to electrical engineering. Electronic instrumentation, signal analysis, and computer aided data processing were the primary areas emphasized. This was followed by strong interest in biomechanics and biomaterial, areas that are critical for the development of both external and implantable orthopedic devices. Most recently, departments are expanding into areas of cellular and molecular engineering, taking advantage of the revolutionary advances in basic biology. Of particular interest is tissue engineering, a field that uses biological materials, such as specially designed living cells, to replace damaged tissues and organs. Chemical engineers are especially well positioned to contribute to this growing area.

Student interest in biomedical engineering is increasing. Although the absolute numbers are still small (less than 3%), biomedical engineering enrollment, as a percentage of total engineering enrollment, is rising. Especially telling of changing student interest is Figure 2, which compares the 1992 enrollment of freshmen, sophomores, juniors and seniors in four different fields of engineering.

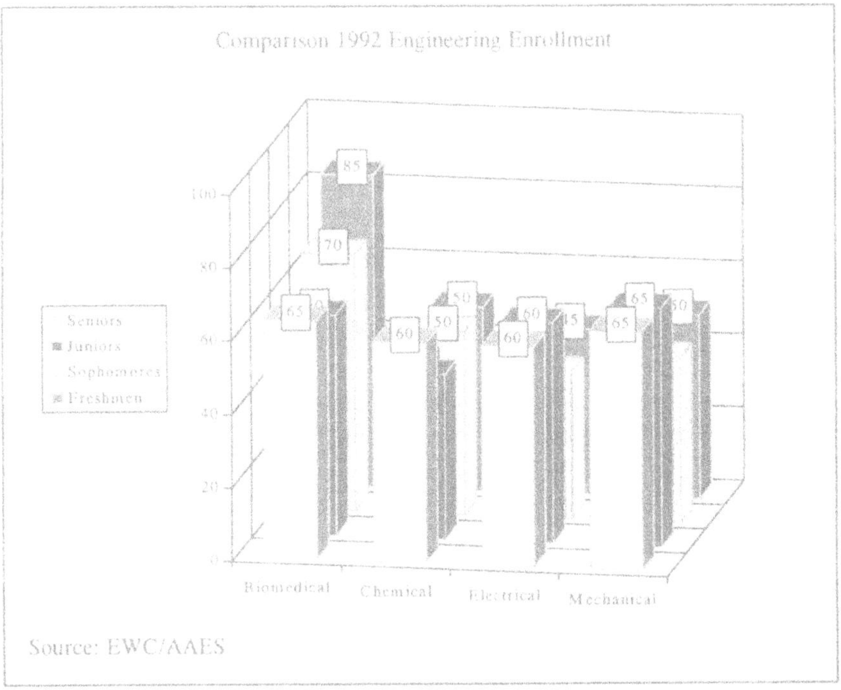

Figure 2. Undergraduate Student Enrollment in Biomedical Engineering Programs
(Figures are normalized to size of senior class)

There are some 40% more freshmen in biomedical engineering than there are seniors, while the number of freshmen in electrical engineering and mechanical engineering is some 40% fewer than the number of seniors. Assuming that the rates at which students graduate in these fields are the same, the figures foretell a major increase in the percentage of biomedical engineers in the engineering profession.

The impact of biomedical engineers is expected to be even higher than the figures would suggest. It is generally found that the academic qualifications of biomedical engineering students, measured in terms grade point average or standardized national test scores, exceed those of students in more traditional fields of engineering. This may reflect the highly challenging nature of biomedical engineering programs, attracting primarily the best qualified students.

Until recently, biomedical engineering education and research has focused in improving the quality of health care without paying much attention to the cost of care. As the demand for containing the cost of health care increases, biomedical engineering is expected to play an increasing role in the development of technology that aims to deliver the same level of care at a lower cost, rather than improving the care at any cost. Educational and research programs in biomedical engineering need to evolve to keep up with changing societal expectations.

5. Technology Transfer to CP countries

The transfer of already existing biomedical engineering technology from the U.S. to CP countries must take into account the differing needs and resources available in the different countries. It must also take into account the ultimate purpose of the technology transfer. The immediate goal of the transfer may be to maintain or improve health care in CP countries, through the use of equipment and systems produced by the U.S. and other NATO countries. A longer range plan would call for the development of capability within the CP countries themselves to manufacture medical equipment that will be used for the health benefit of their own residents. The final goal might be to develop expertise to manufacture equipment that would be exported, bringing economic benefit to the country.

The most important need for achieving any of these three types of technology transfer among countries is the development of appropriate expertise. The short term approach is the exchange of students, teachers, engineers, physicians, public health officials and businessmen. The long term approach needs to include the training of appropriate professionals in the CP countries themselves.

The technology transfer mechanism must provide incentives for both parties. Industrial firms in NATO countries will seek economic benefits, just as CP countries seek to develop their own economic and social services infrastructure. Manufacturers of high technology medical equipment that serves a few very sick patients are less likely to succeed in transferring their technology than manufacturers of equipment that target the health care needs of the broad population. The need for a reliable supply of widely used and relatively simple technological items, such as disposable devices for drug administration, is likely to be greater than the need for complex devices that diagnose or treat rare diseases. In the short term, technology transfer involving these high-volume and high impact health care devices appears to be the most promising.

6. Summary

Biomedical engineering is an expanding field that can contribute to improving health care in a cost effective manner. Success of this field in the U.S. is attributed to the support of basic biomedical engineering research by a variety of governmental and private organizations, a vigorous system for translating basic research results into useful products, and the availability of professionals who understand the principles of both engineering and the life sciences. Major challenges to the field include overcoming regulatory hurdles, and recognizing that society demands care that is not only excellent but is affordable. Transferring health care technology into PC countries needs to recognize the special health care and economic needs of these countries. The development of appropriately trained professionals is an essential early step in the technology transfer process.

19. MODELS IN PRIVATE TECHNOLOGY TRANSFER TO DEVELOPING NATIONS

ROBERT H. RINES
Chairman, Franklin Pierce Law Center
President, Academy of Applied Science
Concord, NH, USA

1. Introduction

A rather neglected area for ready transfer of technology resides not in the much-vaunted, highly expensive projects requiring large industrial or substantial government involvement, but rather in quite simple people-to-people ventures created by the willingness of small higher technology private companies to explore foreign markets heretofore beyond their historic experience or previous know-how.

Particularly in the United States, there exists, and there are continually developing, a myriad of small enterprises spurred by the unique incentives of the American legal concept of inventors rights and the traditional American entrepreneurial spirit that pushes forward and launches many of the major inventions and advances in technology. The term "technology" is here used to embrace new products, techniques and services in all technological and consumer fields, including public health and medicine. More recent examples which we shall discuss more fully herein, include computer software and service; medical, surgical and diagnostic instrumentation; paper converting technology, particularly in the tape, label, printing and chemical adhesive areas; consumer electronic products; and polymer chemistry industrial and consumer products.

The creators of significant advances in this illustrative list are largely independent American inventors and entrepreneurs and their backers, some stemming from university settings, who started new companies or merged into earlier-developed small entrepreneurial companies to launch their new technologies.

G. Bugliarello et al. (eds.), East-West Technology Transfer, 245-253.

It has indeed been reported that an inordinate number of the breakthrough inventions in nearly all fields of endeavor in America have historically, and still presently, come from the individual or small company inventors, and not from the large corporate or even large research institutions [6; 5; 7]. Some of the more current examples include the "CAT-Scan," the "Pacemaker," the "MRI," and "Windows."

While it is beyond the scope of this paper to delve into the reasons for this source of prodigious invention and entrepreneurship, when one reflects on what makes America different - including its constitutional protection of the real inventors and not just the first filer to push a piece of paper into a patent Office - and on the paranoia of the larger American corporate sector for instant profits and cosmetically thrilling bottom lines that forbid much new research risk-taking, some clues are readily apparent.

Suffice it for present purposes to limit ourselves to the technologies of this class of smaller and often high technology groups.

Underlying the development of four highly inventive pilot programs bearing upon technology transfer to developing countries, none of which is probably known to any of the readers of this article, is a personal conviction and prejudice of the writer that no government - my own included - has demonstrated any real competence in responsively, usefully, effectively or reasonably dealing with the accomplishment, let alone the incentivizing, of transferring technology to private sector businesses anywhere, and certainly not in developing countries.

And it is a sad commentary that in my land, undoubtedly the most prodigious, free and individualistic society the world has ever known, there are so many continuing unfortunate and growing roadblocks to entrepreneuring and particularly to the small innovators.

Unenlightened and unskilled tampering with the historic rights of innovators that specifically underlie and are directly responsible for America's inventive and new company successes, is the current game of some political "jokesters" who believe they are going to improve the trading capabilities of our multinational companies, many of which lack the leadership, inventiveness and even know-how to capture world markets.

In my own specialty, the almost total inability to respond to the real needs of the innovative community by our dinosaur legal system is a giant roadblock as well.

I shall review a new mechanism for promoting technology transfer to small and medium size private enterprises. This mechanism asks little or nothing of our respective governments, save to get out of our way in achieving person-to-person new business relationships.

2. International Private Technology Transfer Sessions: The Academy of Applied Science - Oxford Model

The Academy, a non-profit educational and technology-stimulating private institution, now headquartered in Concord, New Hampshire, has historically been graced on its Board of Governors with, among others, a myriad of first-generation high technology inventors - entrepreneurs responsible for launching new and state-of-the-art technologies and businesses in diverse fields. Several came from university roots; and others developed from independent or small inventor communities.

One of the common and almost universal characteristics of such entrepreneurs, as quite strongly contrasted to the umpteenth generations managers of many current multinational enterprises, is a strong concern and feeling for other would-be innovators - and particularly those of less developed lands. The struggles are still fresh in the minds of the first generation entrepreneurs, and they remember their roots and trials. Many of those who have inherited large corporate operations, on the other hand, know little or nothing of this world.

The statesmanship of such entrepreneurs, moreover, reflects recognition that people-to-people private relationships and joint venturing are an important contribution to have the world understand that Americans are a good and caring people and excellent business partners. Additionally, the promise of finding a possible non-competing and supplemental potential return on their technology abroad that would otherwise lie fallow, made some of our Academy members very anxious to explore innovative mechanisms for effective technology transfer to technologically developing countries.

The strategy evolved for this model experiment involved several steps:

- First, to identify a technology system need that could have a significant commercial impact in the developing country, and hopefully, would have the potential for an extra-national export or foreign trade as well;
- Secondly, to select a technology which fell within the purview of the business of one or more Academy members whose technologies melded to create a required overall system, and who could jointly afford and share the risk;

- Thirdly, to identify genuine potential businessmen and women in specific countries who were serious about prompt deals, who possessed at least basic technical and financial resources, and who could handle the politics of their respective governments in getting permissions to import, make payments, and set up their own business; and
- Last, to select a site with an appropriate atmosphere and an adequate agenda and time to meet, teach, demonstrate (hands on) and negotiate deals right then and there.

The technology we first selected was that of manufacturing high grade adhesive backed paper tapes and labels, it being quite evident that the total dependencies on other countries for modern product labelling was intolerable if developing country products were to compete in western markets. A beer or cosmetic label of black and white or only one color is hardly appealing to foreign customers flooded with high-quality gold and silver imprint and multicolored labelling.

Within the Academy "family," there were:

- the preeminent (though small) innovative company manufacturer of paper handling and modern adhesive application equipment (Acumeter Laboratories, Inc., under Frederic S. McIntyre);
- the leading (though small) innovative company manufacturer of electron beam adhesive and ink curing equipment (Energy Sciences Inc., under Jack Weisman);
- their associated suppliers of paper, modern pressure-sensitive and other adhesives and electron-beam curable inks;
- suppliers of allied (again small) printing equipment already designed to fit with the above-named equipments to provide a complete system.

At biannual international paper converting trade shows, conversations had been held and cards exchanged at the Acumeter, Energy Sciences and other booths, and with the paper converting trade organizations, and there had been letters of inquiry that served as a starting point to identify serious and competent possible recipients of technology transfer in several developing countries. These contacts were later sharpened by correspondence and telephone; potential business partners from over twenty countries were identified and ready to participate - many from former British colonies.

This latter fact led us to select Oxford University (St. Catherine's College) as the site of a technology transfer happening. The though was that a respected and trusted British academic institutional site would create the teaching atmosphere, the willingness to live and learn together as colleagues and the credibility of high purpose and expectation of developing real projects, as that would be quite distinct from the commercial crassness and circus atmosphere of a convention or trade fair [1].

Invitations were sent, with subscription fees high enough (covering housing and meals at the College) to insure seriousness of purpose. The company participants set their equipment and prepared lectures, hands-on demonstrations and practice, private interviews to negotiate deals, and social functions.

Within a few months, three contracts were completed; and within a year, equipments were delivered and installed and tape-and-label private business started.

KUALA LUMPUR

The Academy's Oxford model, with variations, was tried again by the Academy in November, 1984 in Kuala Lumpur, Malaysia at the invitation of the Printing and Packaging International Conference [9]. However, this did not have such spectacular or immediate success, since the atmosphere resembled that of a convention and, additionally, the Academy was not able to carry out all the steps of the Oxford experiment.

SINGAPORE - BANGLADESH

Again, in Singapore, November of 1986, at the National University Hospital department of ophthalmology, the Academy, in consort with Project Orbis, established an ophthalmic training center for the exchange and teaching of medical technology introducing modern ophthalmic, cryosurgical and laser techniques and approaches for doctors, nurses and equipment technicians. (The Academy knows well that a laser without maintenance know-how and procedures is only a short-lived transfer and even an invitation to misuse.) This time, equipment and library materials donated through the efforts of Dr. Percy Amoils of South Africa and the Academy Board, inventor of the cryosurgical ophthalmic probe, Dr. Steven burns of MIT and the Academy Board, and Academy co-counsel Rob Rines, several New England hospitals including the Massachusetts Eye and Ear Infirmary, the Concord, New Hampshire Hospital, the Harvard Countway Medical Library, were physically transferred to the Islamic Eye hospital in Bangladesh - a favorite project of the Academy's good friend, the late Justice Abu Sayeed Chowdhury, first president of Bangladesh. This project was under the direction of the late Academy Vice President Carol M. Rines and the late Executive Director, Howard S. Curtis.

The Academy continues to be ready to work with others in developing countries who wish to explore further this type of active person-to-person technology transfer technique for their countries.

3. Teaching the Know-How of Technology Transfer

Unlike Japan, Germany and the former USSR, America has not earmarked funds to train people from other countries in its system for protecting intellectual property and effecting technology transfer, or to help them set up patent, copyright, trademark and other compatible systems of legal protection and technology transfer in their own countries.

As a result, the U.S. missed an opportunity: the chance to persuade - by demonstration and example instead of rhetoric or threat -key people from other countries, that the U.S. approach to protecting intellectual property and trading is both practical and preferable.

As part of a philosophy in a shrinking world, the Franklin Pierce Law Center, also of Concord, New Hampshire, and its Patent, Trademark and Copyright (PTC) Research Foundation, together with the Academy, moved into the breach and have been making aggressive efforts as a private instrument of national policy, to: 1) familiarize business people, lawyers and government officials from developing and other countries with how the U.S. system of intellectual property protection works and how it compares with other such systems in the world; 2) apprise individuals from our economic competitors, such as the Pacific Rim countries, of the importance of adequate protection of intellectual property; and 3) train persons in the government and business sectors of developing countries in the principles of technology transfer and in the understating of the economic harm which comes from counterfeiting and piracy.

Since the writer's 1985 negotiations in China, the Law center commenced development of an intellectual property and technology transfer Master's degree, diploma and summer programs, initially for administrators and practitioners of China and now other developing and developed foreign countries, as well as American and foreign industrial private sector representatives, academic and law school students, and faculty.

4. PACT - New Technology Co-Venturing With the Academy and Law Center

This resource is also being applied to a patenting-licensing-technology transfer program called PACT (initially meaning the Promotion of American and Chinese technology, but now enlarged to embrace Promotion of Advanced Commercial Technology), administered by the Academy of Applied Science for the mutual benefit of the Law Center and the Academy.

When President Nixon dissolved the private-government National Inventors Council (NIC) [2], the Academy was instrumental in securing its transfer under Chairman Charles Stark Draper to the Law Center and Academy. PACT became a natural outgrowth of the NIC as part of its activities, particularly as it has come to aid not only Chinese universities and ministries in protecting and licensing or otherwise commercializing their inventions and technologies, but also faculty and graduate students of American and foreign universities and an occasional independent inventor or small company.

Though privately and inadequately funded through altruistic volunteer professional and business assistance, PACT has succeeded in supporting some two dozen new technologies (including some inventions from developing countries) to free patenting and other intellectual property protecting services, licensing, business planning and other commercialization services, in return for a "piece of the action" for the primary benefit of the educational activities of the Academy and the Law Center. This effort also affords law students and the Law Center a "laboratory" for drafting patents, licenses and other legal documents and participating with real clients in the technology transfer process, though always under responsible legal supervision and final control [8].

This program has also resulted in the spawning of new high technology companies and, though considerably less than a decade old, is now starting to reap success and financial returns.

The U.S. government, through its Small Business Administration and National Science Foundation programs, and private foundations and philanthropists, have been persuaded to contribute significant funding to try to incentivize (promote) entrepreneurship in, we believe, far less promising and largely unproven directions. However, there has been no support to help PACT grow or even to spread the PACT model. Thus we are limited in the number of technologies from developing countries for which PACT may provide such joint venture assistance. Nonetheless, PACT continues to entertain the approach of worthy applicants.

Currently PACT has a number of promising technologies for licensing or joint venturing in or with developing countries, including oil well recovery improvements that obviate paraffin clogging, highly novel and realistic stone-simulating plastic surfaces, herbally-derived plant and crop stimulating nutrients, new medical diagnostic instruments, new packaging materials, self-compensating hydrostatic machine tool bearings and long-life submersible pumps, novel electronic consumer items, remote wireless lighting and appliance controls, and new processes for the production of thermoplastic polyolefins, among others.

5. Negotiation Assistance and Conflict Resolution

The Franklin Pierce Law Center and the Academy of Applied Sciences have been hard at work in designing a center (ACCORD) for conflict obviation and resolution of disputes that will, for a fee, assist parties in approaching other parties to explore joint venturing, licensing and other facets of technology transfer, with the aid of experienced neutrals or facilitators.

Among these facilitator are professionals with highly developed mediation skills, particularly in technical subject matter, including patent and other intellectual property and technology transfer areas, not only for aiding parties get together to perform their own negotiations, but also for helping to avoid disputes and to resolve disputes that have already arisen. The Law Center and the Academy, indeed, have been at the early forefront of urging alternatives to the legal system for rapidly and economically resolving disputes [3; 4].

ACCORD is now "open for business" at the Franklin Pierce Law Center under the auspices of its PTC Research Foundation and the Academy. The goal is a) to totally bypass the need for the use of courts in the U.S. or other countries for resolving disputes involving technology transfer and other technical subject matter; and b) even more significantly, to help parties negotiate joint venturing and technology transfer activities *for themselves*, with user-friendly facilitation - either at the Law Center or anywhere that the parties may choose, under any guidelines the parties may feel comfortable in setting up.

References

1. (1983) *Adhesive Age*, **September**, 46-48.

2. Hayes, J. (1993) Inventors' heyday: the national inventors council, *Inventors' Digest*, **May/June**, 16, 32.

3. (1976) *IDEA - The Journal of Law and Technology* **18**, 1-142.

4. (1984) *IDEA - The Journal of Law and Technology* **29**, 235.

5. Jewkes, J. (1959) *The Sources of Invention*, MacMillan.

6. Rabinow, J. (1976) Are patents needed?, *IDEA - The Journal of Law and Technology* **18,** 19-35.

7. Rines, R. H. (1969) *Create or Perish - The Case For Inventions and Patents*, Acropolis Press.

8. Rines, R. H. and Shaw, R. (1992) The PTC research foundation - past, present and future, *IDEA, The Journal of Law and Technology* **32**, 261-262.

9. (1984) Mind for technology, *Malaysia New Straits Times*, **November 6**.

APPENDIX I - WORKSHOP PROGRAM

1st Day

9:00 a.m.	**Welcome & Introduction**: *co-directors* (**Alferov**, **Moore**, and **Pak**)
9:15	**Welcome**: *Chairman, Local Organizing Committee* (**Pak**)
	Chairman: **Jubier (NATO)**
9:25	**Newman (U.S.)**
	Legal Framework of the Industrial Economy. The Laws of Intellectual Property - Economic Incentives in Development
10:10	**Pak (Turkey)**
	The Turkish Experience
10:30	**Rambaut (Deputy Assistant Secretary General of NATO)**
	NATO's Science and Environment Program
10:55	*Break*
11:10	**Alferov (Russia)**
	Science and Technology Policy in Russia - A View from the Russian Academy of Sciences
11:55	**Moore (U.S.)**
	Aspects of Technology Transfer: U.S. Policy in Practice
12:40 p.m.	*Lunch*
2:00	*Chairman:* **Alferov (Russia)**
	deJong (Netherlands)
	A View from a Market Economy
2:45	**Macioti (EC, Italy)**
	European Union (EU) Relations with Central and Eastern Europe and with the Commonwealth of Independent States (CIS): the Example of Central Asia
3:30	**Rines (U.S.)**
	Training Patent Lawyers and Engineers
4:15	*Break*
6:00	*Adjournment*
7:00	*Dinner*
	Speaker: **T. Terzioglu, President of TÜBİTAK**

2nd Day

8:15 a.m.	**Organizing Committee**: Review of Previous Day *Chairman:* **Pak (Turkey)**
8:30	**Rabkin (Canada)** Technology Transfer with the Former USSR: History, Problems and Opportunities
9:15	**Alaverdov (Russia)** The Russian Federal Space Program up to the Year 2000
10:00	**Salaev (Azerbaijan)** Issues in Azerbaijan
11:00	*Break*
11:15	**Daukeev (Kazakhstan)** Technology Transfer Problems for the Republic of Kazakhstan
12:00 p.m.	**Forsberg (Sweden)** Swedish Personnel and Leadership Experiences in Technology Transfer
12:45	*Lunch*
2:00	*Chairman:* **Moore (U.S.)** **Bratersky (Russia)** Social and Political Impact on Russia of the Transfer of Technology from NATO Countries
2:45	**Poholkov (Russia)** The Personnel Needs of Siberian Industries and Institutions for Effective Technology Transfer
3:30	**Kuusi (Finland)** Finnish Experiences in Technology Transfer
4:15	*Break*
4:30	**S. Arzhakov (Russia)** Some Aspects of Technology Transfer between Russia and Western Countries
5:15	**Pachadzhanov (Tajikistan)** Issues in Tajikistan
6:00	**Katona (US)** Biomedical Engineering in the U.S. from Basic Research to Commercial Products and Technology Transfer
6:45	*Adjournment*

7:30	*Dinner*

3rd Day

9:00 a.m.	*Chairman:* **deJong (Netherlands)**
	Radosevic (UK)
	The Eastern European Latecomer Firm and Technology Transfer: From "Muddling Through" to "Catching Up"
10:15	*Break*
10:30	**Team Workshops**
	Team A: Leaders: **Bratersky (Russia)** and **deJong (Netherlands)**
	Technology Transfer, Human Resources in CP countries (specific skills needed - legal, managerial, industrial, etc., who should be trained, where and how)
	Team B: Leaders: **Alferov (Russia)** and **Moore (US)**
	Role of institutions and industries in NATO countries in contributing to preparation of human resources for technology in CP countries and between CP countries and NATO countries
1:15 p.m.	*Lunch*
2:45 p.m.	**Continuation of Team Workshops**
4:00	*Break*
4:15	**Continuation**
5:00	**Team Leaders**
	Tentative Outline of Conference Report
6:30	**Discussion of Tentative Outline**
7:15	*Adjournment*
7:45	*Dinner*
	Speaker: **T. Titiz (Turkey), Member of Parliament**

4th Day

9:00 a.m.	**Conference Organizing Committee** and **Team Leaders** Draft of Tentative Outline
9:30	**Discussion of Draft**
10:45	*Break*
11:00	**Conference Organizing Committee** Final Remarks
12:00 p.m.	*Lunch* *Remarks:* **Pak (Turkey)**, *Conference Co-Chairman*
1:30	*Conference Adjournment*

APPENDIX II - LIST OF PARTICIPANTS AND AUTHORS

Key Speakers

Prof. G.A. Abilsiitov
Minister of Science and Technology
Kazakhstan

Dr. V. Alaverdov
First Deputy of Director General
Russian Space Agency
Russia

Prof. Zhores Alferov
Vice President
Russian Academy of Sciences
5, Universitetskaya nab.
St. Petersburg 199034
Russia

Prof. Sergei A. Arzhakov
Polymer Department, Faculty of Chemistry
Lomonosov Moscow State University
Lenin Hills, Moscow 119899
Russia

Prof. Ilgiz Aytmatov
President
Academy of Sciences
Kirgizistan

Dr. G. Batyrbekov
Director General
National Nuclear Center
Kazakhstan

Dr. Maxim Bratersky
Director, International Programs
Russian Public Policy Center
Moscow
Russia

Prof. George Bugliarello
Chancellor
Polytechnic University
6 Metrotech Center
Brooklyn, NY 11201
USA

Prof. Dias K. Daukeev
Deputy Minister of Science and New Technologies
Masanchi str. 57a
Almaty 480012
Kazakhstan

Prof. W.A. deJong
129 Gevers Deynootweg
NL-2586 HL Den Haag
The Netherlands

Prof. Vincenzo Di Cataldo
Facoltà di Legge
Universita di Catonia
Catonia
Italy

Dr. Hans G. Forsberg
President
Royal Swedish Academy of
Engineering Sciences
Box 5073
S-102 42 Stockholm 5
Sweden

Prof. A. Hedjamamedov
President
Academy of Science
Turkmenistan

Dr. Peter Katona
Vice President
The Whitaker Foundation
1700 N. Moore St., Suite 2200
Rosslyn, VA 22209
USA

Dr. Juhani Kuusi
Director General
Technology Development Centre
TEKES
Malminkatu 34
Helsinki
Finland

Dr. Manfredo Macioti (Ret.)
Advisor, European Commission
Rue G Stocq, 16
Ixelles, B-1050 Brussels
Belgium

Prof. John Moore
Director, International Institute
George Mason University
4001 N. Fairfax Dr., Suite 450
Arlington, VA 22203-1616
USA

Honorable Pauline Newman
Circuit Judge
U.S. Court of Appeals for the Federal
Circuit
The National Courts Building
717 Madison Place, NW
Washington, DC 20439
USA

Prof. O. Odekov
Director of Institute of Geology
Turkmenistan

Prof. Daler N. Pachadzhanov
Vice-President
Academy of Sciencesof Tajikistan
Nikitin Institude of Chemistry
Aini 299/2
734063 Dushanbe
Tajikistan

Prof. Namik K. Pak
Vice President of TÜBİTAK
The Scientific and Technical Research Council of Turkey
Atatürk Bulvari, No. 221
Kavaklidere
06100 Ankara
Turkey

Prof. Yury P. Poholkov
Rector
Tomsk Polytechnic University
30 Lenina Ave.
Tomsk 634004
Russia

Dr. Slavo Radosevic
Science Policy Research Unit
University of Sussex
Mantell Building
Palmer, Brighton BN1 9RF
England

Dr. Robert Rines
Chairman
Franklin Pierce Law Center
Academy of Applied Science
65 India Row
Concord, NH 03301
USA

Prof. Eldar Salaev
President
Academy of Sciences
Azerbaijan

Mr. William C. Salmon
National Academy of Engineering
2101 Constitution Ave., NW
Washington, DC 20418
USA

Prof. O.M. Sultangazin
National Academy of Sciences
21 Ulitsa Shevchenko
Almaty
Kazakhstan 480021

Prof. N.R. Yousurbekov
Commissioner for Science and Technology
Uzbekhistan

Other Participants

Güller Adigüzel
Ministry of Industry & Commerce
Ankara
Turkey

Ali Riza Akçay
NETAS Alemdag Cad Ümraniye
Istanbul
Turkey

Sedat Apaydin
Ministry of Industry & Commerce
Ankara
Turkey

Prof. Maxim Arzhakov
Polymer Chemistry Department
Lomonosov Moscow State University
Moscow 119899
Russia

Özden Aslan
TAI (Turkish Aerospace Ind.)
Akinci, Ankara
Turkey

Senol Ataman
TÜBÌTAK
Atatürk Bulvari No. 221
Kavaklidere, Ankara
Turkey

Halime Atamer
TÜBÌTAK
Atatürk Bulvari No. 221
Kavaklidere, Ankara
Turkey

Dursun Ayan
Atatürk Merkezi, Atatürk Bul. No. 225
K.dere 06690, Ankara
Turkey

Emel Aydinalp
Duyu Sok. No. 17/3
Çankaya, Ankara
Turkey

Sevki Bakirci
General Directorate of
Turkish Maritime
Karaköy, Istanbul
Turkey

Vladimir Barinov
First Sec., Russian Embassy
Karyagdi Sok. No. 5
Ankara
Turkey

Sema Basintas
Ankara University
Faculty of Linguistics,
History and Geography
Ankara
Turkey

Tarik Baykara
Materials Research Dept.
TÜBİTAK Marmara Research Center
PK. 21 Gebze Kocaeli
Turkey

Dr. Srym Bukeychanov
President
New Technology Centre
112 Mate Zalka str.
Almaty 480062
Kazakhstan

Arif Çaglar
Hacettepe University, Department of Chemical Engineering
Beytepe, Ankara
Turkey

Mustafa Dagli
TÜBİTAK
Atatürk Bulvari No. 221
Kavaklidere, Ankara
Turkey

Oya Ersan
TÜBİTAK
Atatürk Bulvari No. 221
Kavaklidere, Ankara
Turkey

Luigi Fontana Giusti
Ambassador, Italian Embassy
Ankara
Turkey

Dr. C.H. Glenday
Head Europe Office
National Science Foundation (US)
France

H. Aykut Göker
TÜBİTAK
Atatürk Bulvari No. 221
Kavaklidere, Ankara
Turkey

Nuran Günöven
TÜBİTAK
Atatürk Bulvari No. 221
Kavaklidere, Ankara
Turkey

Ersan Gürlük
Ministry of Industry and Commerce
Maltepe, Ankara
Turkey

Dr. Alain Jubier
Fellowships Program Director
NATO Scientific Affairs Division
1110 Brussels
Belgium

Haluk Korkmazyürek
Dept. of Armament & Defense Research of the General Staff of Turkey
06100 Bakanliklar, Ankara
Turkey

Duran Leblebìcì
Istanbul Technical University
Ayazaga Kampüsü
80626 Istanbul
Turkey

Nese Lüleç
TÜBÌTAK
Atatürk Bulvari No. 221
Kavaklidere, Ankara
Turkey

Vladimir Mirnov
METU Physics Dept.
Ankara
Turkey

Ing. Teresa Murino
University of Naples
Corso Vittorio Emanuele 110/2
80121 Napoli
Italy

Serpil Olgüç
Turkish Cement Factory (ÇITOSAN)
Eskisehir Yolu 7 Km, Ankara
Turkey

Nevzat Özgüven
General Director
Turkish Cement Factory (ÇITOSAN)
Eskisehir Yolu, Ankara
Turkey

Dr. Yakov M. Rabkin
Department d'Histoire
Universite de Montréal
C.P. 6128, Station Centre-Ville
Montréal, QC
H3C 3J7 Canada

Dr. Paul Rambaut
Deputy Assistant Secretary General for
Scientific and Environmental Affairs
NATO
B-1110 Brussels
Belgium

Dr. Sefik Süzer
Bilkent University
Dept. of Chemistry
Ankara
Turkey

H. Tanriyar
Deputy Director
Paper and Pulp Industry (SEKA)
Ìzmìt
Turkey

Bülent Tekin
Paper and Pulp Ind. (SEKA) Dalaman
Company
Turkey

Ahmet Tezel
MKE
Kirikkale
Turkey

Ersin Tulunay
Secretary of the Research Grant
Committee of Electrics,
Electronic & Informatics
TÜBÌTAK
Atatürk Bulvari No. 221
Kavaklidere, Ankara
Turkey

Ömür Türksoy
TÜBÌTAK
Atatürk Bulvari No. 221
Kavaklidere, Ankara
Turkey

Nevin Vahapoglu
Ministry of Industry and Commerce
Directorate of Research and
Development
Tandogan, Ankara
Turkey

INDEX

A

B

C

F

G

J

K

M

N

O

P

Q

R

S

T

V

www.ingramcontent.com/pod-product-compliance
Ingram Content Group UK Ltd.
Pitfield, Milton Keynes, MK11 3LW, UK
UKHW021353110926
15107UKWH00004B/13
* 9 7 8 9 4 0 0 9 0 1 5 2 0 *